OTHER BOOKS BY MIE PUBLISHING

Find Anyone Fast
Checking Out Lawyers
Secrets of Finding Unclaimed Money
They Also Served: Military Biographies of Uncommon Americans

How to Locate Anyone Who Is or Has Been in the Military

Armed Forces Locator Guide

8th Edition

Lt. Col. Richard S. Johnson, (Ret.)
Debra Johnson Knox
Private Investigators

MIE PUBLISHING

MIE PUBLISHING
PO Box 17118
Spartanburg, SC 29301
(800) 937-2133
E-mail: thelocator@aol.com
http://www.militaryusa.com

Library of Congress Cataloging-in-Publication Data:

Johnson, Richard S., 1933–1999
How to locate anyone who is or has been in the military: Armed Forces locator guide / Richard S. Johnson, Debra Johnson Knox. — 8th ed.

p. cm.
Includes index
ISBN 1-877639-50-8

1. United States—Armed Forces Registers. 2. Veterans—United States—Societies, etc. Directories. I. Knox, Debra Johnson. II. Title.

U11.U5J54   1999
355'.0025 73—dc21   99-18103
                                                      CIP

Dedication

This edition is dedicated to my father,

Lt. Col. Richard S. Johnson,
June 20, 1933 – February 2, 1999,

the original author and inspiration for this book.
Thank you Dad for your love and for your service
to your country.

—Debra Johnson Knox

Acknowledgments

We wish to acknowledge the enormous contributions and support made by everyone associated with this project. It is an overwhelming task for only one or two people to update and research all this information. The help of others makes the job much easier and more pleasant. The list of people includes Dick Bielen, Karen Bianchi, and Tom Ninkovich for his endless support, advice, editing and interior design. And George Foster of Foster & Foster for his wonderful patriotic cover design.

Disclaimer

This book is designed to provide information and is sold with the understanding that the publisher and authors are not engaged in rendering legal or other professional services.

Every effort has been made to make this book as complete and accurate as possible. There may be mistakes, either typographical or in content. Therefore, this book should be used as a general guide.

The authors or MIE Publishing shall have neither liability nor responsibility to any person regarding any loss or damage caused or alleged to be caused directly or indirectly by the information contained in this book.

Foreword

Lt. Col. Richard Johnson has provided a useful and welcome service to all men and women who have been privileged to wear the military uniforms of our nation.

It is my opinion that virtually every veteran of our military services, in peace or war, does at some time want to contact a buddy with whom he or she served. Until now, that has been unusually difficult. But now, thanks to Colonel Johnson, it can be expeditiously accomplished.

> —William C. Westmoreland
> General, United States Army, Retired
> Charleston, South Carolina

Preface

Since the first edition of this book was printed in 1988, we couldn't image the scope and impact this book would have on people and their lives. It has successfully helped thousands of people reunite after serving together in WWII, Korea, and Vietnam. Hundreds of people have used it to locate their birth fathers who served in the military, and it's helped countless of others in many other ways. We are grateful that this book could make a difference.

In this, the 8th edition, we have given you a more detailed and comprehensive book. Through the years we have noticed that more and more people are using this book who don't have any military background. Therefore, we have tried to spell out the information more clearly. For example, we have given you definitions of Active Duty, Retired, Reserve and Veteran for those who don't know exactly what these terms mean. We've also included as much Internet information as was available at the time of printing. Pertinent Internet information is given at the end of each chapter and includes screen dumps.

Today there are over 70 million people who have served in the military since World War I. Over two million men and women are currently serving on active duty. Retired military members total 1.9 million. Chances are that someone you're searching for has a military connection.

Why is it important to your search to find out if there is a military connection? Simply because of the information that is contained in military records — important identifying information such as a complete legal name, date of birth, marital status, duty assignments, etc. Our nation is a nation of record keepers and this is definitely true of the military. We have seen many searches solved simply because the person being sought served at one time in the military.

We hope very much that this book will help you in many ways. Good Luck!

Table of Contents

Chapter *1*

Locating Active Duty Military

The term *active duty* indicates a person who is currently serving in either the Air Force, Army, Coast Guard, Marine Corps or Navy.

Most people enter the service on active duty after completing high school or college. Enlisted military usually enter the service at ages 17–19. Officers enter after graduating college, usually at ages 21–25.

Locating an Active Duty Military Member

Each branch of the military operates an Armed Forces World-Wide Locator. The locator will either forward a letter to an active duty member or provide the current unit of assignment, if the person is stationed in the United States. For security reasons, overseas unit of assignment and identification of personnel assigned to a deployable unit or ship are not releasable information.

In case of an emergency, the best and most effective means to locate an active duty military member anywhere in the United States or overseas, is to contact your local American Red Cross chapter. Keep in mind that it must be an urgent situation. Child support collection or contacting an old friend are not considered emergencies.

In order to use the World-Wide Locators you must supply enough information to identify the person being sought. Information could include the name, rank, Social Security number, branch and type of service (e.g., active duty Air Force), date of birth, sex, officer or enlisted (if actual rank is not known), date entered service, and last duty assignment.

If you wish to have a *letter forwarded*, place the letter in a sealed, stamped envelope. Put your name and return address in the upper left-hand corner. In the center of the envelope, put the person's rank and full name. Write the Social Security number or date of birth under the name. On a separate sheet of paper, list all available information about the person.

All World-Wide Locators except the Coast Guard charge $3.50 for unit of assignment or forwarding letters to active duty military personnel. The Coast Guard does not charge a fee. A written verification of active duty status is $5.20 for all branches, including the Coast Guard. Checks or money orders should be made payable to "U.S. Treasurer." The Air Force requests their checks be made payable to "DAO-DE RAFB."

*Active duty and retired military, immediate family members (mother, father, grandmother, grandfather, brother or sister), and county, state or federal agencies are not required to pay the $3.50 fee. All civilians or civilian businesses must request information in writing and pay the appropriate fee.

Air Force:
U.S. Air Force World-Wide Locator
AFPC-MSIMDL
550 "C" Street West, Suite 50
Randolph AFB, TX 78150-4752
(210) 652-5775, (210) 652-5774 (recording)
($3.50 fee) Hours: 7:30 am to 4:30 pm, Central Time.

The Air Force locator will forward only one letter per request, and will not provide overseas unit of assignment. They will only provide a unit of assignment for those on active duty serving stateside who are not assigned to a deployable unit. Requests with more than one address per letter will be returned without action. Include a self-addressed stamped envelope with request for the unit assignment. The locator will explain if the individual is separated from the Air Force. This office has base assignment information on Air Force personnel since 1971. A Social Security number is not mandatory to locate active duty Air Force. Make sure you include as much information as known about the person, such as rank (or officer/enlisted), previous base assignments, approximate age, and home of record. Responses to requests for information should not take longer than 10 days. Make checks payable to "DAO-DE RAFB."

Army:
  World-Wide Locator
  U.S. Army Enlisted Records
      and Evaluation Center
  8899 East 56th Street
  Indianapolis, IN 46249-5301
  (703) 325-3732
  ($3.50 fee) Hours: 7:30 am to 4:00 pm, Eastern Time.

The Army locator furnishes military addresses for individuals currently on active duty in the Army and for the Department of Army civilians. Information cannot be furnished without the request containing the individual's full name and Social Security number *or* the full name and date of birth. A reply should be received in 7 to 10 working days. This office maintains separation data (date and place of separation) for two years.

If you have an *emergency* and need to contact someone on active duty in the Army, you may call the Total Army Personnel Command Staff Duty Officer at (703) 325-8851. This office has the microfiche of all individuals currently on active duty in the Army. It is available 24 hours a day.

Coast Guard:
Commandant
(CGPC-ADM-3)
U.S. Coast Guard
2100 Second Street, S.W.
Washington, DC 20593-0001
(202) 267-1340, (202) 267-4310 Fax
(no fee) Hours: 8:00 am to 4:00 pm, Eastern Time.

The Coast Guard will provide ship or station of assignment, and unit telephone number of active duty personnel. They do not charge the $3.50 fee. The fee for written verification is $5.20.

Marine Corps:
U.S. Marine Corps — CMC
(MMSB-10)
2008 Elliot Road, Room 201
Quantico, VA 22134-5030
(703) 784-3942, (703) 784-5792 Fax
($3.50 fee) Hours: 8:00 am to 4:30 pm, Eastern Time.

Navy:
Department of Navy
Navy Personnel Command
NPC-0210
5720 Integrity Drive
Millington, TN 38055-0212
(901) 874-3388, (901) 874-2660 Fax
($3.50 fee) Hours: 8:00 am to 4:30 pm, Eastern Time.

Military Installations, Base/Post Locators

If you think you know the base or post to which the person is assigned, contact the base directly by using Appendix A (Directories of Military Installations). Simply call the information phone number for the installation and ask for the military personnel locator. When calling, ask for the base locator. (In many cases, the information operator is also the base locator.) The base locator can check their computer or printout of those stationed at that particular installation. If they have the person listed, ask for the unit assignment, and unit telephone number. Note: Some bases have closed their locators and refer all inquiries to the World-Wide Locator for that particular branch of the service.

Many active duty military live on base. If they are single and live on base in barracks, dormitories or quarters, they can be contacted through the Charge of Quarters of their unit, after normal duty hours. Some married non-commissioned officers or officers live on base in quarters, and have their name, address, and telephone number listed with the city directory assistance. If they do not live on base, then the chances are they live in close proximity to the base. Always check with the information operator for neighboring areas.

Locating Active Duty Military Stationed Overseas

It's difficult to track down someone on active duty stationed overseas. Due to security reasons, no branch of the armed forces releases overseas assignments, or gives names of those assigned to deployable units. However, there are a few avenues to keep in mind when someone is stationed overseas. If the person is married, there is a possibility that the family is still living stateside and may have a listed telephone number. A computer search of nationwide phone books will sometimes give an overseas address. The following is an example: Unit 1111, Box 2222, APO, AE 09102. This address can be interpreted using Appendix A (U.S. Military Installations, Overseas). Searching by zip code shows it's for Patton Barracks in Heidleberg Germany. Then check Appendix A (Phone Numbers of Overseas Military Installations) to obtain the overseas telephone number.

Child Support Collection

The county or state child support collection office should fax a request on their agency letterhead to the appropriate World-Wide Locator. The locator will not charge the agency a fee, and should respond with the current unit of assignment.

Internet Sources for Locating Active Duty Military

www.militaryusa.com
www.militarycity.com
Both of these Internet sites contain a listing of active duty military stationed in the United States for all branches of the service. Personnel serving overseas or aboard ships are not contained in the lists. You must become a registered user and pay a fee to use these websites.

The information contained in these files includes first name, middle name or middle initial, last name, rank, date of entry into the service, branch of service, complete address of assignment (including unit assigned, base, state, and zip code), and estimated date of discharge. These databases do not contain Social Security numbers or dates of birth.

These military databases are extremely useful, especially if you have limited information on an individual. The World-Wide Locators will not "hunt" for the right person for you; you have to supply them with enough identifying information. If you do not have a Social Security number for the person you are looking for, and he has a common name, it may be very difficult for the locator to find the right person. However, these databases allow you to search all branches of military by name. So, if you are searching for a person who happens to have a common name, you can find out how many people there are with that name in all branches of the service. They are also helpful with common names if you happen know the middle name. For example, these databases may show the only "John Henry Smith" serving on active duty in the Army.

Once the unit of assignment is obtained from the list, you can use Appendix A (Directories of Military Installations) to call the base. Ask for the actual unit telephone number. The address given is also a correct mailing address. Just add the name and rank to the first line for a complete address.

Please be aware that these databases can be over a year old, depending on how often they are updated.

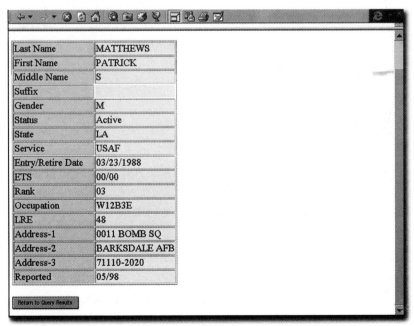

Example of an active duty search on www.militaryusa.com.

Summary: Locating active duty military is not very difficult. Remember, if it's an actual emergency, contact the American Red Cross. If you have several people on active duty to locate, or have limited information, use the Internet databases; they will save you time and money. When using the Armed Forces World-Wide Locators, keep in mind to supply as much identifying information about the person as possible. Not supplying enough information or giving incorrect data will only prolong your search.

Chapter 2

Locating Reserve and National Guard

Each branch of the Armed Forces has a reserve component, such as the Air Force Reserve, Air National Guard, Army Reserve, Army National Guard, Coast Guard Reserve, Marine Corps Reserve, and the Navy Reserve. There is active and inactive reserve status. The active reserve status is when the reservist is part of a unit and required to attend training one weekend per month and two weeks of active duty training per year. They are sometimes referred to as "weekend warriors." Many members of the reserve components go to service schools for periods of a few weeks — up to a year. They are considered to be on active duty, but are not listed on the active duty roster when they attend these schools. However, they may be listed with the base locators. There are also reservists who are on continuous active duty.

Members of the reserve components wear the same uniform as active duty personnel, and they have the same insignias and ranks. A large percentage of the reserve forces once served on active duty prior to joining the reserves, and therefore may be listed with the Department of Veterans Affairs. It's also true that someone on active duty may have previously served in a reserve component. The President can call reserve units to active duty when the need arises. Reserve units recently served in Haiti, Bosnia, and the Persian Gulf War.

The National Guard consists of the Army National Guard and the Air National Guard. These guard units are under the command of a state governor. However, if called to active duty, they fall under the command of the appropriate armed forces. Army National Guard members can be located through the appropriate state adjutant general's office. See Appendix B (Directory of State Resources) for the address and telephone number. Air National Guard members can be contacted in the same manner as the Air Force Reserve.

"Inactive reserve" means that the person is in the reserves but is not assigned to a unit. Such a person does not attend training and does not receive pay. If a locator has an address for an inactive reservist, it's a home address and not a unit address. They will only forward a letter and will not release any information to the public.

Locating Air Force Reserve and Air National Guard

The Air Force World-Wide Locator will forward only one letter per request, and will not provide overseas unit of assignment. They will only provide a unit of assignment for those serving within the U.S. who are not assigned to a deployable unit. Requests with more than one address per letter will be returned without action. Include a self-addressed stamped envelope with request for unit assignment. The locator will explain if the person has separated from the Air Force. A Social Security number is not mandatory to locate Air Force Reserve or Air National Guard. Make sure you include identifying information, such as name, rank (officer or enlisted), previous base assignments, approximate age, or home of record. Requests should not take longer than 10 days. Make checks payable to "DAO-DE RAFB."

U.S. Air Force World-Wide Locator
AFPC-MSIMDL
550 "C" Street West, Suite 50
Randolph AFB, TX 78150-4752
(210) 652-5775, (210) 652-5774 Recording
($3.50 fee*) Hours: 7:30 am to 4:30 pm, Central Time.

*Active duty and retired military, immediate family members (mother, father, grandmother, grandfather, brother and sister), county, state or federal agencies are not required to pay the $3.50 fee. All civilians or civilian businesses must request information in writing and pay the fee.

Locating Army Reserve and Inactive Army Reserve

The Army Reserve Personnel Command in St. Louis is no longer operating their reserve or inactive reserve locator. You should use the Internet reserve database from *militarycity.com* or *militaryusa.com*. See the Internet section at the end of this chapter.

Locating Coast Guard Reserve

Commandant
(CGPC-ADM-3)
2100 2nd Street, S.W.
Washington, DC 20593-0001
(202) 267-1340, (202) 267-4310 Fax
(No fee) 8:00 am to 4:00 pm, Eastern Time.

Will provide unit of assignment by telephone. For more than one name, submit in writing.

Locating Marine Corps Reserve

Commandant
Headquarters U.S. Marine Corps
MMSB10
2008 Elliot Road, #201
Quantico, VA 22134-5030   (703) 784-3942

($3.50 fee) Hours: 8:00 am to 4:30 pm, Eastern Time. Please submit all requests in writing.

Marine Corps: Individual Ready Reserve, Fleet Marine Corps Reserve, or Inactive Reserve

Marine Corps Reserve Support Command
15303 Andrews Road
Kansas City, MO 64147-1202
(800) 255-5082, (816) 843-3395
(No fee) Hours: 6:00 am to 4:30 pm, Central Time. Please submit all requests in writing.

Locating Navy Active Reserve

Department of Navy
Navy Personnel Command (NPC-312)
5720 Integrity Drive
Millington, TN 38055-3120
(901) 874-3388, (901) 874-2660 Fax
($3.50 fee) Hours: 7:30 am to 4:30 pm, Eastern Time. Please submit all requests in writing.

Navy Individual Ready Reserve and Inactive Reserve

Commanding Officer (N3)
Naval Reserve Personnel Center
4400 Dauphine Street
New Orleans, LA 70149-7800
(800) 535-2699
($3.50 fee) Hours: 7:00 am to 3:00 pm, Central Time.
Will only forward a letter. Do not put a return address on the letter to be forwarded.

Locating Army National Guard

Army National Guard members should be contacted through the appropriate state adjutants general office. See

Appendix B (Directory of State Resources) for the address and telephone numbers. They will only forward a letter and do not charge a fee.

Military Records for Reserve and National Guard

Officers Registers may be available for reserve components and National Guard. These only contain information on officers and not enlisted personnel. These Registers may be available at military libraries or civilian libraries in cities that have a large military population. They contain biographical information about officers including full name, rank, date of birth, military service number or Social Security number, education, promotions, etc. See Chapter 5 (Military Records) for more information on Officers Registers and where to access information.

Using the Department of Veterans Affairs

Members of the reserves and National Guard who have served at some time on active duty are veterans and therefore eligible for veteran's benefits. The Department of Veterans Affairs may have them listed in their records. If their file contains a current address they will only forward a letter. See Chapter 4 (Locating Veterans). Contact them at (800) 827-1000.

Internet Sites for Locating Reserve and National Guard

www.militaryusa.com
www.militarycity.com

Both of these Internet sites have the databases of those serving in a reserve unit, inactive reserve status, and National Guard. Information contained in these databases include the last name, first name, middle name, rank, sex, pay grade, branch of service, service component, specialty code, date of rank, separation date, and unit address. Unit address is only listed for those attached to a unit; inactive reservists have no unit address. These databases do not contain Social Security numbers or dates of birth. Following are examples of active reserve and inactive reserve personnel.

Summary: Locating active reserve and National Guard is similar to locating active duty military. Use the above listed locators and be sure to give all identifying information about the person. It may be difficult if the person is in a reserve component *and* serving on active duty. If this is the case, we suggest contacting both the active duty and reserve locators. Even though the person is serving on active duty status, he may be listed only with the reserve locator.

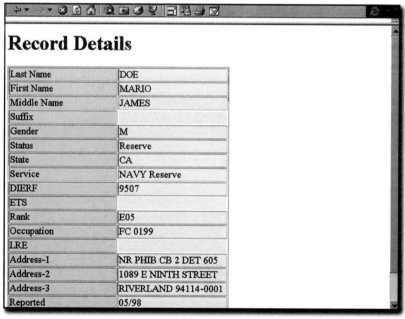

Record Details

Last Name	DOE
First Name	MARIO
Middle Name	JAMES
Suffix	
Gender	M
Status	Reserve
State	CA
Service	NAVY Reserve
DIERF	9507
ETS	
Rank	E05
Occupation	FC 0199
LRE	
Address-1	NR PHIB CB 2 DET 605
Address-2	1089 E NINTH STREET
Address-3	RIVERLAND 94114-0001
Reported	05/98

Example of active reserve search on www.militaryusa.com.

Chapter 3

Locating Retired Military

The term *retired military* indicates a person who is receiving retired pay from one of the branches of the military for any of the following reasons:

Length of service retirement: A person may retire after serving 20 or more years of active duty. Recently, due to budget constraints, some personnel have been allowed to retire with only 15 years of service.

Disability retirement: A person serving on active duty who has severe disabilities from injuries or medical conditions may be placed on either the *temporary duty retirement list* or the *permanent duty retirement list* (both of which comprise the *active duty retirement list*). Those on temporary duty retirement can be in this status for up to five years. After that period they can be moved to the permanent duty retirement list, medically discharged (without retirement benefits), or returned to active duty.

Reserve retirement: A member of the reserve or National Guard who has completed 20 or more years of satisfactory reserve or active duty service, may retire from the reserves. They don't receive any benefits or retirement pay, nor do they appear on the retired list until they reach the age of 60. They are known as "Gray Area Retirees." Once the person has turned 60, he is transferred to retired military status, and as such would receive retired military benefits and pay.

★ **TIP**: If a person entered the service on active duty at an early age (e.g., right after completing high school) and served 20 years, it's very possible that he could retire at age 37. If the person entered the service after completing college, then the age of retirement could be around 42–45. If the person retired after 15 years of active duty service, the age of retirement could be 32–40 years of age.

Locating Retired Military Personnel

Each branch of the service except the Army has a Retired Locator similar to the one for locating active duty military. The armed forces Retired Locators will forward letters to retired members. However, they are prohibited from releasing addresses. Retired military no longer have a military address, and therefore their addresses are protected under the Privacy Act. All branches also have retired pay centers that may forward a letter in the same manner as the World-Wide Locators. This includes anyone who retired from active duty, the reserve, or National Guard.

To use the Retired Locators you must have enough information for the locator to identify the person being sought. Information could include the name (no nicknames), rank, Social Security number (not all require this), previous duty assignments, date of birth or age, date of retirement, etc. If you wish to have a letter forwarded, place the letter in a sealed, stamped envelope. Put your name, and return address in the upper left-hand corner. In the center of the envelope put the rank and the full name of the person you are trying to locate. Then write the Social Security number or date of birth under the name. On a separate sheet of paper write everything known about the person so the locator can identify the correct individual. Then place your letter in another larger envelope and address it to the appropriate Retired Locator. Don't forget to enclose the search fee.

Air Force: Retired from Active Duty, Air Force Reserve, or Air National Guard

U.S. Air Force World-Wide Locator
AFPC-MSIMDL
550 "C" Street West, Suite 50
Randolph AFB, TX 78150-4752
(210) 652-5775, (210) 652-5774 Recording
($3.50 fee) Hours: 7:30 am to 4:30 pm, Central Time.

The Air Force locator will forward only one letter per request. Requests for more than one address per letter will be returned without action. Make checks payable to "DAO-DE RAFB."

Army: Retired from Active Duty, Reserve, or Army National Guard

The Army Retired Locator is no longer operating. The best method to locate a retired Army member is to use Internet databases, computer searches, or the Defense Finance and Accounting Service. See ahead in this chapter.

Coast Guard: Retired from Active Duty or Reserve

Coast Guard Human Resources Service
& Information Center
444 S.E. Quincy Street
Topeka, KS 66683-3591
(785) 357-3415, (785) 295-2639 Fax
(No fee) Hours: 6:30 am to 5:00 pm, Central Time.

Marine Corps: Retired from Active Duty or Marine Corps Reserve

HQ U.S. Marine Corps
Manpower & Reserve Affairs (MMSR-6)
3280 Russell Road
Quantico, VA 22134-5103
(703) 784-9310, (703) 784-9434 Fax
(No fee) Hours: 7:30 am to 4:30 pm, Eastern Time.

Navy: Retired from Active Duty or Navy Reserve

Commanding Officer
Naval Reserve Personnel Center
4400 Dauphine Street
New Orleans, LA 70149-7800
(504) 678-5400, (504) 678-6934 Fax
(800) 535-2699
($3.50 fee, made payable to "U.S. Treasurer")
Hours: 7:00 am to 3:30 pm, Central Time.
Do not put a return address on letter to be forwarded.

★ **TIP**: The Social Security number of a retired officer or warrant officer may be found in Officers Registers. These are books published each year by the various branches of the military, and contain biographical information on officers and warrant officers. See Chapter 5 (Military Records) for further details on accessing Officers Registers.

Locating Retired Military through Defense Finance and Accounting Services

If the Retired Locator is unable to identify the person, you may then contact the appropriate Defense Finance and Accounting Office. These centers maintain files of all retired military members (active duty, reserve and National Guard), and Survivor Benefit Plan annuitants (widows, widowers and some dependent children). They can reveal to third parties the names and rank/rate of retired members and annuitants. They will also forward a letter in a manner similar to the Retired Locators. The Social Security number is usually required. No fees are charged for these services. Addresses are below:

Air Force, Army, Marine Corps & Navy Retired Military
   (Retired Pay Center):

Defense Finance and Accounting Services
PO Box 99191
Cleveland, OH 44199-1126
(800) 321-1080, (216) 522-5955
(800) 469-6559 Fax

Air Force, Army, Marine Corps & Navy Retired Military
   (Survivor Benefit Plan Annuitants):

Defense Finance and Accounting Services
6760 E. Irvington Place
Denver, CO 80279-6000
(800) 435-3396, (303) 676-6552
(800) 982-8459 Fax

Coast Guard Retired Military:

Human Resources and Information Center
Retiree and Annuitant Services
444 S.E. Quincy Street
Topeka, KS 66683-3591
(800) 772-8724, (785) 295-2639 Fax

Locating Widows/Widowers of Retired Military Members

It's possible to have a letter forwarded to a widow or widower of a person who has retired from the armed forces (active duty, reserve or National Guard). If the widow or widower is receiving survivor's benefits from any branch of the military, the benefactor's address may be in the files of the appropriate finance center. Keep in mind that not all spouses receive these benefits. The finance center will not release the person's address but they may forward a letter in the same manner as for retired military. Contact the appropriate finance center (see above). A Social Security number may be needed to identify the correct records.

Armed Forces Retirement Homes

There are two military retirement homes: the U.S. Naval Home and the U.S. Soldiers' and Airmen's Home. A person must either be retired or have met the military requirements to reside in these two facilities.

U.S. Naval Home	(800) 332-3527
1800 Beach Drive	(601) 228-4013 Fax
Gulfport, MS 39507-1587	
www.afrh.com	
500 residents	

U.S. Soldier's and Airmen's Home	(800) 422-9988
3700 N. Capitol Street, N.W.	(202) 722-3492 Fax
Washington, DC 20317-0001	
www.afrh.com	
1,075 residents	

Internet Sources for Locating Retired Military

www.militarycity.com
www.militaryusa.com

Both of these websites have information about retired personnel. *Militarycity.com* has a list of those who have retired from the Air Force, Army, Marine Corps and Navy since 1980. This information includes the first name, middle name or initial, last name, sex, home of record, pay grade/rank, branch of service, service component, specialty code, prior service, date of retirement, and reason for separation (e.g., retired).

Militaryusa.com contains the complete list of those retired from the Air Force, Army, Marine Corps, Coast Guard, and Navy. Anyone who is currently on the retired rosters for any of the mentioned branches should be listed in this database. It contains over 1.9 million retired military entries. Information available includes complete name, rank, home of record (or state only, if available), and date of retirement.

Neither of these databases will have the home address of a retired person. They also do not contain Social Security numbers or dates of birth. We suggest that if a home of record is included in the file, use one of the Internet telephone directories to look for a listed telephone number for that state.

If the person does not come up on either of these databases, then there are usually two reasons: the person is not retired from the military, or the person is deceased and has been taken off the retired list.

You must pay a fee and become a registered user to access these sites. Be aware that these databases can be over a year old, depending on how often they are updated.

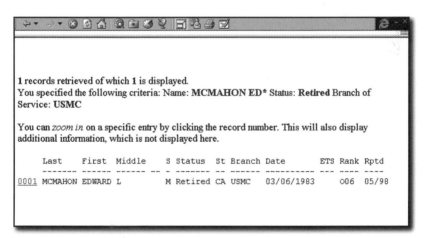

Example of retired military search on name and branch of service. From www.militaryusa.com.

★ **TIP**: Dates of retirement for active duty should be the first day of a month, for example 5/1/96. If the date is in the middle of the month, this could mean the person retired from a reserve component or from disability retirement.

Retirement Service Officers

Retirement service officers handle retirement affairs for military installations. They usually have a mailing list of the retired military that are living in their surrounding area. It's the officer's job to notify retirees of upcoming events, and give them updates on retiree issues. Some even send out newsletters. The Army has paid staff retirement service officers for most of the large Army installations in the United States and overseas. Other branches of the service have volunteers that handle these duties. Simply contact the military installation and ask for the retirement service officer.

Locating Retired Military Living Overseas

Some retired military live overseas. Reasons for this can include: those who married spouses from other countries, those who have taken a civilian job overseas, or those who have simply decided to move back to a foreign country after having served there during their military career. Whatever the reason, tracking down such an address can be difficult. The first suggestion is to have a letter forwarded by the Retired Locator. If the overseas base is known, contact the retirement service officer for that particular installation. Search for parents, children, or other family members who may not have gone overseas with the person.

The retired pay centers may not be of much help in this situation because it's possible that the retired person is having his paychecks deposited directly into a military bank in the United States. This means that the bank may not have an overseas address to even forward a letter.

In case of emergency, the American Red Cross does assist in locating retired military who are living overseas. Contact your local chapter listed in the telephone directory.

★ **TIP**: Many people do not understand the word "retirement" as it applies to the military. They assume if the person they are searching for is of retirement age (65 or so), that the person has retired from the military. However, the person may simply be a veteran who served a few years and was discharged, not retired. Remember, most people have to serve 15–20 years of active duty, reserve, or National Guard duty to receive retirement status from any branch of the military.

Chapter *4*

Locating Veterans

A *veteran* is a person who, at one time, served on active duty in one or more branches of the armed forces.

In this chapter, we focus on veterans — those who didn't stay in the military to retire but did serve at some time. A veteran is much more difficult to locate than an active duty or retired military person because their military connection was in the past — sometimes in the distant past. There are approximately 25 million living veterans today. In this chapter, you'll find some of the best and easiest methods to track them down.

Using the Department of Veterans Affairs

The Department of Veterans Affairs is normally very cooperative in providing assistance in locating veterans. They have a listing of all veterans who were discharged since 1974. However, they have addresses only for those who have at some time applied for VA benefits, such as education assistance, medical care, disability compensation, pensions, home loans, and VA insurance. If an address is listed, it is the address given when the veteran last obtained or applied for benefits. If a veteran was discharged prior to 1974, he will be listed only if he applied for benefits at some time.

The VA will forward a letter in a similar manner as the armed forces World-Wide Locators. But before attempting to have a letter forwarded, it's recommended that you first find out if they have any information on the veteran. Contact your nearest VA regional office by calling (800) 827-1000. You will automatically be connected with the closest VA Regional Office. Explain to the counselor who answers your call that you wish to verify if a veteran is listed in their records. Be sure to say that you intend to have a letter forwarded and that you are not asking them to release information to you.

Give the counselor the veteran's full name and service number or Social Security number, or full name and date of birth, and the state that they entered the service from (if known). Confirm that they have the right person by giving the counselor details of the person's military service: time period served, rank or other available information. If the veteran is listed, ask for their VA claim number. This should be placed on the letter for forwarding purposes (see below). You may also be able to obtain some of the following information: service number, date of birth, if the veteran used educational benefits, and what colleges he attended.

The VA is required to tell you the location of the veteran's file, whether it is in a Regional Office or in a record holding area. If the file is not over three or four years old, the veteran is probably living within 300 miles of the Regional Office where the file is located. Use the Internet or CD-ROM telephone directories to complete your search. See Chapter 12 (Computer & Internet Searches).

To have a *letter forwarded*, place your correspondence in an unsealed, stamped envelope with a return address. Put the veteran's name and VA claim number on the front of the envelope. Next, prepare a short fact sheet and state that you're requesting that the VA forward this letter to the veteran indicated on the sheet. Place the letter and fact sheet in a larger envelope and mail to the VA Regional Office you spoke with over the telephone. If they cannot identify the veteran, they will return your letter. See Appendix B (Directory of State Resources) for addresses of Regional Offices.

If the Department of Veterans Affairs can't find the individual listed in their files, then contact the Veterans Affairs Insurance Office:

Department of Veterans Affairs
PO Box 8079
Philadelphia, PA 19101
(800) 669-8477

For veterans who have been separated from the military for less than five years, contact:

Servicemen Group Life Insurance
213 Washington Street
Newark, NJ 07102-2999
(800) 419-1473

The above offices have insurance information in their files that is not readily available in the Regional Offices.

If the VA counselor you're dealing with is somewhat difficult or uncooperative, hang up and dial again. You'll probably receive a different counselor on the phone. Be persistent, but be courteous and eventually you will obtain some important identifying data that will enable you to locate the person.

How to Obtain a Veteran's Social Security Number

It may be possible to acquire a Social Security number for a veteran if the person applied for VA benefits after April 1973. Send a check for $2 made payable to the Department of Veterans Affairs to the address listed below. State in your letter that you would like the veteran's VA claim number (do not ask for the veteran's Social Security number). If the claim number has nine digits then it's also the veteran's Social Security number. Once you have the Social Security number in hand, you can use a professional computer search (see Chapter 12) to locate the person quickly. Mail the request to the following address:

Department of Veterans Affairs
Records Management Processing Center
PO Box 5020
St. Louis, MO 63115

★ **TIP**: Social Security numbers are available for officers who served in any branch. Check the Officer's Registers for the appropriate year. See Chapter 5 (Military Records) for more details.

Using the National Personnel Records Center

The National Personnel Records Center (NPRC) will forward correspondence to a veteran's last known address. That is usually the one given when the person separated from active duty or when a reserve commitment was completed. You must meet one of the following reasons for the NPRC to forward your correspondence.

- Requester's VA or Social Security benefits are dependent on contacting the veteran.
- The veteran's VA benefits may be affected in some manner.
- Forwarding is in the veteran's or next of kin's interest, e.g., estate settlement.
- The veteran may have fathered a child.
- A financial institution's legitimate effort to collect a debt.

A search fee of $3.50 is required only when the forwarding of correspondence is *not* in the veteran's best interest, e.g., debt collection. The check should be made payable to "Treasurer of the U.S."

The NPRC will place your letter to the veteran in another envelope and will write the veteran's name and last known address on it. In the event the letter is not delivered (meaning the address is no longer valid), it will be returned to the NPRC and you will *not* be notified.

If a person has written to the NPRC for assistance in locating a veteran who does not meet one of the above listed requirements, the writer will be told to contact the nearest Department of Veterans Affairs Regional Office or the Records Processing Management Center.

National Personnel Records Center
9700 Page Ave.
St. Louis, MO 63132

☆ **TIP**: The NPRC will probably not have a current address for a veteran unless the person has recently requested copies of his records. But don't overlook this method if the reason for locating the veteran is valid.

*In July 1973 a fire at the National Personnel Records Center destroyed about 80% of the records for Army personnel discharge between November 1, 1912, and January 1, 1960. About 75% of the records for Air Force personnel with surnames from Hubbard through "Z" who were discharged between September 25, 1947, and January 1, 1964, were also destroyed. Some alternative information may be available from records of the state Adjutants General. See Appendix B (Directory of State Resources) or Chapter 5 (Military Records) and state Veterans Affairs offices. There are currently over 70 million records at the National Personnel Records Center.

Locating Former Coast Guard

The U.S. Coast Guard will forward letters to former members of the Coast Guard using their last known address. A fee of $3.50 applies.

Commandant
CGPC-ADM-3
2100 2nd Street, S.W.
Washington, DC 20593-0001
(202) 267-1340, (202) 267-4985 Fax

Locating Veterans Who Belong to Associations

Military, patriotic and veterans organizations will usually assist in locating members. Although they normally won't release a home address, they will usually forward a letter. This service varies by organization — some only provide this service for their members. Most of the larger groups have a newsletter, newspaper or magazine where you can place an "in search of" announcement or advertise a reunion.

The addresses, phone numbers, and websites for the larger organizations are listed in Appendix D. When contacting them, remember to give as much identifying information about the veteran as possible. Most groups do not charge a fee.

Locating Former Military Pilots and Doctors

Due to the high cost of education, many men and women entered the service to learn to fly or become physicians. Once their term ended they either stayed in to retire or left the service to go into private practice or to fly for a commercial airline. The licensing requirements of these professions makes doctors and pilots very easy to locate. Use the Internet databases listed below.

Certified Pilots. *www.landings.com*
The "landings" website is a mega-source of aviation infor-

mation covering the U.S., Canada and the United Kingdom. First, get into the site; then click on "Search Engines" to access the database and much more.

This database contains over 600,000 names of pilots certified by the Federal Aviation Administration. Search by full name or last name only (if unique) and receive the complete legal name of the pilot, current address, date of last medical exam, type of pilot certificate, rating, and the FAA region to which they are assigned.

Doctors. *www.ama-assn.org*

Search for one of the 650,000 physicians licensed in the U.S. by using this American Medical Association site. It provides the physician's office location, office telephone number, gender, medical school, year of graduation, residency training, and specialty. It will tell you if he is board certified or a member of the AMA.

Search by name or specialty. One possible problem: if all you have is a name, you'll have to search state by state. But again, it's a free and accessible resource.

Attorneys

www.wld.com (West's Legal Directory)

www.martindale.com (Martindale-Hubbell Lawyer Locator)

West's Legal Directory and Martindale-Hubbel Lawyer Locator are sites to find lawyers and law firms. Search by the person's name or law firm. Information returned includes firm name, type of practice (sole practitioner, etc.), business address, telephone/fax numbers, the year the attorney was born, undergraduate school and law school attended, type of law practiced (family, criminal, etc.), and a list of his business partners. It covers the entire United States and many foreign countries. Former military lawyers, after leaving the service or retiring, might go into private practice.

Locating Former Military Chaplains

Because military chaplains were usually officers, check the Officers Registers. See Chapter 5 (Military Records). If you know the military base that the chaplain was assigned to, contact that base and speak with the base librarian or historian. There may be documents that contain more information about the church or chaplain.

> Military Chaplains Association
> PO Box 42660
> Washington, DC 20015-0660
> (202) 574-2423, (202) 574-2423 Fax

> Catholic Chaplains Archdiocese
>   for the Military Services
> PO Box 4469
> Washington, DC 20017
> (301) 853-0400

Has information on active duty, retired, reserve and Department of Veterans Affairs Catholic chaplains.

The Air Force and the Marine Corps both published books detailing lists of chaplains and other biographical information: *Air Force Chaplains* (4 volumes) and *Chaplains With Marines in Vietnam, 1962-1971*.

Locating Civil Service Employees

Thousands of veterans and retired military are employed by the federal Civil Service because of military experience and hiring preference. The Office of Personnel Management operates a centralized service that will locate most Civil Service employees. However, they will not locate employees of the judicial and congressional offices, U.S. Postal Service, TVA, General Accounting Office, FBI, DEA and other intelligence agencies.

The only information that is permitted to be released is the name and address of the individual's employing agency, the location of his actual place of employment, or the address of the agency's personnel office. The latter will provide the address of the work site, if their policy permits.

To request a search, submit the name and Social Security number. Allow two weeks for replies to written requests.

U.S. Office of Personnel Management
1900 "E" Street, N.W., Room 7494
Washington, DC 20415

The American War Library

This organization has put together a database of current and former military personnel that contains 21 million names. Their data is received from veterans, family members, and a variety of other sources, and can be searched to locate someone, or even verify military service.

The American War Library
16907 Brighton Avenue
Gardena, CA 90247
(310) 532-0634 phone/fax
www.amervets.com

Army Quartermaster Roll Call

The U.S. Army Quartermaster Museum at Fort Lee, Virginia, is home to the Quartermaster Roll Call which archives names, places of birth, dates of service, units of assignment, and highest ranks or grades held. Fort Lee is the home of the Quartermaster Corps.

U.S. Army Quartermaster Museum
ATTN: Quartermaster Roll Call
PO Box A
Fort Lee, VA 23801

Internet Sites for Locating Veterans

www.militarycity.com

Militarycity.com has a retiree and veteran database and a veteran's registry. Their retiree and veteran database lists those who have separated from the service since 1980. It supplies the name, rank, branch of service, date left the service, and reason (e.g., "retired" or "term expired"). The registry is searchable, although it's up the person registering to give out his address and other identifying information.

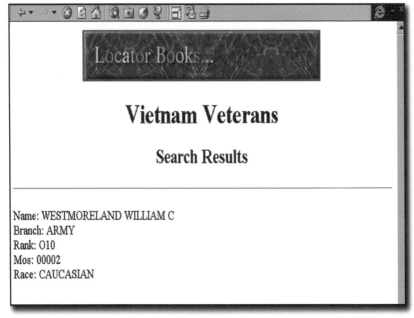

Sample of militaryusa.com search.

www.militaryusa.com

This Internet site has a searchable database of 2.7 million Vietnam veterans who served in Southeast Asia. It lists the name, rank, branch of service, and race. There is no fee to access this data. It's searchable by name.

www.fredsplace.org

This is a mega-site for former U.S. Coast Guard personnel,

and includes an e-mail directory of Coast Guard veterans. It gives the veteran's name, rank, component, place stationed or ship assignment, and years of service. Click on the name and it takes you to the e-mail address.

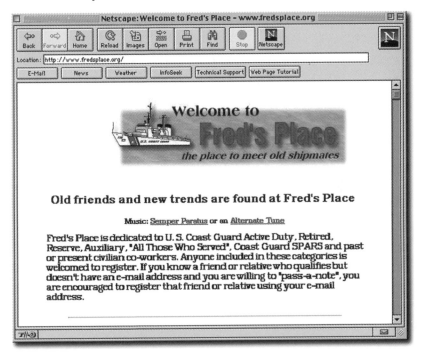

www.lonesailor.org

This is the site for the U.S. Navy Memorial Foundation. Their "Navy Log Online" lists present or former members of the sea services. The data includes the veteran's name, date of birth, hometown, rank, service dates, and branch of service. The most complete records even have a photograph. The number of veterans listed is close to 250,000.

How to Locate Veterans to Substantiate a VA Claim

To complete a VA claim, it may be necessary to locate other veterans you served with to get statements concerning old injuries or wounds. Follow the guidelines below:

Request copies of your entire military personnel file and medical records from the National Personnel Records Center. Do not mention "VA Claim" on your request for medical records. See Chapter 5 (Military Records).

Contact a Veterans Service Officer of an accredited national veteran's organization such as the American Legion, Disabled American Veterans, Veterans of Foreign Wars or AMVETS. They are trained professionals and can assist in obtaining rosters, ship muster rolls, or military records which can help back up your claim. There are no fees for their services and it's not required that you join their organization. See your local telephone book or check with the national headquarters. See Appendix D for a listing of veteran's groups.

Once you've received the unit rosters, prepare a letter to all personnel listed. Use the VA Records Processing Management Center to forward the letter for $2 per name. Ask them to respond in writing or via e-mail if they have any recollections of your injury. See Chapter 8 (Locating Veterans for a Reunion).

Contact the officers listed in the rosters. Check the various Officers Registers for date of birth or Social Security number. See Chapter 5 (Military Records). Use computer searches to locate their current whereabouts. See Chapter 12 (Computer & Internet Searches). Ask them if they have any memory of the incident.

Check with *www.vets.org* or *www.militaryusa.com* for reunion listings of your former group. Attend the reunion or publish an ad in their newsletter or magazine stating that you need to find people who served with you at a particular time.

Collect all the statements and military records and go back to the Veterans Service Officer. He should take it from there and assist you in processing your claim.

Chapter 5

Military Records

A record exists somewhere for every single person who was ever in the U.S. military. Simply because these records exist, the average person can solve difficult cases. A wide range of important identifying information can be obtained from a variety of military records, including personnel records, morning reports, unit or ship rosters, draft records, etc. Useful information in these records includes correct spelling of the name, middle name or initial, date of birth, hometown, duty station, etc. By accumulating these records, information is built up bit by bit until you find the person you're looking for.

Individual Military Personnel Records

Ways to request military personnel records:

1. Request copies of your own military record.
2. Request copies of your deceased relative's military record, stating that you're next of kin.
3. Request copies of another person's military record, asking for releasable information under the Freedom of Information Act.
4. Obtain a court order to access another person's military record.

Requests for records should be submitted using a Standard Form 180 (see Appendix H or "Standard Form 180," later in this chapter) or by typewritten letter if the form is not available. There is usually no fee for this type of request. It should be sent to the appropriate address listed later in this section.

Active Duty Military Personnel Records. It's possible to access releasable information from active duty records. However, be aware that this releasable information is different than what the National Personnel Records Center deems releasable in the records that they maintain. The armed forces do not release date of birth, official photograph, records of courts-martial, medical information, Social Security number or present address of active duty personnel. But they do consider the following data to be releasable from active duty records: name, rank or grade, duty status, date of rank, salary, geographic location of duty assignments, approved future assignments, source of commission (officers), military and civilian education level, promotion sequence number, military job code, and awards and decorations.

Air Force:

Active Duty, Temporary Disability Retired List, or General Officers Retired with Pay. (Also National Guard serving in the Air Force on Active Duty.)

Air Force Personnel Center
HQ AFPC/DPRP
500 "C" Street West, Ste. 19
Randolph AFB, TX 78150-4721

Army:

Active Duty Enlisted, or Temporary Disability Retired List for Enlisted. (Also National Guard serving in the Army on Active Duty.)

Commander USAEREC
Attn: PCRE-F
8899 E. 56th Street
Indianapolis, IN 46249-5301

Army:
Active Duty Officer, or Temporary Disability Retired List for Officers. (Also National Guard serving in the Army on Active Duty.)

U.S. Total Army Personnel
Command
200 Stoval Street
Alexandria, VA 22332-0400

Coast Guard:
Active Duty, Reserve, or Temporary Disability Retired List.

Commander CGPC-Admin 3
U.S. Coast Guard
2100 2nd Street, S.W.
Washington, DC 20593-0001

Marine Corps:
Active Duty, Selected Marine Corps Reserve, or Temporary Disability Retired List.

Headquarters, U.S. Marine Corps
Personnel Management Support Branch
(MMSB-10)
2008 Elliot Road
Quantico, VA 22134-5030

Navy:
Active Duty, Reserve, or Temporary Disability Retired List.

Bureau of Naval Personnel
Pers-313D
2 Navy Annex
Washington, DC 20370-3130

Retired, Discharged, and Deceased Military Personnel Records. All branches of the military send their records for retired, discharged or deceased military personnel to the NPRC. They are sent within three to six months after the member is separated from the service.

The NPRC will release name, rank or grade, duty status, date of rank, salary, geographic location of duty assignments, approved future assignments, source of commission (officers), military and civilian education level, promotion sequence number, military job code (or MOS), awards and decorations, date of birth, an official photograph (if available), dependent's names, sex and age, and a military service number. They *do not* give out Social Security numbers. Use the Standard Form 180 when requesting these records. See Appendix H.

Army, Air Force, Coast Guard, Marine Corps and Navy:

National Personnel Records Center
(Military Personnel Records)
9700 Page Avenue
St. Louis, MO 63132-5100
www.nara.gov/regional/stlouis.html

Private Researcher for NPRC Records. U.S. Locator Service (not affiliated with the government) can quickly obtain records from the National Personnel Records Center and the Army Reserve Personnel Center. All requests are properly prepared and hand-carried to the appropriate Center, thus assuring that records are received in the quickest manner possible. They can obtain Reports of Separation, and complete copies of personnel and medical records. This service is available only for those individuals who are requesting their own records, or for next of kin, if the veteran is deceased. See forms in the back of this book.

U.S. Locator Service
PO Box 2577
St. Louis, MO 63114-2577
(314) 423-0860 phone/fax
uslocator@earthlink.net

Standard Form 180. A sample of Standard Form 180 is available in Appendix H to copy. Copies may also be found at any state or federal veterans office.

The National Archives has implemented a fax-on-demand system for SF 180. Call from a fax machine and dial (301) 713-6905. Request document number 2255.

The following telephone numbers are message machines. Leave your name and address or send a written request by fax. A Standard Form 180 will be mailed.

Army	(314) 538-4261
Air Force	(314) 538-4243
Marine Corps & Navy	(314) 538-4141
Or request by fax:	(314) 538-4175 Fax

The National Personnel Records Center's Computer Index. The NPRC in St. Louis has a computer index database that contains names and ranks of approximately 70 million veterans who served since WWI. It's possible to request a listing by name citing the Freedom of Information Act. Information returned includes the last name, first name, middle name or initial, and branch of service; they will not release service numbers or Social Security numbers. This is simply because they can't easily distinguish which numbers are service numbers (which are releasable) and which are Social Security numbers (which are not releasable).

This can prove helpful when trying to determine if an individual actually served, or to obtain more identifying information such as a middle name or initial. It's not recommended for common names.

Various Military Rosters and Reports

There are several types of official documents that military units create, usually on a daily basis, to keep track of personnel and duty assignments. These include morning reports, unit rosters, deck logs, muster rolls, and unit diaries. These are all explained in more detail further in this chapter.

These documents can be the answer to many searches, especially if the complete name is not known. Once you have the person's full name and service number, you can request his military records and obtain a date of birth.

Anyone can obtain copies of unit rosters or ship's muster rolls by requesting them from the National Personnel Records Center, the National Archives, or the appropriate Armed Forces. If the roster is needed to support a Veterans Affairs claim, there is usually no charge. If not, records cost a minimum of $8.30 (deposit) an hour plus a search cost of $13.25 per hour. This charge is for all research other than VA claims. Requests for rosters or muster rolls specifically for reunion planning receive low priority and take more time to process. It's also possible to make a request citing the "Freedom of Information Act." In this case, there is no fee charged by the National Personnel Records Center or the National Archives. However, a small fee is still charged by the Armed Forces. See "Addresses" further in this chapter.

When submitting a request, you must specifically identify the type of document you want, clearly identify the unit or ship, and give the month and year you are looking for. Units should be identified by the company, battery or troop, and battalion or regiment (i.e., 46th Quartermaster Company; Company B, 127th Infantry, USS Enterprise).

Army Records

A *unit roster* contains a list of men and women who served in a military unit at a certain point in time. The rosters have the rank, last name, first name, middle initial, service number and sometimes a hometown.

```
MISCELLANEOUS
REPORT FORM                          ●              ●
                                                                         SHEET        (
                                                                                      OF      SHEETS
  SERIAL          NAME OF INDIVIDUAL        RANK  P  C ARM OR   SUB UNIT  PARENT UNIT  CURRENT COM. OR.          STATUS
  NUMBER                                    OR    L    SERVICE                         ENLISTMENT DATE  DUTY
                                           GRADE  S    OF       NO  TYPE  NUMBER  TYPE  GR   MO  YEAR    DESIG  DAY  MO  YEAR
                                                  T  N INDIVIDUAL

MONTHLY  PERSONNEL  ROSTER  AUG  31  1941
17TH  PUR  SQ  INT  4TH  COMP  GP
     FORT  STOTSENBURG

6772072KING  CLARENCE  J         M  SG  1AC  1708      406130639      7  7081

6833158KINDER  JAMES  W          1  SG  1AC  1708      406  91039      417081

6826235DAY  JACK  E              T  SG  1AC  1708      406  20640    1  5061
6827530MAROZAS  WILLIAM  B       T  SG  1AC  1708      406210141    1  5061
6802401WRIGHT  WILLIAM  R        T  SG  1AC  1708      406290639    1  5061

6832531ARLIN  MARTIN             S  SG  1AC  1708      406160839    1  5061
6731418BROWN  DOUGLAS  E         S  SG  1AC  1708      406  20839  7423071
6800800BROWN  JOHN  F            S  SG  1AC  1708      406  70840    1  5061
1160113CLAWSON  FLOYD            S  SG  1AC  1708      406280139    1  5061
6280719CANADY  BRUCE  T          S  SG  1AC  1708      406  41838    1  5061
6534085CARABIN  EUGENE  R        S  SG  1AC  1708      406120740    7  2071
6828281CHISM  FRANK  J           S  SG  1AC  1708      406161039    1  5061
6828888CACKLEY  JOSEPH  H        S  SG  1AC  1708      406130540    1  5061
6795737ELKES  FREDERICK  H       S  SG  1AC  1708      406  10740    1  5061
6550623FLYNN  JOHN  M            S  SG  1AC  1708      406270939    1  5061
6460729HOLEMAN  DAVID  E         S  SG  1AC  1708      406230141    1  5061
6831855HOLCOMB  ELLIS  J         S  SG  1AC  1708      406  41039    1  5061
```

Sample of Army unit roster from 1941. Important data includes service number, rank, name, date and place of report.

Morning reports were produced on a daily basis by Army and Air Force units to show any important changes in the availability or status of personnel. This would include initial assignment of a person to the unit, sick days, hospitalization, absence without leave, ordinary leave, killed, wounded or missing in action, change in rank or occupational code speciality, and reassignment out of the unit. Depending on the year, entries might show full name, rank and service number. These reports can be used to prove hospitalization, presence in a unit or location on a certain date, or in the absence of a roster, identify other members of a unit.

Note: Most Army organizations discontinued morning reports in 1974; some discontinued them in 1972 and others in 1980. Personnel Data Cards (DA Form 2475-2) replaced morning reports after that time. Then in 1987, Personnel Data Cards were discontinued. Now the Army's document for recording unit assignment is the Zero Balance Report. These reports are kept by the unit for one year and then retired to the National Personnel Records Center.

Army morning reports and personnel rosters from November 1, 1912, to 1974 are available from the National Personnel Records Center. All rosters from Army and Army Air Force units were destroyed for the years 1944, 1945 and 1946.

The Army Reserve Personnel Center has copies of unit rosters of Army Reserve units from 1917 to the present.

Army Staff Daily Journals, After-Action Reports and Operation Reports (lessons learned) for WWII, Korea and Vietnam are held at the National Archives at College Park, MD.

See "Addresses" further in this chapter.

Air Force Records

Air Force *morning reports* (see definition in previous section) from September 1947 to June 30, 1966, are available from the National Personnel Records Center. After that time, morning reports were discontinued for the Air Force. We've been unable to track how the Air Force kept up with units after that time. See "Addresses" further in this chapter.

Note: The Air Force never prepared unit rosters.

Navy Records

A *ship's muster roll* shows the rank, last name, first name, middle initial, and service number of all enlisted persons aboard a ship. A *ship's deck log* will usually list the officers assigned to the ship.

Navy muster rolls were for ships only, and include the names of enlisted members only. 1940–1967 muster rolls are available from the Textual Reference Branch of the National

Archives at College Park, Maryland. 1968 to present are available from the Naval Historical Center. Send to attention of Ship's Deck Log Section.

Navy deck logs contain a listing of all officers aboard a ship. Deck logs from 1940–1967 are available form the Textual Reference Branch of the National Archives at College Park, Maryland. Deck logs from 1968 to present are available from the Naval Historical Center. Send to attention of Ship's Deck Log Section. See "Addresses" further in this chapter.

Coast Guard Records

Muster rolls from 1914 to present for vessels, districts, lifeboat stations, miscellaneous units, and recruiting stations are available from the National Archives at College Park, Maryland. These show dates of enlistment, duty stations, changes in ratings, transfers, absences, surrenders, deliveries, separations, and leave.

War Diaries for Coast Guard units and vessels from 1942–1945 and *Personnel Rosters/Diaries* from 1915–1975 are available from the Washington National Records Center. These show location and status of personnel in Coast Guard units. See "Addresses" further in this chapter.

Marine Corps Records

The Marine Corps Historical Center holds Marine Corps *muster rolls/unit diaries* from WWI to 1965. The term "muster roll" changed to "unit diary" sometime after WWII. These documents show duty stations, dates of enlistments, dates received on board, changes in ratings, transfers, absences, surrenders, separations, deliveries, and leave.

The National Personnel Records Center has muster rolls and unit dairies from 1893 through 1977 on microfilm, and muster rolls for Reserve districts for 1948 through 1977.

The Marine Corps Headquarters, Unit Diaries Section, has unit diaries from WWI to present. Request muster rolls or unit diaries by stating a specific month and year. See "Addresses" further in this chapter.

National Guard Records

Rosters of National Guard units that served on active duty during WWII, in some cases, may be obtained form the appropriate state Adjutant General's office, state military historical office, state military museums, National Guard Association or from the appropriate military reunion organization. Rosters are also available from the National Personnel Records Center (except for 1944–46.) Refer to Appendix C (State-Held Military Records) or Appendix B (Directory of State Resources).

Addresses

Army Reserve Personnel Center
9700 Page Avenue
St. Louis, MO 63132

Marine Corps Historical Center
Washington Navy Yard
901 "M" Street, S.E., Bldg. 58
Washington, DC 20374-5040
(202) 433-3840
www.usmc.mil

Marine Corps Headquarters
Records Correspondence Section
2008 Elliot Road
Quantico, VA 22134-5030
www.mmsb.usmc.mil

National Personnel Records Center (MPR)
9700 Page Avenue
St. Louis, MO 63132-5100
www.nara.gov/regional/stlouis.html

National Archives and Records Administration
7th Street and Pennsylvania Ave, N.W.
Washington, DC 20408
(202) 501-5400
www.nara.gov/nara/dc/archives1_info.html

National Archives at College Park (Archives II)
8601 Adelphi Road
College Park, MD 20740-6001
(301) 713-6800
www.nara.gov/nara/dc/archives2_info.html

Naval Historical Center
Washington Navy Yard
901 "M" Street, S.E., Bldg. 57
Washington, DC 20374
(202) 433-2210
www.history.navy.mil

Washington National Records Center
4205 Suitland Road
Suitland, MD 20746-8001
(301) 457-7000, (301) 457-7117 Fax
www.nara/gov/records.wnrc

Selective Service System Records

Draft Registration Cards of men who registered for the draft under the Selective Service Act, and information from ledger books are available to the public. These records list name, date of birth, draft classification, date to report for induction, and in some cases, date of separation. Records were maintained from 1940 to 1975. These records are archived in various Federal Records Centers (by state and county). All requests for information must be made through the national headquarters. You may also check Appendix C (State-Held Military Records) for those records maintained at the state level.

National Headquarters
Selective Service System
1550 Wilson Blvd, Suite 400
Arlington, VA 22209-2426
(703) 235-2555, (703) 235-2212 Fax

Unit or Ship Histories

These types of historical records are usually not available from government sources. In most cases, a veteran or historian has written them using official government documents. However, they can provide an enormous amount of information that can eventually help locate a person. Histories for larger units can include a large amount of biographical background on a veteran; some even contain photographs.

Army and Air Force Unit Histories. James Controvich maintains the most comprehensive bibliography available concerning Army and Air Force unit and organization histories. His library has numerous references concerning army officers including Army Officer Registers and directories. He charges $10 to research a unit history or research an entry in one the Officers Registers. He can be reached most nights after 8:00 pm, Eastern Time. He also requests that authors and associations inform him when new histories are published.

James T. Controvich
97 Mayfield Street
Springfield, MA 01108-3535
(413) 734-4856

Ship Histories. The following company sells histories of all Navy and Army transports, and most Coast Guard and Liberty ships. They have partial, up-to-date crew rosters of the ships and have lists of sunken ships. Lists are free with purchase of a ship's history.

Seaweed Ship's Histories
PO Box 154
Sisterville, WV 26175
(800) 732-9333, (304) 652-1525 phone/fax
www.uss-seaweed.com

Military Historical Offices

The following list of military historical organizations can be of great help in providing unit and ship historical information. While most can't search for a specific person, they usually have names of unit and ship commanders, Officers Registers, key personnel, and other people who have been of some importance to a unit or ship. These people, if living, may be helpful in locating others.

Other data held by historical organizations include station lists, unit directories, and order of battle information. All of these can assist in determining the location of a ship or unit on a particular date, or provide a list of units or ships that were in a certain city or port on a certain date.

Air Force:

Air Force Museum Foundation
PO Box 1903
Wright-Patterson AFB, OH 45433
(513) 258-1218

Air Force Historical Support Office
500 Duncan Avenue, Box 94
Bolling AFB, DC 20332-1111
(202) 404-2264   *www.afhistory.hq.af.mil*

Air Force Historical Research Agency
600 Chennault Circle
Maxwell AFB, AL 36112-6424
(334) 953-2966   *www.au.af.mil/afhra*

Army:

U.S. Army Center of Military History
103 Third Avenue, Bldg. 35
Ft. Lesley J. McNair
Washington, DC 20319
(202) 685-2194
www.army.mil/cmh-pg

U.S. Army Military History Institute
Bldg. 22, Upton Hall
Carlisle Barracks
Carlisle, PA 17013-5008
(717) 245-3611
http://carlisle-www.army.mil/usamhi

Coast Guard:

Coast Guard Historian's Office
2100 Second Street, SW, Room 4601
Washington, DC 20593

Coast Guard Academy Museum
U.S. Coast Guard Academy
15 Mohegan Avenue
New London, CT 06320
Note: Unlike the other academy libraries, the Coast Guard
Academy library serves as the main library for the Coast Guard
and is willing to perform research for anyone.

Marine Corps:

Marine Corps Historical Center
Washington Navy Yard
901 "M" Street, SE, Bldg. 58
Washington, DC 20374-5040
(202) 433-3840
www.usmc.mil

Navy:
Naval Historical Center
Washington Navy Yard
901 "M"Street, SE, Bldg. 57
Washington, DC 20374
(202) 433-2210   *www.history.navy.mil*

National Guard Bureau
Historical Services
5109 Leesburg Parkway Freeway
Falls Church, VA 22041

Military Post/Base Libraries

Most large military installations have a library and perhaps a base historian. These can be of help in determining the
units stationed at that base at a certain time. It's possible they
have records such as unit histories, morning reports, muster
rolls, unit diaries, journals, and yearbooks. If the base is still
operating, see Appendix A (Directories of Military Installations) for a phone number. When calling, ask for the librarian
first. He will know if there's a separate base historian.

Other Military Libraries

U.S. Air Force Academy Library
5130 Community Center Drive
Colorado Springs, CO 80840

U.S. Coast Guard Academy Library
U.S. Coast Guard Academy
15 Mohegan Avenue
New London, CT 06320

U.S. Military Academy Library
U.S. Military Academy
757 Washington Road
West Point, NY 12990

U.S. Naval Academy Library
Nimitz Library
U.S. Naval Academy
589 McNair Road
Annapolis, MD 21402

Marine Corps Research Center Library
2040 Broadway Street
Quantico, VA 22134-5107
(703) 784-4348
www.mcu.quantico.usmc.mil

National Guard Association Library
1 Massachusetts Ave, N.W.
Washington, DC 20001
(202) 789-0031
www.ngaus.org

Pentagon Library
6605 Army Pentagon
Washington, DC 20310
(703) 697-4301
www.hqda.army.mil/library

Air Force Non-Commissioned Officer's Academy Library
481 Williamson Street
Maxwell AFB
Gunter Annex, AL 36114
(334) 416-3103
www.au.af.mil/au/aul/school/sncoa/academy.htm

Military Historians and Researchers

Following is a list of historians who can perform research for a fee. They may be helpful with unit histories, ship histories, or finding a list of units for a particular installation.

Air Force & Army:

James T. Controvich (see address later in this chapter)

Coast Guard:
Coast Guard Historian's Office
2100 Second Street, SW, Room 4601
Washington, DC 20593
(We could not find a private Coast Guard historian, so it's recommended that you send questions to the current Coast Guard Historian's office. They don't charge for their services.)

Marine Corps:
Dr. Jack Shulimson
2307 Haddon Place
Bowie, MD 20716
(301) 262-0956, jshulinson@aol.com
(This is a retired historian from the Marine Corps Historical Center. He was head of the Marine Corps History Writing Unit and Senior Vietnam Historian and is the author of many books dealing with the Marines in Vietnam.)

Navy:
Archival Research International
1539 Foxhall Road, N.W.
Washington, DC 20007-2067
(202) 338-4249, (202) 338-9134 Fax
www.militaryunits.com

Officers Registers

Military Officers Registers provide a variety of useful information about officers and warrant officers. These books were published every year or two by various branches of the service and include biographical data such as name, date of birth, and service number or Social Security number (depending on the year). They come under many different titles. When requesting these publications, ask for an Officers Register and specify the year. We've listed the various sources for these records, but it's first recommended that you contact your local government depository library first. The sources we've listed require a small research fee and requests should be submitted in writing.

Air Force. *U.S. Air Force Register: Annual List of Commissioned Officers, Active and Retired.* Includes service number (pre mid-1969) or Social Security number and date of birth. The Denver Public Library has the years 1949–1972, 1979, 1982 and 1984. See the end of this section for addresses.

Army. *U.S. Army Register.* Yearly lists of active, reserve and retired officers. Lists service number (pre mid-1969) or Social Security Number and date of birth. Pre-1969 active lists include date of birth and military training. Denver Public Library has years 1934–1953. James Controvich has years 1900–1972. Ft. Sam Houston Library has an incomplete set, missing several years during WWII. The San Antonio Public Library has a complete set dating from 1800 to present. See the end of this section for addresses.

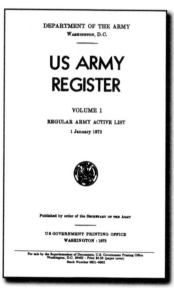

DEPARTMENT OF THE ARMY
Washington, D.C.

US ARMY REGISTER

VOLUME I

REGULAR ARMY ACTIVE LIST

1 January 1972

Published by order of the Secretary of the Army

US GOVERNMENT PRINTING OFFICE
WASHINGTON : 1972

For sale by the Superintendent of Documents, U.S. Government Printing Office
Washington, D.C. 20402 - Price $4.50 (paper cover)
Book Number 0821-0065

REGULAR ARMY ACTIVE LIST

NAME	SSN	BASIC BRANCH	TEMP GRADE	DATE OF RANK YR MO DA	BASIC PAY ENTRY DATE YR MO DA	PERM GRADE	DATE OF RANK YR MO DA	SOURCE OF COMM	BASIC DATE YR MO DA	CIV ED LEVEL	MIL ED LEVEL	DATE OF BIRTH YR MO DA
AXSON HARRY B JR		IN	1LT	71 11 05	70 07 30	2LT	70 11 05	05	70 11 05	5	7	48 09 20
AXTENS FRANK M B		MS	LTC	68 04 08	51 11 05	MAJ	67 10 22	07	53 10 22	5	5	29 01 07
AYALA ISAAC		MS	CPT	67 03 08	67 06 02	2LT	68 09 09	D5	68 09 09	2	7	40 03 20
AYCOCK DANIEL D		IN	2LT	71 06 09	71 05 16	2LT	71 06 09	85	71 06 09	5	7	47 10 14
AYCOCK HERBERT L			LTC	68 09 06	46 06 21	MAJ	65 10 27	07	51 10 27	8	6	28 03 03
AVEROI EVALT		MC	MAJ	69 09 10	64 02 21	CPT	68 12 25	D5	61 12 25	3	7	38 08 18
AYERS DONALD R		AR	1LT	71 09 23	70 06 06	2LT	70 09 23	81	70 09 23	5	7	47 11 11
AYERS DONNA M		AN	LTC	69 12 15	50 11 03	MAJ	68 04 30	D5	54 04 30	6	7	28 02 10
AYERS ROBERT E		EN	LTC	67 10 20	53 06 02	MAJ	67 06 02	A1	53 06 02	2	3	31 04 30
AYERS THEODORE F		SC	LTC	68 02 26	53 07 31	MAJ	68 07 01	0T	54 07 01	5	6	30 08 12
AYERS THOMAS D		IN	COL	70 06 12	49 09 21	MAJ	66 06 03	A1	52 06 03	2	3	28 01 30
AYERS THOMAS III		IN	MAJ	68 12 05	62 06 04	CPT	69 06 04	D2	62 06 04	5	6	39 11 10
AYKROYD ALBERT M		MI	COL	62 04 24	41 06 09	COL	69 01 01	07	41 12 07	5	5	16 05 13
AYKROYD DOUGLAS S		AR	CPT	71 07 15	69 06 04	2LT	69 06 04	A1	69 06 04	5	7	47 03 02
AYLOR ROBERT L		IN	CPT	69 01 08	67 01 08	1LT	70 01 08	D2	67 01 08	5	6	44 09 14
AYLWARD JAMES J JR		AG	LTC	71 10 15	57 06 04	MAJ	71 09 13	D5	57 09 13	5	6	34 04 11
AYLWARD JAMES J JR		AG	CW4	59 01 27	41 11 12	CW4	66 11 01	F6	61 11 01	8	4	13 12 15
AYOTTE RONALD J		IN	LTC	69 07 22	55 06 18	MAJ	69 08 13	0T	55 08 13	2	5	34 05 15
AYRES GLENN R		JA	CPT	68 06 07	65 06 12	2LT	69 03 07	81	65 03 07	5	6	37 03 02
AYRES HAROLD B		IN	COL	56 06 08	41 05 21	COL	66 12 07	07	41 12 07	2	3	19 01 25

(In the SSN column, vertically: *For privacy reasons, these SSNs have been erased for this book, but they appear in the actual Registries.*)

The cover of a U.S. Army Officers Register from 1972 (above) and a sample of the contents.

Coast Guard. *Register of Officers (Coast Guard)*. Published annually. Lists officers and warrant officers with date of birth and service number. Later editions include cadets at the U.S. Coast Guard Academy and list Social Security numbers. Best source for these publications is the Coast Guard Academy Museum or the Coast Guard Historian's Office. They have all years. See end of this section for addresses.

Marine Corps & Navy. *Register of Commissioned and Warrant Officers—Navy and Marine Corps and Reserve Officers on Active Duty—of the United States Naval Reserve; Register of Retired Commissioned and Warrant Officers, Regular and Reserve of the United States Navy and Marine Corps*. Annual lists that include service numbers (pre-1972) or Social Security numbers and date of birth. Denver Public Library has years 1910–1968, 1970–1974, 1976, 1978–1986 and 1991. See the end of this section for addresses.

Air National Guard & National Guard. *General Officers of the Army and Air National Guard*. Lists officers in the Air and Army National Guard Reserve and contains some biographical information. The National Guard Library has the entire set. The Denver Public Library has years 1953–1954, 1956–1959 for Air National Guard Registers. See below for addresses.

James T. Controvich
97 Mayfield Street
Springfield, MA 01108-3535
(413) 734-4856
*Research fee is $10. Contact him after 8 pm Eastern Time.

Coast Guard Academy Museum
U.S. Coast Guard Academy
15 Mohegan Avenue
New London, CT 06320

Coast Guard Historian's Office
2100 Second Street, S.W., Room 4601
Washington, DC 20593

Denver Public Library
Western History Genealogy
10 West 14th Avenue Parkway
Denver, CO 80204

National Guard Association Library
1 Massachusetts Ave, N.W.
Washington, DC 20001
(202) 789-0031
www.ngaus.org

San Antonio Public Library
ATTN: Government Documents
600 Soledad
San Antonio, TX 78205
*Requests a small donation to cover research costs.

Military Criminal Records

These offices handle criminal investigations for the military. Check with the appropriate office and ask what information is obtainable and releasable to the public.

Air Force:

Headquarters AFOSI
1535 Command Drive, Ste. C301
Andrews AFB, MD 20762-7001
(240) 857-9101

Army:

Department of Army
U.S. Army Criminal Investigation Command
6010 6th Street
Ft. Belvoir, VA 22060-5585
(703) 806-0431

Coast Guard:
Director
Coast Guard Investigative Service
4200 Wilson Blvd #740
Arlington, VA 22203
(202) 493-6600

Marine Corps and Navy:
Naval Criminal Investigative Service
Washington Navy Yard, Bldg 111
716 Sicard Street, S.E. #2000
Washington, DC 20388-5380

Courts-Martial Records

A variety of courts-martial records are available citing the Freedom of Information Act. Please check with the appropriate branch of service to see what records are available.

Air Force:
AFLSA/JAJM
112 Luke Avenue
Bolling AFB
Washington, DC 20332-8000
(202) 767-1539

Army:
Army Court of Criminal Appeals
Clerk of Courts
U.S. Army Judiciary
5611 Columbia Pike
Falls Church, VA 22041-5013
(703) 681-6780

Coast Guard:
U.S. Coast Guard Court of Criminal Appeals
ATTN: GL3
2100 2nd Street, S.W.
Washington, DC 20593-0001
(202) 267-0045

Marine Corps and Navy:
Officer in Charge
Marine Corps/Navy Appellate Review Activity
901 "M" Street, S.E.
Washington Navy Yard, Bldg 111
Washington, DC 20374
(202) 433-4651

Miscellaneous:
Criminal Investigation Division Agents Association, Inc.
3613 Concord Court
Augusta, GA 30906
www.onin.com/cidaa

Daniel E. White Investigations
2920 South Grand, Ste 154
Spokane, WA 99203
(509) 459-6904, (509) 459-6905 Fax
dannopi@aol.com
Mr. White is a former Army CID agent and retired from
the military in 1988.

Military Prison

Fort Leavenworth Prison houses 700 inmates from all
branches of the service. It will perform a search by name only.
In many cases, inmates legally change their name. In such
cases, the prison keeps a cross-reference file with both names
listed. Reason for incarceration and date of incarceration is
releasable; but date of release and date of parole are not. The

records are held at the prison for approximately 20 years and then turned over to the National Personnel Records Center in St. Louis, Missouri.

United States Disciplinary Barracks
300 McPherson Avenue
Ft. Leavenworth, KS 66027
(913) 684-4629

Chapter 6

Locating Women Veterans

Women veterans are usually more difficult to locate than their male counterparts because they often marry and assume a new last name. If the woman's current name is known, then you can locate her in the same way as male veterans. If you do not know the woman's new name, the search can be more difficult.

When trying to locate a woman veteran, it's very important to have as much identifying information as possible. Identifying information can include service number or Social Security number, complete date of birth or year of birth, branch of service, former unit or base assigned, rank, and former addresses.

Women Serving on Active Duty

Women who are serving on active duty in any branch of the military can be contacted using the armed forces World-Wide Locators. Chapter 1 (Locating Active Duty Military) has the addresses and information for all locators. Active duty women stationed in the United States can also be located using the Internet active duty military lists. One of these *(www.militaryusa.com)* has the capability to search using the first name only. So, if the current last name is not available, this is a great way to find it. Use other sources of identifying information such as branch of service, rank, home of record, and middle name to narrow the search.

Women Retired from the Military

Retired military women can be contacted using the armed forces Retired Locators (however, the Army Retired Locator is no longer operating). See Chapter 3 (Locating Retired Military). There are two websites for determining if a woman has retired from the military: *www.militarycity.com* and *www.militaryusa.com*. *Militarycity.com* has a list of those who retired since 1980 but does not include the Coast Guard. *Militaryusa.com* has the complete retired list, including Coast Guard, and can be searched by first name only and branch of service. Narrow the search by branch of service, rank, hometown, and approximate date of retirement. Remember, most retirees need 15–20 years of service to qualify for retirement.

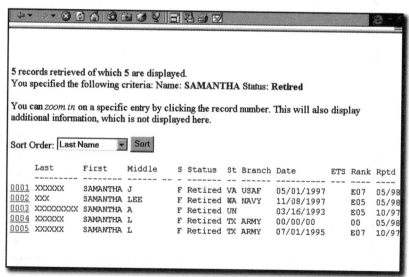

Example of a first name, retired military search for all branches of the service on www.militaryusa.com.

Using the Department of Veterans Affairs

The Department of Veterans Affairs (formerly the Veterans Administration) will probably have the woman's married name if she is receiving veterans benefits. They will be able to identify her using a maiden name, and Social Security number, military service number, date of birth, or Veterans Affairs claim number. If the Veterans Affairs counselor can identify her in the database, ask for her current name and the location of her file. She should live within 300 miles of the Veterans Affairs Regional Office that has her file, but only if she has a current file. With the current name or file location, check with directory assistance, or use one of the Internet telephone directories to search for a listed telephone number. Remember, the telephone might be listed in her husband's name, so search using only the last name.

★ **TIP**: If Veterans Affairs has a current file and address for her, they might not release any additional information. However, always ask them if they have a current address so that you may have a letter forwarded to her through their office.

Using the Social Security Administration

Women are required to let the Social Security Administration know of any name change. When this occurs, they are not issued a new Social Security number; their current number is updated. Therefore, they should be able to pull up information on a woman by her maiden name and her complete date of birth. If the maiden name if very uncommon, they might be able to use the name only.

When contacting the Social Security Administration, ask them if they have a report of death, or if they have a current file so you can have a letter forwarded. See Chapter 13 (Other Methods). It's against the Privacy Act for them to release personal information to you except report of death.

Women Veterans Who are Pilots, Lawyers or Doctors

Women who served in the military to become doctors, lawyers or pilots can be found using several easy methods. If they are still active duty, use the above listed sources to locate them. If by chance they have already left the service, and now are in private practice or flying for a commercial airline, there are several Internet sites that can locate them quickly. See the Internet section at the end of this chapter for more details.

Military Records

The National Personnel Records Center enters names of veterans into their index using the person's name when discharged (after separation from either active duty or the reserves). They will forward a letter to a woman veteran under certain circumstances. See Chapter 5 (Military Records) for details.

If you need more identifying information, such as a date of birth, it should be listed in the military records. Individual military records can be requested citing the Freedom of Information Act. However, you will need a name and military service number or Social Security number to acquire the records. The military records usually contain a date of birth which is considered releasable information. A name and date of birth can then be used to find her through the Social Security Administration, the Department of Veterans Affairs, or professional computer searches. See Chapter 4 (Locating Veterans), Chapter 12 (Computer & Internet Searches), and Chapter 13 (Other Methods).

★ **TIP**: Individual military records might be necessary to obtain more identifying information. However, they will take around 3–6 months to receive. Freedom of Information Act requests are considered low priority for the National Personnel Records Center. See a sample request form and Form 180 in Appendix H.

Officers Registers

One source of quick and easy information is the Officers Registers. These books were published yearly by each branch of the service. They include only officers and not enlisted personnel. Biographical information includes the full name, rank, Social Security number or military service number, schools attended, and date of birth. See Chapter 5 (Military Records) for more details and a list of where these Registers can be found.

Veterans Organizations

Hundreds of thousands of women veterans are members of major veterans organizations such as the Veterans of Foreign Wars, Disabled American Veterans, the American Legion, and others. These women can often be located through these organizations. See Appendix D (Directory of Military and Patriotic Organizations) for a list of major associations. Always ask these organizations if women are listed by their maiden or their married name.

Women's Memorials

There are two memorials honoring women who served in the military: Women in Military Service for America and the Vietnam Women's Memorial Project.

Women in Military Service for America (WIMSA)

The Women in Military Service Memorial Foundation seeks women veterans to include in its computer database. Authorized by Congress in 1986, the Memorial is located at the main entrance to Arlington National Cemetery, and includes a computer registry of 150,000 women to date. The database includes photographs of women in uniform with narratives of their most memorable experiences. They are registered by both maiden and married name and their hometown.

Please assist the Memorial by identifying women veterans for inclusion in the registry. The organization does not release the addresses of individuals registered with the Memorial, but can on a limited basis forward correspondence. There is no cost for this service, however, donations are accepted. For information on registration and how to donate:

Women in Military Service for America Memorial
    Foundation, Inc. (WIMSA)
5510 Columbia Pike Street #302
Arlington, VA 22204
(800) 222-2294, (703) 533-1155, (703) 931-4208 Fax
www.wimsa.org

Vietnam Women's Memorial Project, Inc.

On November 11, 1993, the Vietnam Women's Memorial Project dedicated the first memorial in the nation's capital honoring military and civilian women who served our country. The bronze statue portrays three women and a wounded male soldier, and stands near the wall of names at the Vietnam Veterans Memorial in Washington DC. Its quiet grace, strength, and dignity reflect that of the thousands of women who served during the Vietnam War.

This memorial welcomes home Vietnam women veterans. The project thanks women who throughout the ages have tended to the wounded, and provided support wherever and whenever they could. The project puts women veterans in touch with ongoing research on the after-effects of wars — sociological, psychological and epidemiological.

Their database contains 9,500 names of women veterans and civilians who served in Vietnam. They will forward letters on a limited basis. Contact them to register or make a donation.

Vietnam Women's Memorial Project, Inc.
2001 "S" Street, N.W., Suite 302
Washington, DC 20009
(202) 328-7253, (202) 986-3636 Fax
www.vwmp.org

Determining If a Woman Veteran is Deceased

Chapter 9 (Is a Veteran Deceased?) provides excellent information that pertains to women veterans. However, in many cases the current last name of a woman is not known. It's possible to search on the first name only, using the Social Security Death Index. Using the complete date of birth and the first name only, run this search on the death index, either on the Internet at *www.ancestry.com* or on CD-ROM (available at most libraries). If the name is common, you may receive a long list. If the first name is uncommon, your list will be much smaller. To narrow the list, it helps to know in which state the

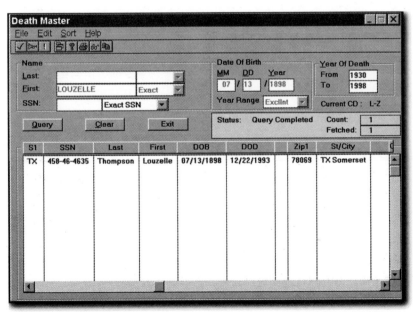

Result of Social Security Death Index search on CD-ROM, using first name and date of birth.

person was issued their Social Security number or in which state they died. Then obtain a copy of the obituary by contacting the local newspaper or library where the person died.

★ **TIP**: Don't forget to run the deceased woman's Social Security number through the Department of Veterans Affairs to see if they have her listed as a veteran.

Commercial Computer Searches for Locating Women

There are many computer search companies that can assist in your search. They subscribe to special computer databases that help locate people by using names, Social Security numbers, dates of birth or former addresses. However, some companies may be reluctant to do searches concerning women due to the recent rise in stalking crimes. Many of these companies are requiring the woman's permission before releasing any information to the public. Check with the company policy before pursuing a computer search for a woman.

A *date of birth computer search* uses a woman's first name and complete date of birth. The computer lists everyone in the database with a matching first name and date of birth. The report includes first name, last name, city, state, and date of birth, and may provide a street address and phone number. It's the most effective computer search to determine someone's current last name and address. This type of search can save hours of time and money. See Chapter 12 (Computer & Internet Searches).

★ **TIP**: If the first name is not very common, the search will give only a few matches. However, if the name is common, the results will be much larger.

Internet Sources for Locating Women Veterans

www.ancestry.com
Ancestry's website contains the Social Security Death In-

dex and is available free to the public. They give you the ability to do a "first name only" search, or a "first name and date of birth" search. When a complete date of birth isn't available, only uncommon first names will give useable results.

www.militaryusa.com

This site contains the active duty, reserve, and complete retired military databases. The active duty database lists only those serving in the U.S. and does not contain names for those serving overseas or in deployable units. All these databases can be searched by first name only. You must become a registered user and pay a fee to access this information.

www.militarycity.com

Active duty, reserve, and those who left the service since 1980 are listed on this website. However, you must use a last name to perform a search. Their veteran database lists those who have retired since 1980 or have had their terms expire. You must become a registered user and pay a fee to access this information.

www.ama-assn.org

Search for one of the 650,000 physicians licensed in the U.S. by using this American Medical Association site. It provides the physician's office location, office telephone number, gender, medical school, year of graduation, residency training, and specialty. It will tell you if she is board certified and if she is a member of the AMA. It has the option to search by first name only. No fee is required.

You can search by name or specialty. One possible problem: you have to specify a state. This means if all you have is a name, you'll have to search state by state if you don't already know which state she is in.

www.landings.com

The "landings" website is a mega-source of aviation information covering the U.S., Canada, and the United Kingdom. On this site you can do a search using the woman's first name. First, get into the site; then use their search engines to access the databases, and much more. This site has listings of over 600,000 pilots licensed by the FAA. No fee is required.

www.martindale.com or *www.wld.com*

These are the Martindale-Hubbell Lawyer Locator and West's Legal Directory sites to find lawyers and law firms. Search by the person's name or law firm. Information returned includes firm name, type of practice (sole practitioner, etc.), business address, telephone/fax numbers, year of birth, undergraduate school and law school attended, type of law practiced (family, criminal, etc.), and a list of business partners. It covers the entire United States and many foreign countries. You have the option of searching by first name only. No fee is required.

Chapter 7

Verifying Military Service

Millions of veterans served with valor and distinction, and their service is an essential underpinning of the freedoms we enjoy today. But thousands of people make false claims about their military service. If you have any reason to doubt a person's claim to military service, this chapter can help you find out the truth.

Skepticism can arise because an individual boldly claims to have received awards for valor, been promoted to an unusually high rank, or have been assigned to a special unit such as the Navy Seals or Special Forces. Sometimes they say they were involved in secretive operations. The usual story is that these missions and jobs were so highly classified that no verifiable record exists. Occasionally, someone will claim to have been a prisoner of war. Considering the suffering experienced by real POWs, this is one of the ugliest lies a person can tell.

Most veterans and retired military personnel speak of their accomplishments with a mixture of pride and appropriate discretion. It's usually the fakes who are braggarts.

Why would apparently reasonable people make false or exaggerated claims? Many want to impress girlfriends, family, friends, coworkers or members of veterans organizations. Others seek VA benefits such as disability compensation, education benefits, medical treatment in VA hospitals, or admission to VA nursing homes. Some make false claims about their service to gain civil service hiring preferences for federal and state jobs. Others want the personalized license plates available to Purple Heart recipients. At least one person posed as a veteran so he could be buried in a national cemetery.

So how do you verify that a veteran is telling the truth or is qualified for the job he or she has applied for? How do you check out and expose the phonies? All of the methods and connections you need are in this book. There is some information that cannot be obtained from military records because of national security concerns, but these cases are few and far between.

Before you begin to search for information, you will need the person's:

- legal name
- service number and/or Social Security number
- branch of service
- date of birth (if possible)

Verifying Active Duty Military Service

Several options are available for determining whether or not someone is currently serving in the Air Force, Army, Coast Guard, Marine Corps or Navy. These options include the World-Wide Locators, the Internet, and base/post locators.

If you have the person's legal name, branch of service, Social Security number or date of birth, the World-Wide Locator for the appropriate branch of service will verify his active duty status within seven to 10 days of receiving your written request. If the person is serving within the United States, the World-Wide Locator will also provide you with the current unit of assignment. If the individual is serving outside the U.S. or is in a deployable unit or ship, the locator will only provide verification of active duty status. There is a $5.20 fee for written verification for all branches. See Chapter 1 (Locating Active Duty) for addresses of World-Wide Locators.

Using Internet Sources to Find Active Duty Military.

www.militaryusa.com and *www.militarycity.com*

To use the databases in these websites, you must register and pay a fee. There are listings for the Air Force, Army, Navy and Marine Corps. Coast Guard information is available for active duty but may be limited for retired military. Data shown includes name (with complete middle names listed when known), home of record, date of entry, estimated date of discharge, rank, date of rank, and military assignment (which includes the installation and unit assigned).

Using Base or Post Locators. If you suspect a person is stationed or serving at a particular military base, you may speed things up by contacting that installation's base or post locator and asking if the individual is stationed there. If the person in question has a common name, the locator will need a Social Security number or more underlying information such as rank or date or birth.

When you're unsure of the name of the base but know the city or region where it's located, find the bases in that area by referring to Appendix A and contact each one.

Verifying Retired Military

We have seen many cases of people falsely claiming to be retired from the military. Most military retirees served 15 to 20 years in order to qualify for a pension and other retirement benefits. It's not difficult to check an individual's retired military status. You can contact the appropriate retired military locator (there is one for each branch of service), the retired pay center (again, one for each branch) or check the Internet (see below). If a person served in the reserves, he will not be placed on the retired list until age 60. Please read Chapter 3 (Locating Retired Military) for additional information.

To use a retired military locator or pay center, you need the person's legal name and Social Security number, or name and date of birth. If the name is unusual, the name only may be enough. Otherwise, your best options are the Internet sites.

Using Internet Sources to Find Retired Military.

www.militaryusa.com and *www.militarycity.com*

Militaryusa's website contains the name, rank, branch of service, date of retirement, and home of record. Information for all branches is available except Coast Guard. Militarycity has a database of people who have left the service since 1980 and that includes those who retired. These databases do not contain Social Security numbers or dates of birth.

Verifying Veteran Status

For the purposes of this chapter, a veteran is an individual who at some time served in the military, but not for the number of years required to achieve retirement status. When a person leaves the service, it's called "separating from service." The date he left is the "separation date."

Verifying whether or not a person is a veteran is not as simple as verifying active duty or retired status. There is no database that contains a list of the 70 million veterans who served since WWI. It's extremely important to have as much identifying information as possible. If a person claims military service in WWII, Korea or Vietnam, a military service number may be needed. There are several avenues you can use to verify military service, including the Department of Veterans Affairs, military records, Officers Registers, Internet sites and veterans organizations.

Using the Department of Veterans Affairs. The VA's mission is to serve veterans. It is not a locator service, nor is it set up to verify information for the general public. Nonetheless, the records of millions of veterans are entered into the VA's database, and the information in these records is extremely useful in verifying possible military service. Veterans who served before 1974 are listed if they have used or applied for any type of veteran's benefits. Veterans who served between 1974 and the present are listed in the VA's files, even if they never applied for benefits.

It's possible to access some of this information, but you must know the right questions to ask. If you call and ask to verify a person's military service, you will be told, "Sorry, we can't help." If, on the other hand, you request a report of death or ask the VA staff to check for a file so that a letter may be forwarded, you may learn whether an individual did serve in the armed forces and whether he is likely to be alive. Keep in mind that if there is no information available on someone who served prior to 1974, it does not mean that the person in question is lying about being a veteran. It simply means that person may not have applied for benefits.

To contact the VA, call (800) 827-1000. This number will connect you with the closest Regional Office. For a list of Regional Offices, see Appendix B (Directory of State Resources).

Obtaining Military Records of Veterans. The most conclusive way to verify a claim of military service is to obtain the person's military file. By citing the Freedom of Information Act, you can get the file from the National Personnel Records Center. You must have enough identifying information so that the NPRC can determine for sure that there is or isn't a record. Necessary information includes name, service number or Social Security number, or name and date of birth. However, due to the fire at the NPRC in 1973, some records were burned.

If the records were burned, keep searching — there are other documents such as unit rosters, morning reports, and VA records that can substantiate military service. See Chapter 5 (Military Records). See FOIA form in Appendix H.

At minimum, you must provide a name and date of birth. If the individual served at any time from WWII until the late 1960s, a military service number may be needed. After the late 1960s, a Social Security number is required. Only releasable information will be sent to you. Releasable information from military records includes:

- Name
- Rank/grade
- Duty status (active, retired, etc.)
- Date of rank
- Military service number
- Date of birth
- Dependents (including name, sex and date of birth)
- Gross salary
- Locations of duty assignments
- Future assignments (approved)
- Source of commission (for officers)
- Military and civilian education level
- Promotion sequence number
- Awards and decorations
- Official photograph (if available)
- Record of court martial trials (unless classified)
- City/town and state of last known residence
- Date of last known residence
- Places of induction and separation

Social Security number, medical information, and present address are not considered releasable information.

To request a person's military records, complete Standard Form 180 and state that this is a "Freedom of Information Act" request. See Appendix H for Form 180 and example of request. These requests are low priority for the NPRC and may take 3 to 6 months for a response. Mail the form to:

National Personnel Records Center
9700 Page Avenue
St. Louis, MO 63132

Other Military Records. The military keeps numerous files, logs and reports. Many of these are available to the public and can be used to verify military service. Please see Chapter 5 (Military Records) for detailed information on acquiring unit rosters, ship muster rolls, morning reports, unit histories, yearbooks, cruise books, ship's logs, order of battle information, and troop lists.

Internet Sources for Verifying Veteran Status. There are quite a few military and veteran registers available on the Internet. Registers can be found for all wars and for many major battles. However, please use caution when using these registers. Not all of them require proof of service when registering.

www.amervets.com
The American War Library has put together a database of current and former military personnel that contains 21 million names. Their data is received from veterans, family members or a variety of other sources and can be searched to verify military service. They do require a discharge paper for their verified records. A verified record has a color-bar or service medal ribbon showing that military service was checked.

www.militarycity.com
This is the only Internet site containing veteran information, and it lists more than 10 million names of those who have left active duty since 1980. It's searchable by name, branch of service, and rank. Social Security numbers and dates of birth are not available.

www.militaryusa.com

This database contains the names of more than 2.3 million people who served in Southeast Asia during the Vietnam War. It's not 100 percent accurate, but is excellent for verifying claims of Vietnam service when used in conjunction with other resources. You can only search by name, so if the name is common it's difficult to know if you have the right person.

Officers Registers. Prior to 1981, each military branch published detailed biographical information on officers and warrant officers. If you are searching for information about someone who claims to have been an officer prior to 1981, these published logs, which were published annually for active duty, reserve and retired officers, can be extremely useful. Editions published before 1968 contain name, rank, military service number, date of birth, colleges and universities attended and some assignment information. Later editions (1968–80) list name, rank, Social Security number, date of birth and other service data. Please refer to Chapter 5 (Military Records) for information on how to find these Registers.

Military Academies. Verification of graduation from any of the military academies is easily available. Contact the Office of the Registrar at the appropriate institution and ask whether or not the person in question is a graduate. There are also yearbooks available for each graduating class. Once you learn the year of graduation, you may contact the academy library for further information. Academy addresses and phone numbers are as follows:

U.S. Air Force Academy
Colorado Springs, CO 80840
(719) 333-1110
www.usafa.af.mil

U.S. Coast Guard Academy
New London, CT 06320
(860) 444-8444
www.cga.edu

U.S. Military Academy
West Point, NY 10996
(914) 938-4011
www.usma.army.mil

U.S. Naval Academy
Annapolis, MD 21402
(410) 293-1000
www.nadn.navy.mil

Special Forces and Elite Military Organizations. Many "fake" veterans claim outrageous accomplishments, including being part of the elite Navy Seals or Special Forces. Here are a few resources that can be used to check out these claims.

The Navy Seal Museum has a complete list of all those who completed Navy Seal training.

UDT/Seal Museum
3300 N. A1A
Ft. Pierce, FL 34949
(561) 595-5845

Radix Press compiles the names of those who served in Special Forces units in Southeast Asia. The names are gathered from military records. Although this list is not 100% accurate, it may provide some assistance.

Radix Press
2314 Cheshire Lane
Houston, TX 77018
(713) 683-9076

Special Forces Association
PO Box 41436
Fayetteville, NC 28309-1436

U.S. Army Ranger Association, Inc.
PO Box 52126
Ft. Benning, GA 31995-2126
www.ranger.org

Air Commando Association
2502 W. Highway 98
Mary Esther, FL 32569
http://home.earthlink.net/~aircommando1

U.S. Marine Corps Force Recon Association
3784-B Mission Avenue #1775
Oceanside, CA 92054
www.clearpages.com/forcerecon

Summary. If your investigation reveals that the person in question has lied to you, be careful to not confront him with your proof. The situation could become dangerous.

Our experience with these cases is that even when shown data refuting a claim, the individual frequently says the records were destroyed because the missions were so highly classified. Do not let this sway you. This is most likely a last-ditch effort to maintain his story. There should be some record of military service. There are *very* few missions or operations so highly classified that no record of military service exists.

Chapter 8

Locating Veterans for a Reunion

There are approximately 7,000 military reunions held every year in the U.S. Although the majority are WWII reunions, Korea, Vietnam and even other military eras are now being represented.

The most difficult part of any reunion is finding the people. This chapter outlines and emphasizes the necessary steps for locating veterans for reunions. However, it should be used in conjunction with the rest of the book.

Steps for Reunion Planners

Military service numbers were used as identifying numbers by all branches of the military until the late sixties and early seventies. After that time, Social Security numbers were used. Don't confuse these two numbers; they are separate numbers, issued by two different government agencies. It's not possible to derive a service number from a Social Security number.

We mention this because finding veterans using Social Security numbers is much easier than finding them using service numbers. This is because Social Security numbers are in almost all databases, not just military-related databases. In fact, it's wise to obtain Social Security numbers from all those in your group who have been "found." That way it's easier to keep track of them in case they move without notifying you.

It may be a daunting and somewhat "hopeless" job to find *every one* of the veterans assigned to a particular unit or ship. But it *is possible!* Through the years, we have worked with reunions groups, small and large, to help with this task. The 11th Armored Cavalry's Veterans of Vietnam and Cambodia located over 16,000 of their former members in three years. Several WWII groups have located all of their members, even though it's much more difficult to locate veterans using only name and military service number.

We've outlined here the most important steps and methods to use when searching for large numbers of veterans for a reunion. Remember to use this chapter in conjunction with the other chapters that go into more detail.

First and Foremost: Who's in Charge?

Someone has to be in charge of locating people. This person should have very good organizational skills because it's very important to keep track of the various steps that have been used to find someone. Don't waste time and money performing the same searches over and over again. We suggest that one person be in charge and then break out a list of 20 names or so and farm those out to others in the group. But it should be the main responsibility of the "General" (person in charge) to keep a master listing.

Locating people can get expensive. Using this book will save time and money, and hopefully prevent some mistakes, but don't think that finding every one for the upcoming reunion is solely your financial responsibility. The reunion group should fund this effort in some manner.

Ready, Set, GO!

Now that you have your committee organized, money and this book in hand, lets go to work. We will list the appropriate steps for locating veterans who served using service numbers as well as those who served using Social Security numbers.

Rosters

Rosters are the key elements. Obtain a unit roster or ship muster roll from the National Personnel Records Center, National Archives, or appropriate military service. See Chapter 5 (Military Records). Rosters contain the name, rank and service number of all members. However, the Army rosters from 1944, 1945, and 1946 were destroyed. For those years, create a roster from morning reports. See Chapter 5 (Military Records). Combine these reports to accumulate a "master list" with legal names, service numbers, and ranks. Make additional columns for addresses, dates of birth, dates of death, and places of death so this information can be entered as it is received.

★ **TIP**: For those who served with Social Security numbers instead of service numbers, the unit rosters or ship musters contain the name, rank and Social Security number of enlisted and sometimes officers assigned to that unit or ship on the date the document was prepared. However, the Social Security number will be marked out. Occasionally the marking can be removed to reveal the number.

Who Has Passed Away?

It may be difficult to discover that a military buddy has died, but if the reunion is WWII era, this should be one of the first steps taken. Use the Social Security Death Index, war casualty databases, and the Department of Veterans Affairs to find out which individuals have passed away. Although, it's much easier to search the Death Index using a Social Security number, it's also searchable by name and approximate age. If any possibilities match, cross check the Social Security number and date of birth against the Veterans Affairs records. Send your list to the Department of Veterans Affairs. They will notify you which veterans are deceased (see later in this chapter.) Make note of the deceased veterans in your master database. See Chapter 9 (Is a Veteran Deceased?).

National Telephone Directories

Go through your master list and pull the names that are relatively uncommon — not "Smith," "Jones," or "Johnson." Now use the National Telephone Directories on the Internet or on CD-ROM and check these names. If the person's complete name doesn't appear, then search using the last name only. For an unusual last name, contact some of the people listed; it's possible they could be related and would know the whereabouts of the veteran. See Chapter 12 (Computer & Internet Searches).

Officers

Search your master database for a list of officers. Acquire entries for the officers from the appropriate service's Officers Registers. The data should include their name, rank, date of birth, and service number or Social Security number. See Chapter 5 (Military Records).

Retired Military

Have the Retired Locator of the appropriate branch of service forward letters to individuals who have retired. Or use *www.militarycity.com* or *www.militaryusa.com* to access retired military data. See Chapter 3 (Locating Retired Military).

Reserve Military

Is it possible that any of the veterans stayed in a reserve component? If so, check with the appropriate reserve locators or use the Internet databases at *www.militarycity.com* or *www.militaryusa.com*. See Chapter 2 (Locating Reserve and National Guard).

Check with each individual who has been found to see if he knows addresses or locations of other missing members. Ask them to search their own files, footlockers, scrapbooks, and letters for any military orders. Orders (unit orders, reassignment orders, orders for promotions, awards, etc.) are valuable because they contain the correct spelling of the names, service numbers, and may have Social Security numbers listed. Have your group's members send in copies and enter these into the master list.

If you know the city and state where the veteran entered the service, contact the postmaster, newspaper, mayor, historical organizations, veteran organizations, churches, schools and reunion groups of that city or town and ask if they have the current location of the veteran or his family.

Some of the individuals you are trying to locate may belong to veterans organizations such as Veterans of Foreign Wars, Disabled American Veterans, The American Legion, AMVETS, The Retired Officers Association, Non-Commissioned Officers Association, Fleet Reserve Association, Marine Corps League, etc. Headquarters for these associations can only search by name but the local posts can be a better source of information. These are smaller groups and would be more familiar with their own rosters. See Appendix D (Directory of Military and Patriotic Organizations).

Contact any appropriate high school, college or university alumni associations. Ask if they will forward a letter announcing the reunion. Be sure to include on the announcement that the veteran should respond even if not planning to attend the reunion. This way you can be sure to include them on your master list as "found."

Military Records

For those veterans on your master list who have common names and have only service numbers (not Social Security numbers), request their military records through the Freedom of Information Act. These military records contain a complete date of birth. However, this process can take up to six months. Keep in mind that some records were burned in the 1973 fire at the National Personnel Records Center, the repository for these military records. Once you receive dates of birth, use the other methods listed to find out their current location or if they have died. See Chapter 5 (Military Records).

Computer Searches

At this point you should have found the majority of the people. To find the rest, call in a professional searcher who has access to proprietary computer databases. These searches can be performed using a name and date of birth, a name and Social Security number, or sometimes a name and approximate age. Searches are expensive and that's why they shouldn't be your first choice. When requesting price information from private investigators, researchers, or locator services, let them know that it's for a reunion and how many names are to be searched. Quantity discounts may be available. See Chapter 12 (Computer & Internet Searches).

Using the Department of Veterans Affairs

From your master list, pull the remaining names, ranks, and service numbers or Social Security numbers. Make a print out of this information to send to the Department of Veterans Affairs, following the instructions listed below.

The Department of Veterans Affairs Records Management Center is located in St. Louis, Missouri, and is responsible for researching large groups of veterans. Their policy states that they will forward letters to veterans for reunion notification or to secure statements substantiating veterans disability claims. They can work from copies of unit rosters, ship's muster rolls, or computer lists that contain names and service numbers or names and Social Security numbers. This service is open to the public, not just to veterans.

☆ **TIP**: Don't confuse the Department of Veterans Affairs Records Management Center with the National Personnel Records Center. Although they are both located in St. Louis, Missouri, they are separate agencies.

There are two ways to acquire information from the Records Management Center. One is a "request for information" and the other is to "have letters forwarded." The two methods are explained below.

For either method, prepare from your master list a separate list that includes the name, service number or Social Security number, branch of service and rank (if available). This is the sheet that will be sent to the VA Records Management Center. If a service number or Social Security number is not available for a particular veteran, they suggest including the date of birth or place of entry into the service (city and state). If the name is unique, then name only is sufficient.

For ten names or less there is no fee charged. For over ten names, send a check for $2 per name made payable to the "Department of Veterans Affairs."

Request for information. The Records Management Center will research the names and provide the following data:

• VA file number or VA claim number
• Folder location (the VA Regional Office that has the file)
• Veteran deceased (will provide date of death, if available)
• No record (VA can't identify the veteran)

The information will be returned to you along with instructions on how to have letters forwarded to veterans through the Records Management Center.

Have letters forwarded. The other avenue to utilize the services of the VA Records Management Center is to send letters, list of names, identifying information and payment together. Request that they research the names and forward the letters. This process usually takes about four weeks. They will let you know which letters were forwarded and which names could not be found. If a letter is returned to the center as undeliverable, you will not be notified.

Dept. of Veterans Affairs, Records Management Center
PO Box 5020
St. Louis, MO 63115
(314) 538-4500

News Releases

Some people may be found if they simply respond to an article or notice about the reunion in a newspaper or magazine. It's extremely important to get information about your reunion into print.

Prepare a good news release or reunion notice. Make it brief, but be sure to include your organization, branch of service, the war or period of time, name, address and telephone number of the reunion organizer, date and place of the reunion. Send reunion notices or news releases (at least 6 months in advance) to all appropriate veterans organizations and request that they be published in their magazines, bulletins or newsletters. See Appendix D (Directory of Military and Patriotic Organizations).

Continue advertising the reunion:

• Have members send news releases to local newspapers.

```
            101st Mess Kit Repair Battalion
                    555 Nowhere Street
                 Sometown, USA 22222-2222
                    U.S. Army  - WWII
```

For Immediate Release
Contact: John S. Doe, (555) 555-5555

The United States Army (WWII) 101st Mess Kit Repair Battalion will hold its first reunion on September 5, 2003, at the Waldorf Astoria Hotel in New York City. Former members, widows, children, or relatives are asked to contact John Doe, Reunion Organizer, at 123 Maple Street, Anytown, USA 11111, (555) 555-5555.

```
                    - End -
```

Sample press release.

- Use specialty advertising such as bumper stickers, T-shirts, baseball caps, badges, etc., which show your organization, telephone number, and date of reunion.

- Post a page on the World Wide Web advertising your reunion. Link the site with as many military and veterans organizations as possible. Put notices of your reunion on computer bulletin boards.

- Use the websites listed for the large veteran's organizations listed in Appendix D (Directory of Military and Patriotic Organizations).

- Check with *www.usmc.mil/reunions*

Veterans Electronic Telecommunication Service (VETS)

VETS is an organization that maintains a database on over 15,000 military reunions. Search reunion listings on their Internet site or register an upcoming reunion. There's no charge for either service.

VETS
PO Box 901
Columbia, MO 65205
(573) 474-4444 (recording)
www.vets.org

National Reunion Registry

The National Reunion Registry is a means of publicizing military reunions and conventions. Their database currently contains over 7,300 organizational listings. Each listing shows the unit name; name, address, telephone number of the reunion planner; and the date and location of the next reunion. There's no charge for reunion planners to register or update information about their planned or proposed reunions. Entries and updates can be sent in by mail, fax, or on the Internet at *www.militaryusa.com*.

National Reunion Registry
PO Box 17118
Spartanburg, SC 29301
(864) 595-0813 Fax
www.militaryusa.com

Reunions for Grenada, Panama, Bosnia and the Persian Gulf War

If you were involved in any of these military activities or have friends or relatives who were, preparation for a future military reunion should be done now. Don't wait until 50 years have gone by to start looking for people and planning a reunion. Start making preparations by creating a master list and gathering information. Send out postcards asking if the veterans would be interested in a reunion, and if so, when. Use the steps listed in this chapter to help start the process.

Summary. Military reunions are a great time for friends to get together and reminisce. Veterans who served together, especially in wartime, establish special bonds. We know that preparing and planning a military reunion offers many challenges, but those who have been through this experience tell us that reunions are some of the best times they have ever had. Good luck and here's to 100% attendance.

Chapter 9

Is a Veteran Deceased?

Verifying that a veteran is deceased is not difficult and can save you time if you're searching for an older person, or for someone who served during a war and you're not sure if he survived that war. The Department of Veterans Affairs, the Social Security Administration, and military casualty offices all have excellent records pertaining to deceased veterans.

When a person dies, the family, the funeral home, or certain government offices are responsible for reporting the death to the Social Security Administration. If the person is a veteran, the Department of Veterans Affairs is usually informed. However, keep in mind that this is not done 100% of the time.

There are now many ways to determine if a veteran is deceased. In this chapter we explain all available sources as well as how to contact the next of kin of a military casualty.

Using the Social Security Administration

The Social Security Administration is usually very helpful when asked if a person has died. Contact them at (800) 772-1213 or your local office. Furnish a name and complete date of birth. It's also helpful if you have the names of the person's parents but this isn't always necessary. If they can locate the person in their records, they will release the date of death and place where benefit payments were sent. With this information you can look for a copy of the obituary from the local library or newspaper. The Social Security Administration has information on all individuals, not just veterans.

Social Security Death Index. This database is a listing of over 60 million deceased, as reported to the Social Security Administration. It's available on CD-ROM (try your library) and on the Internet (*www.ancestry.com*) and is one of the best sources to check for death information. The database contains last name, first name, Social Security number, date of birth, date of death, and the place where Social Security sent death benefits. However, a person is not listed if benefits were not sent. *One disadvantage of this file is that it doesn't contain middle initials.*

Using the Department of Veterans Affairs

When searching for a veteran of any age, it's always a good idea to check with the Department of Veterans Affairs. They do *not* have all deceased veterans listed in their files, but it's a free resource and can sometimes solve a search quickly.

When contacting Veterans Affairs, ask them to check their records for a report of death. They will ask for the person's name and military service number or Social Security number. Give them all available information. If they can identify the person in their records, and they *do* have a report of death, ask them for the date of death, place of death, and place of burial. Contact the Department of Veterans Affairs at (800) 827-1000.

★ **TIP**: If you've found a possible match on the Social Security Death Index and want to find out if that person is a veteran, call Veterans Affairs to have the name and Social Security number run against their files. Ask the counselor for a report of death for this person. If you know the middle name, ask if it's the same in their files. The Social Security Administration is also helpful in verifying a middle name. This can be extremely important if the person has a common name such as "John Smith."

Veterans Who Died During Wars

If you're searching for a someone who served in the military during wartime and haven't heard from him since, it may be a good idea to check the various wartime casualty databases. These databases contain name, rank, branch of service, date of casualty, place of casualty, and some include hometown and date of birth. These are available from a variety of sources, including the Internet (see the Internet section and other sources later in this chapter).

WWII Casualties. Over 400,000 Americans died during WWII. In 1946, the War Department and the U.S. Navy Department published listings of men and women who were killed in action, died of wounds, or lost their lives as a result of WWII. The War Department's publication is entitled the

The cover of the WWII Honor List of Dead and Missing for the state of Illinois and a sample of the contents.

World War II Honor List of Dead and Missing. The Navy Department put out two publications: The *State Summary of War Casualties* and *Combat Connected Casualties, World War II.* See below.

World War II Honor List of Dead and Missing. The inclusive dates for these books are May 27, 1941, to January 31, 1946, and include only Army personnel. Each book covers one state and is then organized by county. However, there is an alphabetical index by name in the back of each book. The book includes last name, first name, middle initial (and Jr. or Sr., if applicable), military service number, rank, and type of casualty (KIA = Killed in Action, DOW = Died of Wounds, DNB = Died Non-Battle).

State Summary of War Casualties (broken down by state) and *Combat Connected Casualties, World War II* (two volume set: Alabama–Montana and Nebraska–Wyoming). These books list those

State Summary of War Casualties

[ILLINOIS]

U. S. NAVY
1946

KILLED IN ACTION, DIED OF WOUNDS, OR LOST LIVES AS RESULT OF OPERATIONAL MOVEMENTS IN WAR ZONES

A

ABBOTT, William Edwin, Aviation Machinist's Mate 3c, USN. Mother, Mrs. Lillian Dell Abbott, 1306 North University, Peoria.

ABEL, John Henry, Torpedoman's Mate 1c, USN. Parents, Mr. and Mrs. John Carl Abel, 545 South Spencer St., Aurora.

ABRAHAMSON, Alexander Julius, Motor Machinist's Mate 2c. USNR. Mother, Mrs. Mary Jane Abrahamson, 4449 W. End Ave., Chicago.

ABRAHAMSON, Chester Elmer, Boatswain's Mate 1c, USN. Mother, Mrs. Anna Abrahamson, 1008 West State St., Geneva.

ABT, John Bernard, Pvt, USMCR. Parents, Mr. and Mrs. Charles Abt, 8630 South Aberdeen St., Chicago.

ADAMS, Malcolm, Radio Technician 1c, USNR. Mother, Mrs. Eunice Adams, 3758 North Wayne Ave., Chicago.

ADAMS, Richard Lee, Seaman 2c, USN. Mother, Mrs. Dorothy May Adams Piscus, 2012 South 13th St., Lawrenceville.

ADAMSON, Harold Arthur, Seaman 2c, USN. Aunt, Mrs. Rosa Adamson, 1224 East Leefland Ave., Decatur.

ADEN, Gene J., Cpl, USMCR. Father, Mr. Herman Aden, 125 Franklin St., East Peoria, Peoria.

AEBY, Jack W., Sgt, USMCR. Wife, Mrs. Jack W. Aeby, 1845 South Kedzie Ave., Chicago.

AGRIMONTI, Louis, Electrician's Mate 2c, USNR. Parents, Mr. and Mrs. Henry Agrimonti, 6235 So.

ALLAN, Arthur M., Jr., Pvt, USMCR. Parents, Mr. and Mrs. Arthur M. Allen, Sr., 200 East 7th St., Pana.

ALLEN, Clifford Edward, Seaman 1c, USN. Mother, Mrs. Laura Allen, 1943 North Larabee Ave., Chicago.

ALLEN, David R., Pvt, USMCR. Wife, Mrs. David R. Allen, 411 Bryan Ave., Danville.

ALLISON, Harry Jones, Aviation Radioman 3c, USNR. Parents, Mr. and Mrs. Royce Allison, Box 105, Chester.

ALLISON, Hugh R., Pvt, USMC. Father, Mr. William Allison, 908 Madison St., Lockport.

ALLSOP, Charles Everett, Pfc, USMCR. Parents, Mr. and Mrs. Charles E. Allsop, Gen. Del., Cowden.

The cover of the **State Summary of War Casualties** *for Illinois (above) and a sample of the contents.*

persons who died while on active duty in the Navy, Marine Corps, and Coast Guard from December 7, 1941, to 1946. They do not include deaths in the United States or deaths which were not attributable directly to the war. They contain those killed in action, died of wounds, or lost lives as a result of operational movements in war zones. Included are last name, first name, middle name, job assignment, rank, branch of service, next of kin's name, and address.

The above books are available from some state historical societies; see Appendix B (Directory of State Resources). The complete set of all 48 states is available from the New York Public Library. Send your request in writing to:

New York Public Library
Center for the Humanities Reference Department
5th Avenue & 42nd Street
New York, NY 10018-2788

★ **TIP**: If you know the home state of the person, have the state library or state historical society check the above mentioned books to see if the person died during WWII. If the state is not known but the service number is, see Appendix G (Military Service Numbers) to determine where he entered the service from. Then search that state (and nearby states) for casualty information.

Korean War Casualties. Approximately 54,000 Americans died during the Korean War, 1950–1957.

The Korean Conflict Casualty File is available on the Internet, Center for Electronic Records or military casualty offices. See ahead in this chapter for information.

The Korean War Casualty File – U.S. Army contains 109,975 records of Army personnel killed or wounded during 1950–1953. There are 27,727 records of those who died during those years. Another 82,248 records are of Army personnel that sustained non-fatal injuries.

Vietnam Veteran Casualties. Over 58,000 Americans died as a result of the Vietnam War. *The Vietnam Veterans Casualty File* is available on the Internet, from the Center for Electronic Records, or from military casualty offices (see ahead in this chapter). The database contains name, rank, date of casualty, branch of service, and date of birth.

Desert Storm Casualties. Three hundred sixty-two men and women died during Desert Shield/Desert Storm from 1990–1991. *The Desert Shield/Desert Storm Casualty File* contains the last name, first name, middle name, rank, branch of service, date of casualty, if the death was due to hostile or nonhostile means, place of casualty, sex, and city/state the veteran was from. This is available from *www.militaryusa.com* and from military casualty offices (see ahead in this chapter).

The Center for Electronic Records.

This department of the National Archives has several military casualty reports:

• The Korean Conflict Casualty File.
• The Southeast Asia Combat Area Casualties File.
• The Korean War Casualty File – U.S. Army.
• The Casualty Information System File. This file contains records of casualties suffered by all U.S. Army personnel and their dependents from 1961 to 1981. Extracts of records for all U.S. Army active duty personnel who have died are available.
• The Vietnam Veterans Casualty File

Center for Electronic Records
National Archives at College Park
8601 Adelphi Road
College Park, MD 20740-6001

(301) 713-6845, (301) 713-6911 Fax
www.nara.gov/nara/electronic
The archives will search for three names without a charge.

Locating Next of Kin of Military Casualties

Names and addresses of next of kin are included in all military casualty reports. However, you must be the next of kin to obtain a complete casualty report. Anyone who is not related must request these records citing the "Freedom of Information Act" in which case the names of next of kin and other restricted information will be withheld.

Presidential Libraries

Presidential libraries may have copies of correspondence sent to the family members of a veteran killed during a war. We have included below the presidential libraries of the Presidents who served during WWII, Korean, Vietnam, and the Persian Gulf Wars.

Franklin D. Roosevelt Library (World War II)
511 Albany Post Road
Hyde Park, NY 12538-1999
(914) 229-8114, (914) 229-0872 Fax

Harry S. Truman Library (Korean War)
500 West U.S. Highway 24
Independence, MO 64050-1798
(816) 833-1400, (816) 833-4368 Fax

Dwight D. Eisenhower Library (Korean War)
200 S.E. 4th Street
Abilene, KS 67410-2900
(785) 263-4751, (785) 263-4218 Fax

John F. Kennedy Library (Vietnam War)
Columbia Point
Boston, MA 02125-3398
(617) 929-4500, (617) 929-4538 Fax

Lyndon B. Johnson Library (Vietnam War)
2313 Red River Street
Austin, TX 78705-5702
(512) 916-5137, (512) 478-9104 Fax

Nixon Presidential Materials Staff (Vietnam War)
National Archives at College Park
8601 Adelphi Road
College Park, MD 20740-6001
(301) 713-6950, (301) 713-6916

George Bush Library (Persian Gulf War)
701 University Drive, East, Suite 300
College Station, TX 77840-9554
(409) 260-9552, (409) 260-9557 Fax

American World War II Orphans Network (AWON)

The American World War II Orphans Network is an organization of sons and daughters of WWII casualties and an
orphan registry. At present they have over 1500 orphans listed
in their database. They provide a locator service to assist orphans, war buddies, and family members to find each other.
This is a nonprofit organization, and registration in their database is free. Send a self-addressed, stamped envelope when
making inquires. Ann Mix, the director, is the author of *Touch-
stones: A Guide to Records, Rights and Resources for Families of
American World War II Casualties*. It can be ordered from AWON
for $19.95.

This Network also has a complete list of WWII casualties.

They will perform a search for a $10 fee which offsets labor costs. Their data includes the name, rank, service number, race, home of record, and burial site. Over 400,000 names are in the database.

American World War II Orphans Network (AWON)
PO Box 4369
Bellingham, WA 98227
(360) 733-1678, (360) 715-8180 Fax
www.awon.org

Locating Family and Friends of Deceased Vietnam Veterans

The Vietnam Veterans Memorial Fund operates "Healing Connection" which assists people who are searching for someone who died in the Vietnam War. There are no fees for this service.

Vietnam Veterans Memorial Fund
1020 14th Street, N.W. #201
Washington, DC 20005
(202) 393-0090, (202) 393-0029 Fax
www.vvmf.org

★ **TIP**: If the name of the veteran is uncommon, use one of the Internet Telephone Directories and search using only the last name. Any matching name could be a relative.

Military Casualty Offices

Air Force:
HQ AFPC/DPWCS
550 "C" Street West, Suite 14
Randolph AFB, TX 78150-6001
(210) 652-5514

Army:
Army Casualty & Memorial Affairs Operation Center
Total Army Personnel Command
TAPC-PED
2461 Eisenhower Avenue
Alexandria, VA 22331-0482
(703) 325-5300

Coast Guard:
Commandant (HSC)
U.S. Coast Guard
2100 2nd Street, S.W.
Washington, DC 20593

Marine Corps:
Headquarters, U.S. Marine Corps
Manpower & Reserve Affairs, MRC
3280 Russell Road
Quantico, VA 22134-5103
(703) 784-9512, (703) 784-9823 Fax
*WWII to present

Navy:
Navy Personnel Command, NPC-621
Casualty Assistance Branch
Millington, TN 38055-6210
(800) 368-3202
*WWII to present

Locating Grave Sites of Veterans Buried Overseas

The American Battle Monuments Commission provides names of 124,914 U.S. war dead of World War I and World War II who are interred in American burial grounds in foreign countries. They also provide the names of over 94,000 U.S. servicemen and women who were missing in action, lost at sea, or buried at sea during both world wars.

American Battle Monuments Commission
Courthouse Plaza II, Suite 500
2300 Clarendon Blvd.
Arlington, VA 22201
(703) 696-6900, (703) 696-6666 Fax
www.abmc.org

Locating Grave Sites of Veterans Buried in the Department of Veterans Affairs Cemeteries

The National Cemetery System of the Department of Veterans Affairs provides limited genealogy services and burial location assistance to the next of kin of deceased veterans. They can research records to determine if a veteran is interred in one of the Veterans Affairs National Cemeteries. You should provide the full name of the veteran, date and place of birth, date and place of death, the state the veteran entered the service from, rank, and military unit. Write to:

Director for Technical Support
National Cemetery System
Department of Veterans Affairs
810 Vermont Avenue, N.W.
Washington, DC 20420
(202) 273-5226, (202) 273-6697 Fax

War Memorials

World War II Memorial
Courthouse Plaza II, Suite 501
2300 Clarendon Blvd.
Arlington, VA 22201
www.wwiimemorial.com

Korean War Veterans Memorial
National Parks Service
900 Ohio Drive, S.W.
Washington, DC 20024-2000
(202) 485-9880

Vietnam Veterans Memorial
1012 14th Street, N.W., #201
Washington, DC 20005
(202) 393-0090, (202) 393-0029 Fax
www.vvmf.org

Internet Sites for Locating Death Information

www.ancestry.com
The Ancestry website has the Social Security Death Index, casualty databases for the Korean and Vietnam Wars, and databases of newspaper obituaries. The Military Records section, which includes the casualty lists, isn't free. You must become a registered user and pay a fee.

The Social Security Death Index is searchable by name only, name and date of birth, or Social Security number. Ancestry gives a searcher the option to send a letter directly to the Social Security Administration requesting the person's original Social Security card application. There is no charge to access the Death Index.

www.nara.gov/nara/electronic
This National Archives Center for Electronic Records website has available at no charge the Korean and Vietnam War casualty lists. The list is by state, and includes the name, rank, hometown, place of death, date of death, date of birth, and type of casualty.

www.no-quarter.org
This site has the most detailed information of all Vietnam casualty lists. It contains the usual information such as name,

rank, etc., but also includes religion, military service number or Social Security number, marital status, reason for casualty, length of service and tour dates. There is no fee to access this database.

www.execpc.com/~dschaaf/mainmenu
Over 1,100 Navy and Marine Corps personnel died aboard the USS Arizona on December 7, 1941. A list of the dead is available on this website. The data contains the last name, first name, middle name, rank, branch of service, and home of record. No fee is charged.

www.militaryusa.com
This a searchable database of the Desert Shield/Desert Storm casualties. Both hostile and nonhostile deaths are included in this list. It does not contain Social Security numbers. There is no charge to access this information.

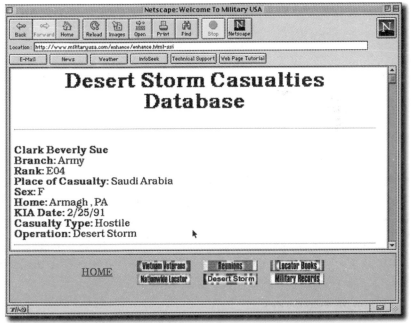

Desert Storm Casualty Database entry on www.militaryusa.com.

Summary: It's always difficult to find out that a friend or loved one has died. But in many cases, perhaps due to age, checking death records should be the first course of action because it can save a lot of time in the long run. With the information given in this chapter we have hopefully made this task easier. When trying to verify a veteran's death, remember that it's very important to have as much identifying information as possible. Sometimes this information must be pieced together from various sources.

Chapter 10

Locating Birth Parents Who Served in the Military

We get hundreds of phone calls each year concerning what is often the most emotionally charged inquiry: the search for birth parents. This type of search is traumatic by nature, especially if the circumstances surrounding the birth were complicated by war. To ensure a successful search, it's important that emotion take a back seat to a logical research process. This chapter offers a detailed look at what information will be necessary as you move through this process.

Although the majority of cases we've seen involve a birth father who has served in the military, we've taken a few cases involving birth mothers. Both situations are discussed in this chapter.

First and foremost, gather all important identifying information available about the birth parent. This should include a legal name (with the middle name or initial), the place and time period where stationed, the branch of service (if known), the date of birth or approximate age, the state of origin, the rank/grade (enlisted or officer), the person's race, a physical description, the military service number or the Social Security number. Use the individual data worksheet available on pages 266–67 to help keep track of your information. In searches for birth parents, it's vital to gather every scrap of information, whether you initially deem this information to be relevant or not. Information may be obtained from adoption agencies, hospitals, doctors, attorneys, friends, family, neighbors, and anyone who may have had contact with the birth parents. Sometimes a small bit of information may be the very thing it takes to solve a case. Records must be searched, and newspaper files are often helpful. Try to find old letters, photographs, phone and address books, medical information, old copies of military orders, pictures of the person in military uniform, etc.

Locating the birth parent of someone who was placed for adoption may at first seem like an impossible task, but this is not always true. Numerous birth parents with military connections have been located with the use of the information in this book.

Records exist for every person who has been in the service. Individual military records show when and where a person was assigned, as well as other identifying information. Most of these records are retrievable, and most may be located through the National Personnel Records Center, the Department of Veterans Affairs, state archives, state historical societies, military and civilian libraries, historical organizations, and military reunion organizations. These records consist of unit rosters, ship muster rolls, Officers Registers, morning reports, ship's logs, troop lists, unit year books, photographs, cruise books, or unit or ship's histories. All of these are excellent sources of information. There are also military records listing where units were stationed, ship homeports, and where the ships traveled.

There is a special office in the National Personnel Records Center that will assist individuals searching for a birth parent if the name of the veteran, location, unit or ship assigned is known. This office will search organizational and individual records to obtain service numbers, dates of birth, and last known address. For assistance, write:

Director
National Personnel Records Center
9700 Page Avenue
St. Louis, MO 63132

Birth parents have been located with information as sketchy as just a first or last name. In other cases, birth parents have been located without a name but with the knowledge of other important facts: maybe a unit, ship, military base, rank, military job, old letter, name of friends, etc. Birth parents with common names (Joe Smith, for instance) have been located in a relatively short period of time because other important information was used.

Each birth parent search is different and there is no set pattern or course on how to proceed with any particular search. Persistence is the most important factor. There is always information, but it may take many attempts to obtain it. Never give up. If you persevere, you will ultimately find the person.

Locating a Birth Parent Who Is on Active Duty

"Active duty" means that the person is still serving in the military. Each of the World-Wide Locators will provide a current unit of assignment if the person is stationed in the U.S. If the person is stationed overseas or in a deployable unit (such as a ship), the locator will only forward a letter. Active duty military lists are also available on the Internet at *www.militaryusa.com* and *www.militarycity.com* for a fee. See Chapter 1 (Locating Active Duty Military).

If your query concerns child support, contact your local county child support agency and ask them to send (on their letterhead) a request for unit assignment to the appropriate military locator. It's also possible to acquire a written verification of active duty status in such a case.

Locating a Birth Parent Who Is Retired Military

It's probable that by the time a child starts looking for a birth parent, the parent has served enough time to have retired or left the service. Remember that military personnel must serve anywhere from 15 to 20 years of active service to retire from the military. Those who have retired from a reserve component will not show up on the retired list until age 60. They can usually be found by contacting the reserve locator or the retired locator. See Chapter 3 (Locating Retired Military) and Chapter 2 (Locating Reserve and National Guard.)

To locate a person who is retired from the military, contact the specific Retired Military Locator or use the Internet retired military list at *www.militaryusa.com*. If the person retired since 1980, check *www.militarycity.com*.

Locating a Birth Parent Who Is a Veteran

This is the most common case we see. Often, a person who was stationed overseas or stateside and fathered a child, eventually left the service. This can make it more difficult to find the person because the military does not know where he is currently living or possibly even if he is still living. But obtaining more information about the person from their military records or other documents can solve these cases.

Military Records

Here we'll discuss military records that can be used to help identify a birth parent. We'll disclose where to obtain these records and how they can be used in a search. Military records are so important in many birth parent cases because they can give you the correct spelling of a name, a military service number or an exact date of birth. All of this can eventually lead to the person's current whereabouts.

Unit or Ship Rosters and Morning Reports. The most important type of military documents are those that contain identifying information. Unit or ship rosters and morning reports contain name, rank and service number. Rosters and morning reports need to be requested for a specific month and year. Be aware that sometimes the older reports are on microfilm and can be of poor quality. It may be smart to request reports from a month before until the month after the date actually needed. See Chapter 5 (Military Records).

Individual Military Personnel Records. Once you've obtained a complete name, rank and service number or Social Security number, you may need to request the person's personnel record from the National Personnel Records Center to acquire a date of birth. A date of birth is considered to be releasable information from the military records held at the NPRC in St. Louis. However, a date of birth is not releasable for active duty personnel.

Using the Department of Veterans Affairs. The Department of Veterans Affairs has in its computer files listings of veterans who have applied for benefits, if they served before 1974. For veterans who served after 1974, the VA has them listed even if they never applied for benefits. The VA is not a locator service, but it will forward a letter to a veteran if the veteran has a current address. Some information held by the VA, including a claim number or military service number, is releasable. Try calling your local VA Regional Office at (800) 827-1000. Ask them first if they have a report of death on the person. If they can pull up the person in their records and there is no record of death, ask them to forward a letter. Or use the VA Records Processing Management Center in St. Louis to acquire more information on the veteran. See Chapter 8 (Locating Veterans for a Reunion).

☆ **TIP**: You may want to be cautious about forwarding letters if searching for a birth parent. If the veteran does not respond then you'll never know if the letter was received or not.

Internet Searches

A wealth of information is available on the Internet, and much of it can be accessed at no charge. If you don't have access to a computer, use the Internet connection at your local library. Run name searches on the various Internet telephone directories (a reference librarian can help with this task if you are unsure how to proceed). If the veteran is a doctor, lawyer or pilot, be sure to check applicable sites for any available listings. See Chapter 4 (Locating Veterans). Most of the large military and veterans associations have websites, and some even have searchable databases of members. See Appendix D (Directory of Military & Patriotic Organizations).

Professional Searchers

If you've done all your homework and found all identifying information for the veteran and you're still not close to finding his current whereabouts, it may be time to call a professional researcher who has access to commercial computer databases. The charges can run from $50 to $200. Make sure you've tracked down as much information as possible. The more identifying information you have on the person, the less money a professional searcher will charge. If the military connection is very strong (if you're searching, for instance, for someone who is retired from the military), make sure you use a searcher who specializes in military cases.

Is He Deceased?

If a veteran served during a war, always check the available casualty lists. It's a free and easy step to take. It's often harder to access WWII casualties than to locate similar lists for Korea, Vietnam or the Gulf Wars. See Chapter 9 (Is a Veteran Deceased?) for more information. If you're searching for a WWII veteran who survived the war, check the Social Security Death Index on the Internet at *www.ancestry.com*. This database is for all people, not just veterans. If you're seeking an older veteran, this is always a smart place to begin.

Birth Mothers

The majority of searches we encounter are for birth fathers, but on occasion we work a case involving a birth mother who served in the military and gave up her child for adoption. This type of case poses a unique set of problems, not the least of which is that the woman might have married and changed her name. But it's possible to track down the right person using military records and computer searches.

As is the case with other searches, it's important to obtain all available identifying information, including where she was stationed, rank, complete name, branch of service and approximate age. We have solved cases using only a first name, approximate age and branch of service, but in each of those cases, the first name was quite unusual. The more common the first name, the less likely you are to find someone using only that name.

Use the Internet military databases if the woman is still serving on active duty, is in the reserves, has retired from the military or has left the military since 1980. If by chance she married before leaving the service, her new last name may be listed in one of these databases. It's possible on some databases to do searches using only a first name. Check out websites at *www.militaryusa.com* or *www.militarycity.com*. If a complete date of birth is known along with a first name, do a first name and date of birth computer search, or use the same information to check the Death Index on *www.ancestry.com*. Refer to Chapter 12 (Computer and Internet Searches) and Chapter 9 (Is a Veteran Deceased?)

Read through this chapter carefully and refer to Chapter 6 (Locating Women Veterans) for detailed information specifically on women.

A Sample Case

A woman in her late thirties contacted us to find her birth father. Her mother was Italian and met her American father while he was in the Army and stationed in Naples. The daughter had only the identifying information given to her by her mother: the father's first and last name, his approximate age, his physical characteristics, his branch of service, and the unconfirmed fact that he said he was from Georgia.

We began the search and found several names that met all the identifying information. The daughter contacted several of the men and asked if they were in Naples in the Army in 1955. She didn't tell them she was looking for her father. Each of these men said either that they weren't in the service or that they served in a different branch. With all possible names crossed out, we had to go back to step one. We needed to acquire a military document to give us more information. We requested a unit roster from the National Personnel Records Center. Although this took some time, it was the key we needed to solve this case. Right there in black and white was the correct spelling of the name: it had only one "n" and not two as the daughter thought. A quick computer search using his name and approximate age supplied us with his current address and telephone number.

She was careful how she approached him when she made first contact. But we are happy to say that all is well and he was very glad to hear from her after so many years.

Of course, not all such stories end with wonderful reunions. Some birth fathers simply deny that they were in the right place at the right time. Military records can usually verify this information without a problem. But even after records are obtained, some birth fathers still deny any relationship ever existed.

The clients we hear from who want to find their birth parents usually want some type of closure, need medical information or just want to know who their parents are. Some seek this knowledge because they've always wondered, and some because they would like information about health problems that may be hereditary. Each case is quite different, and we've seen many different results. We strongly suggest weighing all your thoughts and emotions before embarking on this type of search. Be ready for any kind of reaction. Once you have made these considerations, we wish you the best in your search.

Chapter *11*

Family Histories for Veterans

Families should be extremely proud that one or more of their ancestors served in the military, either during war or peacetime. Researching their military background is a fun and rewarding experience. In this chapter we give you resources and avenues for information that can be used to prepare a family history. Most of the methods discussed in this chapter are brief. Chapter 5 (Military Records) is mentioned throughout this chapter since these records will be the basis for acquiring the information you need.

The following steps are recommended when preparing your family history. These are in addition to normal genealogical research. If you have any difficulty obtaining information, you should contact a professional genealogist who specializes in military records.

First and foremost, gather all identifying information available for the person: complete name, date of birth, date of death, place of birth, what state the person resided in, race, etc. Use the Individual Data Worksheet in Appendix H as a guide.

If you're not sure if a relative ever served in the military, run his identifying information against the Veterans Affairs files, or check the National Personnel Records Center Index. See Chapter 5 (Military Records) for more details.

Request copies of the veteran's military personnel and medical records from the National Personnel Records Center. If the veteran is deceased, you must show proof of death and proof of relationship for the records to be released. The National Personnel Records Center will release complete records only to the next of kin. See Chapter 5 (Military Records). If the veteran served in more than one branch of the service, you must prepare separate requests for each branch.

If records are received back from the National Personnel Records Center, make note of the units, ships, or base assignments. Then request all available unit or ship rosters, unit or ship histories, muster rolls, after action reports, daily staff journals, deck logs, morning reports, and daily journals. If his military records were destroyed in the 1973 fire at the National Personnel Records Center, then these records (which were not destroyed) may help reconstruct some portions of his military service. See Chapter 5 (Military Records).

Check with the National Reunion Registry (see end of this chapter) for a reunion of an organization or ship with which your relative served. Attend the next reunion and talk with those who served with him. Larger reunion groups may have a newsletter where you can place an ad requesting information about your relative. See Chapter 5 (Military Reunions) and Appendix E (Directory of Military Reunion Associations).

Make a list of all the bases where he was assigned. Check against the current list of U.S. military bases and overseas installations. If the base is still open, write a letter addressed to the base historian. Request any historical information about your relative and his unit. There might be some record of him or his unit in the base history, although the chances are better if he was a high-ranking officer. See Appendix A (Directories of Military Installations).

If he ever served as an officer in any branch of the military, check the Officers Registers. They have biographical information, rank, date of birth, military service number or Social Security number, promotion dates, civilian and military schools attended, and awards and decorations received. See Chapter 5 (Military Records).

✭ **TIP**: Most Officers Registers list only regular officers, not reserve officers. Most officers serving in WWII were reserve officers and therefore not listed in these Registers.

If your relative was wounded or killed while on active duty, request from the appropriate military casualty office a copy of the casualty report. See Chapter 9 (Is A Veteran Deceased?). The complete casualty report is only released to next-of-kin.

If your relative was killed in Korea, Vietnam or the Persian Gulf War, obtain a copy of the record from the appropriate Internet war casualty database. Be sure to submit information about the veteran to the correct war memorial. Don't forget about the women's memorials. See Chapter 9 (Is a Veteran Deceased?) and Chapter 6 (Locating Women Veterans).

If your relative was a prisoner of war, acquire copies or excerpts from databases and records kept by the National Archives. The Center for Electronic Records also has data on prisoners of war. See the Internet section in Chapter 9 (Is a Veteran Deceased?).

Did your relative attend one of the military academies? These are the U.S. Military Academy, the U.S. Coast Guard Academy, the U.S. Air Force Academy, and the U.S. Naval Academy. If so, contact the appropriate academy historian and request all releasable information, including yearbooks and photographs. See Chapter 4 (Locating Veterans).

Check with military and patriotic organizations to see if he was a member. See Appendix D (Directory of Military and Patriotic Organizations). If so, ask which post he belonged to and speak directly with other members to learn additional information.

Determine the location or burial site in military cemeteries, Veterans Affairs cemeteries, or overseas American burial grounds. See Chapter 9 (Is a Veteran Deceased?).

Request a copy of his obituary from the local newspaper or library near where he died. Research military newspaper files for articles mentioning your relative.

Internet Sources for Locating Family History Information

www.ancestry.com

Ancestry.com is mentioned several times throughout this book and is a great resource for genealogical information. Ancestry is a company dedicated to genealogy. Their military records section contains many types of military files. Although this book focuses on WWII to present, Ancestry has military records dating back to the Revolutionary War. You must be a registered user and pay a fee to access the military records section of *ancestry.com*.

www.nara.gov/nara/electronic

The National Archives and Records Administration's Center for Electronic Records contains many files pertaining to veterans. Below are a few that may be of interest in preparing a family history.

Korean and Vietnam War Casualty Files. These are the casualty databases for Korea and Vietnam. Refer to Chapter 9 (Is a Veteran Deceased?) for other sites with these lists.

Repatriated American Prisoner of War File. This prisoner of war file contains 122,390 records. It includes the name, military service number, dates of capture and release, prisoner of war camp, date of birth, date of death, period of service, branch of service, dependency information, and days incarcerated. Due to the Privacy Act, certain data is not released.

U.S. Military Personnel Returned Alive–WWII European Theater and *U.S. Military Personnel Returned Alive–WWII Pacific Theater.* There were 85,541 prisoners of war in the European Theater returned alive during WWII, and 19,202 were returned from the Pacific. These files include the name, military service number, grade, branch of service, date reported lost, race, state of residence, date returned to military control, place of detention, if prisoner was on a Japanese ship that sank, or if he died in transport.

www.militaryusa.com
This website run by the National Reunion Registry has a

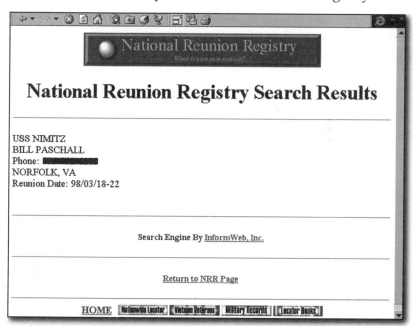

Example of a military reunion listing from the National Reunion Registry at www.militaryusa.com

database of over 7,000 military reunion groups. There's no charge to access this data.

Summary: If you have a question concerning your family history, contact your local county or state genealogical society (see Appendix B). We have hopefully given you many avenues to add military documents, background, and photographs to your family history for those relatives that served in the United States military at any time since WWII.

Chapter 12

Computer & Internet Searches

Chances are that every person in this country is listed in some computer database somewhere. So if you're looking for someone, the question is how to gain computer access. There are two ways: do it yourself or hire someone else to do it. The "do it yourself" method involves looking through CD-ROMs (which you can buy or use for free at the library) or using the Internet (which has some free information but mostly has proprietary databases that require registration and payment). Hiring a professional will cost more per search but will allow access to some high-powered databases that only professionals can subscribe to. We suggest doing as much work as you can by yourself and then hiring a professional.

National Telephone Books on CD-ROM or the Internet

Computer CD-ROMs are much like music CDs, but instead of music they store volumes of text information. More than 100 million names along with addresses, phone numbers and other information can fit on about five disks. National telephone books on CD-ROMs can be found in many computer software stores or through mail-order software companies found in computer magazines. They can cost as little as $80 but the "pro" versions cost up to $250 and are more highly recommended. Many public libraries stock one or more of these CD sets and have the computers and personnel to show you how to use them. Some contain information gleaned only from the white pages of most U.S. phone books. Others also contain information compiled by marketing companies or other information resources. For the most part, they contain only people who have chosen to list their phone numbers. Two of the most common (and best) are Select Phone (800) 992-3766, and Phone Disc (800) 284-8353. Note that these two CD-ROM sets have the same database but different interfaces.

While most searches on these CDs are successful only about 50% of the time, they are still handy resources to have around. One advantage is their flexibility. You can search by name, address or even telephone number. And you can (for example) print out the names, addresses and phone numbers of everyone in a particular neighborhood. You can also print out lists of everyone with a particular surname in any region in the country. You can limit the search to particular cities, states, zip codes or large regions of the United States. This is a popular resource for private investigators, skip tracers, adoption searchers, and reunion organizers. On the next page is a sample CD-ROM search that contains name, address, phone number, and how long the person lived at that address.

Free Internet telephone directories can be found at:

www.four11.com
www.switchboard.com
www.ada.infousa.com
www.infospace.com
www.yahoo.com

Or just go to *www.CyndisList.com/finding.htm* to view a list of phone directories, e-mail directories, and address directories. It's a long list; scroll down.

Years at residence is an estimate only.

Name: **DOE, JOHN M.**   Phone: **(209) 555-1234**
Address: **123 OAK ST**   Years at Residence: **3**
City: **ANYTOWN, CA 93656**

Name: **DOE, JOHN S.**   Phone: **(215) 555-4455**
Address: **6789 LAKEWOOD ST**   Years at Residence: **16-20**
City: **PHILADELPHIA, PA 19021**

Name: **DOE, JONATHAN N.**   Phone: **(206) 555-6789**
Address: **1809 N 43rd ST**   Years at Residence: **21+**
City: **SEATTLE, WA 98103**

Sample CD-ROM search.

Internet sites that have searchable military databases:

www.militaryusa.com

This Internet site has several searchable databases. The databases available for free are the Desert Storm/Desert Shield Casualty List, a database of 2.7 million Vietnam veterans, and the National Reunion Registry which lists over 7,000 military reunions. The fee-based databases include the active duty, reserve, and retired military list.

www.militarycity.com

This site contains a free military veteran registry which is searchable. The fee-based section has active duty, reserve, and a retiree and veteran database of those who have left the service since 1980.

www.ancestry.com

The Social Security Death Index, which contains approximately 100 million names of deceased individuals, is available for free on this site. It does not specify any military or veteran status. The fee-based areas of this site contain the casualty lists for Korea and Vietnam.

www.no-quarter.org

This site has the most detailed information for Vietnam casualties. It contains the usual information such as name, rank, etc., but also includes religion, military service number or Social Security number, marital status, reason for casualty, length of service, and tour dates. There is no fee to access this database.

www.nara.gov/nara/electronic

This National Archives Center for Electronic Records website has available at no charge the Korean and Vietnam War casualty lists. They're listed by state and include the name, rank, hometown, place of death, date of death, date of birth, and type of casualty.

Professional Searchers

If you decide to use an information broker, a specialized locator service or a private investigator, you're likely to pay anywhere from $30 to $200 per search. This can be a bargain if they find the person in the first computer search, but it could drive you to the poor house if you aren't careful. More than 80 percent of the time, a competent researcher will use no more than five commercial database searches to locate someone. The more background information you can provide, the quicker you're likely to score. Always let the researcher know what searches have already been performed and with what results. Don't pay to have the same searches run by different companies. It's a waste of time and money.

Remember, you may be able to get some of the above information for free either on the Internet or at a good library. When you've done all you can do using free resources, then go to a professional.

Professional searches can be successful even if you have surprisingly little information. For example, a search can be made knowing only one of the following:

- Complete legal name
- Last name
- Last name and date of birth
- Name and approximate date of birth
- Name and military background information
- First name and date of birth
- Social Security number
- Former address

Remember that different searches offer different information, different professionals offer different searches, and (to make it more complicated) different states allow different information to be known. If you contact a professional, be sure to ask what search combinations are available for what prices.

Here are some types of professional searches:

Social Security Number Trace. There are many services that provide access to the top portion, or "header," of a person's credit report. They can't give any of the information about bank accounts, credit cards, and delinquent payments, but they can give a lot of identifying information about a person.

One way to access a credit report is by entering a Social Security number. A successful Social Security number search (if he's ever applied for credit) could determine his full name, age, date or year of birth, current and prior addresses, the dates the credit bureau learned of the addresses, sometimes an employer, and sometimes the name of a spouse.

Some professionals automatically check the Social Security number against the Social Security Administration's Death Index. If the person you're looking for has died, you'll also learn the month and year he died.

There are three credit bureaus (Trans Union, CBI-Equifax and TRW) that each maintain their own credit database. Combined, they keep track of more than 300 million credit files and they update them daily. The person you're looking for might very well be listed with all three bureaus. That's why searching the header information is so popular among professionals.

```
TRANS UNION TRACE REPORT

*SOCIAL SECURITY NUMBER TRACE*    123-45-6789
   NAME/SPOUSE                              SSN OWNER
   ADDRESS                                  ADDR RPT DATE

1. DOE, JOHN M                              SUBJECT
   123 OAK ST, ANYTOWN, CA 93656            02/91
   345 PINE ST, OTHERTOWN, OH 44554         12/89
   5678 MAIN ST, SOMETOWN, PA 19933         06/87
**END OF NETWORK TRACE**
COPYRIGHT 1993, TRANS UNION CORPORATION
```

Trans Union Social Security Trace.

Date of Birth Search. Some commercial databases combine information from drivers licenses, voter rolls, marketing files, magazine subscriptions, phone books, city directories, property tax records, credit report headers, state and national death records, and other sources that keep track of people. This kind of search can be efficient because it zeros in on the person's file by combining a date of birth with partial information you may have. These "mega" databases allow you to search with the following information:

- Person's name, date of birth and Social Security number
- Full name and date of birth
- Last name and approximate date of birth

• Last name and exact date of birth
• First name and approximate date of birth (this works best if the first name is unusual)
• First name and exact date of birth

This is the ideal search tool when you know the person's date of birth but, for whatever reason, don't know his current full name. Or if you know the person's name and maybe only a year of birth.

DOE, JOHN M   DOB: 12/1/62   Age: 34

    SSN: 123-45-6789   Phone: (512) 555-1234

Address: 02/09/91
123 OAK ST
ANYTOWN, CA 93656

Example of "name and exact date of birth" search.

Last name: Knox
Complete date of birth: mm/dd/yr
Approximate years of birth: 1955-1960
First name: Martin   Middle initial:

Search results:

KNOX, MARTIN X   KNOX, MARTIN Q
MODESTO   CA   OMAHA NE
01/02/57   12/12/58

KNOX, MARTINA B   KNOX, MARTIN Z
BEND   OR   BOSTON   MA
07/29/55   10/10/59

Example of "name and approximate date of birth" search.

Address Update. Somewhere along the way you may have zeroed in on a person's former address but you still don't have a current address. The folks at Trans Union have put together a magnificent database that can help solve such cases. It's composed of information from various sources, such as city directories, drivers license files, marketing mailing lists, magazine subscription lists, the U.S. Postal Service's change-of-address file, and various other commercial databases. They regularly update the files, so this is a wonderful place to find a more recent address. A person's name and last known address will result in one of three responses:

- The person's name, most current address and telephone number.

- A confirmation that the information you entered is, indeed, the most recent information on file.

- A message that tells you he has moved from the address you provided, but the computer has no record of a more current address.

Sometimes the phone number given in this search is not listed in a phone book or in any of the national telephone directories available on the Internet or on CD-ROM.

The good thing about this type of search is that it can give the names, addresses and phone numbers of up to 20 neighbors, even if the address you have is a single-family dwelling. One of those 20 neighbors is likely to either know something about the person you're looking for or point you toward someone else who might know.

One flaw to this type of search occurs when the address that is entered is an apartment building or complex. The computer will only give the names of neighbors — it won't give any forwarding addresses.

```
TRANS UNION SUBJECT VERIFICATION REPORT
DEPT: ABC INVESTIGATORS

DATE: 03-05-97  TIME: 11:37:56   SUBJECT ID: XX05

XX05A1  DOE, JOHN M  *
123 OAK ST, ANYTOWN, CA 93656  *

TRANS UNION FOR
(I) XXX4022
  **SUBJECT VERIFICATION WITH 5 NEIGHBORS**
ADDRESS
01. SMITH, ALBERT              DOR: 1996      (209) 555-4433
123 OAK ST, ANYTOWN, CA 93656
02. JONES, ROBERT              DOR: 1989      (209) 555-5535
126 OAK ST, ANYTOWN, CA 93656
03. JOHNSON, JOHN    DOR: 1977      (209) 555-1344
125 OAK ST, ANYTOWN, CA 93656
04. DAVIS, JUNE                DOR: 1979      (209) 555-2333
129 OAK ST, ANYTOWN, CA 93656
05. MCELROY, ARNOLD  DOR: 1981      (209) 555-3434
132 OAK ST, ANYTOWN, CA 93656
SUBJECT NOT FOUND, CURRENT OCCUPANT RETURNED
**END OF REPORT**
COPYRIGHT 1993, TRANS UNION CORPORATION
```

Example of an address update search.

Surname Search. If you have nothing more than a name, the surname search may come in quite handy. This search provides a list of names, addresses and telephone numbers of people with that same last name. Even if there's no one in the resulting list with the same first name, you may be able to locate others with that last name in a particular city, county, region or state. Obviously, the more uncommon the name, the fewer people you'll find with that name, and the greater your chances will be of bumping into someone who knows the person you're trying to find. There are some uncommon names that show up only in certain regions across the country. It's very likely they are related. If you can find one person who has researched that family's genealogy, you could very well find a road map that leads directly to the person you want to find.

Residential Telephone Ownership. If, for some reason, you have only a phone number (and not an address or name to attach to it), there are databases that can help you. If the phone number shows up in any of the telephone ownership databases, the name, address and other information usually comes attached. (However, sometimes people filling out credit applications cheat and write down someone else's phone number — oftentimes that of a relative, friend or their place of employment.)

Collection agencies, process servers and private investigators regularly use these databases to find someone's current address. (Also see "National Telephone Books on CD-ROM" earlier in this chapter.)

Property Tax Assessment Search. The index of property tax assessments for most states is on one or more commercial databases. The tax rolls available on-line can include the name of the assessee (usually the owner, but not always), the address of the property, the address where the tax collector sends the bill, the legal description of the property, the assessed value of the land and any buildings on the land, the annual tax assessment, exemptions (such as homeowners exemptions that usually indicate the owner is living on the premises), the year the house was built, the original purchase price, the dates and amounts of any mortgages, and sometimes the number that the recorder assigned to the deed.

Be sure to ask a professional in the state you're focused on if he has access to such a database. There are a few vendors that have information on much of the United States.

PROPERTY OWNERSHIP

ANYTOWN, CA 93656 123 OAK ST

Parcel Number: 1-2345-67890
Short Legal Desc: LOT 55 SHAVER LAKE SUB-DIV
Owner Name: Bank of America
Property Address: 123 OAK ST
ANYTOWN, CA 93656
Mailing Address: 123 OAK ST
ANYTOWN, CA 93656

Assessed Land Value:	Market Land Value:
Assessed Improvements:	Market Improvements:
Assessed Total:	Total Market Value:
Assessment Year: 1995	Most Recent Sale: $155,000
Tax Year: 1994	Prior Sale Price: $145,000
Produced by County: 06/19/95	

Example of a property tax assessment search.

Newspaper Databases. Almost everyone's name ends up in a newspaper at one time — sometimes for things they did that were good, other times for things they did that were bad, and other times because they just happened to be somewhere at the right time. There are a variety of on-line services that provide access to full-text or summaries of newspaper, magazine and broadcast news stories. Hundreds or even thousands of publications can be searched with a single, well-thought-out search strategy. Some professional searchers subscribe to these databases but most on-line services such as America Online and CompuServe have newspaper searches available. Probably the best such databases is Meade Data's Nexis database. Most lawyers have access to Nexis through Meade Data's legal database, Lexis. Many law schools and university libraries also have Nexis accounts.

Nexis, however, is one of the most expensive databases around. That's because it covers so many publications in so many countries. There are other such databases that are less expensive and, predictably, less efficient. Don't forget that more and more newspapers are offering access to their research library information. Some on the Internet are free; others allow you to search the database and see either a summary of the story or the first 15 or 20 words. The catch is they will charge you if you elect to view or order the entire story.

Many newspapers across the United States have research librarians which you can hire to research any topic or name. This can be a good move, especially if you suspect the person you're searching for has lived in a big city for a long time and might have had a profession, hobby, position or affliction that would have made him newsworthy. These searches often find birth or marriage announcements, death announcements or obituaries, or various other (possibly obscure) pieces of information about the person you're trying to find.

Summary. There are many advantages to using professionals. First and most obvious is their ability to search databases that you have no access to or can't afford to subscribe to. But before you drain your savings account, take a look at the Internet sections in each chapter of this book. You might be able to do some of this searching on the Internet for little or no money. Also remember to find as many people on your own (especially for reunions) before paying for searches.

Chapter 13

Other Methods

There are many different ways to locate a person. This chapter outlines other methods that may be used. These do not pertain to finding only military people but can be used to help locate just about anyone.

Government Agencies

Social Security Administration. The Social Security Administration will forward some unsealed letters to people whose names are in their files. This is done for certain humanitarian reasons that are beneficial to the receiver (see below). Letters that are accepted will be forwarded to the employers or directly to the individual if he is drawing Social Security benefits.

Before offering assistance, the Social Security Administration must determine that the person to be contacted would want to receive the letter and would want to reply. They will *not* forward any correspondence unless strong compelling reasons exist. For example:

- A strong humanitarian purpose will be served (e.g., a close relative is seriously ill, is dying or has died).

- A minor is left without parental guidance.
- A defendant in a felony case is seeking a defense witness.
- A parent wishes to locate a child. Consent of the missing person is needed in connection with adoption cases.
- The missing person would want to know the contents of the letter.
- The missing person's disappearance occurred recently enough that SSA could reasonably expect to have a usable mailing address.
- All other possibilities for contacting the missing person have been exhausted.

Submit request in writing citing the following information:

- Missing person's name and Social Security number.
- If the Social Security number is unknown, give date and place of birth, name of parents, name and address of last known employer, or period of employment.
- Reason for wanting to contact the person.
- Last time seen or heard from.
- Other contacts that have been exhausted.

Enclose the letter to be forwarded in an unsealed, stamped envelope. The Social Security Administration will try to find an address in their records for the missing person. If an address is found, they will forward the letter. If they can't forward a letter because a Social Security number can't be found, or the person can't be identified, they will notify you. However, if they can find a person, they won't inform you whether:

- They found an address, or
- They were able to forward the letter.

A "strong compelling reason" may be deemed to exist if a monetary or other consideration is involved and it's reasonable to assume that the missing person does not know it. For example:

- Missing person is beneficiary of an estate.
- Insurance proceeds are due the person.
- An important document is being held.

Under these conditions, the procedures are the same as above except you must include a personal check, cashier's check, or money order payable to the "Social Security Administration" in the amount of $3 per letter to be forwarded.

★ **TIP**: Always ask for a receipt if a payment is made. The clerk may inadvertently write the individual's Social Security number on the receipt. Or if the person has changed her name, the new name may be listed on the receipt.

In the event they were unable to help and you've prepaid a fee, the Treasury Department will refund your money. Mail all correspondence to:

Social Security Administration
Office of Central Records Operations
300 N. Green Street
Baltimore, MD 21201
(800) 722-1213
www.ssa.gov

★ **TIP**: *http://informus.com* is a website that allows you to check the validity of a Social Security number. Is it real or bogus? Run it through this site before submitting a possibly fake Social Security number to the Social Security Administration. It no doubt will save you time and some frustration.

Internal Revenue Service. The Internal Revenue Service will forward letters for humane reasons to people that they can identify with a Social Security number. Humane reasons include:

• Urgent or compelling nature, such as serious illness.
• Imminent death or death of a close relative.
• A person seeking a missing relative.

A reunion or tracing a family tree does not qualify as a humane purpose. The IRS will not forward letters concerning debts. If an address can be found, the letter will be placed in an IRS envelope and the requestor will be advised that the letter is being forwarded in accordance with their current policy. If a letter is forwarded by the IRS and is undeliverable by the post office and returned to the IRS, it will be destroyed and the sender will *not* be notified. They will not divulge the recipient's current address or tax information, and the decision to reply is entirely up to the recipient. Check the telephone book or *www.irs.ustreas.gov* for the nearest IRS office.

The U.S. Postal Service. For many years you could obtain an individual's new address from the U.S. Post Office under the Freedom of Information Act, if the individual had submitted a change-of-address card. This practice was discontinued in April of 1994. However, the U.S. Postal Change-of-Address File is still available to credit bureaus, other information providers, and in many computer databases used by professional searchers. See Chapter 12 (Computer & Internet Searches).

You may still be able to find a person's new address by doing the following: mail a letter to the person's last known address and write "RETURN SERVICE REQUESTED" below the return address. The post office will place a label showing the new address and return your letter to you. You may also put "DO NOT FORWARD" to make sure the post office sees it. Change of address information is retained by the post office for 18 months, but they will forward mail for only 12 months.

Try contacting the postmaster of the town (especially in smaller towns) where the person once lived. It's possible he may know or remember the person. Many small town postmasters have held their job for 30 or 40 years and know the location or relatives of numerous people who once lived there.

www.usps.gov

For address verification or other post office services, check out this post office website. This is a good source to verify an address, or to find the county or the post office that handles that mail. This site will sometimes return the name of an apartment complex or mobile home park.

☆ **TIP**: We've often used the above website to check an address to see if it's valid. In one particular case an address looked very strange. It turned out to be for the local county jail.

Congressional Assistance. If you are not getting results or answers from federal agencies or the military, you can write or call your United States Representative or Senator and ask for their assistance. Federal agencies and the armed forces are very responsive to inquiries from members of Congress. You can expect a quick reply to your letter, usually within two weeks. Include all the information you can about the person you are trying to locate, why you need to contact him, what steps you have taken so far, and the results of these steps.

www.house.gov

This is the website for the House of Representatives. Look up the names, addresses and e-mails for your representative. Try e-mailing first and if no response is received, contact the office by telephone or in writing.

Form of address to use when writing a Congressman:

Honorable [name here]
United States House of Representatives
Washington, DC 20515

www.senate.gov

This is the Senate's website. It lists the Senators' offices, e-mail addresses and mailing addresses.

Form of address to use when writing a Senator:

Honorable [name here]
United States Senate
Washington, DC 20510

County Courthouse and City Hall. Government records such as deeds, marriage licenses, business names, voter registration, licenses, tax records, record of trials (civil or criminal) can be a source of information that can give you current addresses and possibly a Social Security number. Military people often buy real estate near the bases where they are stationed. As they move, they usually rent out the property and the tax bill is mailed to their new address. This information is public record. Check both the courthouse and city hall for tax and deed information. This can be done by mail, in person, or through professional search services (see Chapter 12). In many areas, utility user's (water, gas, electricity, cable television) addresses are available.

★ **TIP**: To find out the county an address is located in, try the post office Internet site at *www.usps.gov*. When an address is entered into this database, the county is listed.

Churches

Churches can be of great assistance in many searches. Most priests, ministers and rabbis have record of the addresses of their current and former members. Churches and synagogues maintain records of membership, baptisms, confirmations, first communions, bar mitzvahs, weddings and funerals. Religious groups have church-sponsored clubs and organizations which can be contacted for information. Try contacting other members of a church that the person attended. Use the Internet yellow pages to acquire a list of churches in the city where the person once lived. If the church is unwilling to release information, they may be helpful by forwarding a letter.

Colleges, Universities and Alumni Associations

The federal Family and Education Rights and Privacy Act allows colleges and universities to release "directory information" to the public without the consent of the students. A student may request that all or part of this information be withheld from the public by making a written request to do so, but few do. "Directory information" includes, but is not limited to, student's name, current address, telephone listing, major, date and place of birth, dates of attendance, degrees and awards received, and previous schools attended. Contact college registrars for this information.

College alumni associations try to keep current addresses of former students, and most will either provide an address or forward a letter. They also publish directories of former students (some list graduates only) with current addresses and employment. If the alumni association will not give out an address, contact the college library which will have a copy of the directory. This normally lists an address and other information. Alumni associations and college libraries have copies of yearbooks which can sometimes provide the individual's legal name, hometown, degree and other information.

Internet users can check the following sites for alumni information: *www.infophil.com, www.alumni.com, www.alumni.net*. These sites link to colleges and high schools around the world and provide support to stay in touch with classmates.

Libraries

Public Libraries. City and county public libraries have a wealth of information for searchers. The same may be true of college, private and other specialized libraries. These resources can be used either in person, by written communication, by telephone or by fax. Visit your local library and ask the librarian for assistance.

Many libraries participate in the Inter–Library Loan and the Online Computer Library Center Programs. With the Inter-Library Loan Program, a distant library sends books and materials to your local library. With the Online Computer Library Center Program you can find out which libraries have what reference materials so you can go to that particular library. Contact a librarian for details.

Most military installations have base libraries and museums that probably have some information about units or ships that were stationed there. Call the information operator of the base concerned to get the telephone number of the base library or museum. See Appendix A (Directories of Military Installations). Ask for help from the library staff.

Family History Centers. The Church of Jesus Christ of Latter Day Saints (Mormons) has the largest genealogical library in the world in Salt Lake City, Utah. It operates numerous local Family History Centers in major cities throughout the world. These local Centers can obtain endless amounts of genealogical information from the main library in Salt Lake City and are extremely helpful to searchers. Many Centers have the Social Security Death Index, local birth and death records, and excellent collections of local telephone books. For additional information, contact the nearest Family History Center or write to:

Church of Jesus Christ of Latter Day Saints
Family History Department
35 North West Temple
Salt Lake City, UT 84150

Regional Government Depository Libraries. Many libraries participate in the Regional Government Depository Library Program. Regional Depository Libraries, which are in every state, are charged with receiving all new government publications authorized for distribution to these libraries.

Smaller libraries that participate in this program can borrow these documents and books from the Depositories. Examples of publications are armed forces Officers Registers, Department of State employee registers and lists, federal government telephone books, U.S. Government pamphlets on such diverse matters as census data, commercial laws, bankruptcy courts, federal tax matters, etc. This is a valuable resource if you are involved with a difficult search. Ask your local librarian how you can use this service to obtain the publications needed. Call the Federal Information Center at (800) 688-9889 for the address and telephone number of the participating library closest to you.

Newspapers

When seeking current or former military people, the following national weekly newspapers may be of some assistance: *Army Times, Navy Times, Navy Times: Marine Corps Edition, Air Force Times,* and *Federal Times.* These are the most popular and most widely read newspapers of Armed Services and Civil Service personnel. *Federal Times* is read primarily by present and former civil servants, a large portion of whom are military veterans, retired military or members of the reserves. These newspapers have locator columns that contain "In Search Of" notices. Following is the publisher for all the above newspapers:

Army Times Publishing Company
6883 Commercial Drive
Springfield, VA 22159
(800) 424-9335
www.militarycity.com

The largest veteran-oriented newspaper in the United States is *Stars and Stripes: The National Tribune.* When seeking a veteran or publicizing a reunion, this publication should be considered:

Stars and Stripes: The National Tribune
PO Box 1803
Washington, DC 20013
(202) 543-4740, (202) 543-0016 Fax
www.stripes.com

A particularly useful newspaper may be the one in the last known town or city where the person lived. Place an advertisement in the personal section of the classifieds, like this:

> **Chief Master Sgt. Joe L. James**
> Urgent, anyone who knows his
> whereabouts call collect (555) 555-5555.

Thousands of people read this section and you may get a response. Or, if your story is very compelling and has a strong human-interest element, write a letter to the editor for possible publication.

The Salvation Army

The Salvation Army conducts searches of missing people for immediate family members only, through their National Missing Person Network. Contact your local Salvation Army Social Service Center for information and a registration form or see their website at *www.salvationarmyusa.org.* There is a $10 fee for this service. There are four U.S. regional headquarters for the Salvation Army that can assist in a search.

Eastern Territory
The Salvation Army
Missing Persons Services
440 West Nyack Road
West Nyack, NY 10994
(914) 620-7200

Southern Territory
The Salvation Army
Missing Persons Services
1424 N.E. Expressway
Atlanta, GA 30329
(404) 728-1331

Western Territory
The Salvation Army
Missing Persons Services
30840 Hawthorne Blvd
Rancho Palos Verdes, CA 90724
(310) 541-4721

Central Territory
The Salvation Army
Missing Persons Services
10 West Algonquin Road
Des Plaines, IL 60016
(847) 294-2000

The Telephone Company

Directory assistance operators (long distance information) can give you valuable information in addition to telephone numbers. They also provide the correct area code for a city and will release addresses for listed telephone numbers. However, remember that directory assistance costs money. Use the free Internet telephone directories as much as possible. See Chapter 12 (Computer & Internet Searches).

Locating Military Dependents

Children of active duty military personnel may have at some point lived overseas with their parents. There are several organizations for those who attended schools in other countries. Not all of these are military schools.

Overseas Brats. Overseas Brats is an umbrella org
tion for over 200 alumni associations of overseas Am
private schools, State Department schools, and Depar
of Defense high schools. Their membership consists of
former students and faculty.

While Overseas Brats does not maintain a list of individual students, they do maintain a list of active alumni associations. Requests for specific alumni associations can be made to:

Overseas Brats
PO Box 29805
San Antonio, TX 78229-0805
(210) 349-1394
www.overseasbrats.com

Military Brats. This organization brings together military brats from around the world. Their website has a free "brat" registry with approximately 20,000 listings and is searchable online. The database contains name, schools attended, year of graduation, and e-mail address.

Military Brats
466 Orange St. #280
Redlands, CA 92374
www.military-brats.com

American Overseas Schools Archives. The American Overseas Schools Archives, under the supervision of the American Overseas Schools Historical Society (AOSHS), was established in 1989. It was organized to collect, record and preserve histories and memorabilia of Department of Defense overseas schools from kindergarten through high school. It includes hundreds of thousands of items such as yearbooks, scrapbooks, curricula, newspapers, magazines and journal articles, photographs, official papers and documents, personal histories and memorabilia of all kinds. AOSHS publishes a quarterly newsletter.

American Overseas Schools Historical Society
PO Box 777
Litchfield Park, AZ 85340
(602) 935-3939, overseasschools@juno.com

Locating People in Prison

All states operate prison locators, usually through the State Department of Corrections. See Appendix B (Directory of State Resources) for phone numbers of state prison locators. If the individual you are looking for is possibly in a federal prison, telephone the U.S. federal prison locator at (202) 307-3126. Aliases may be available. Refer to Chapter 5 (Military Records) if the person may be in the U.S. Disciplinary Barracks (military prison) at Ft. Leavenworth, Kansas. Most prison locators keep records of former inmates for up to ten years. Searches may be completed with name only and do not require a date of birth or Social Security number.

Using Professional Searchers

Some difficult cases may need the help of a professional. These can include private investigators, specialized searchers or attorneys.

The National Association of Investigative Specialists, (NAIS) is a world-wide network of private investigative professionals and agencies. With over 1,500 members, it is one of the largest associations in the world for private investigators.

National Association of Investigative Specialists
PO Box 33244
Austin, TX 78764
(512) 719-3595, (512) 719-3594
www.pimall.com/nais

Darrin Fansler is a private investigator who resides and practices in Germany. He is a former U.S. Army military police investigator. He specializes in locating active and retired U.S. military personnel who were stationed or reside in Germany. He is also available for debt collection and background investigation.

Darrin Fansler
PO Box 27392
Tampa, FL 33685
(813) 963-0499 (information)
011-49-6188-5280 (office in Germany)

Charles Eric Gordon is an attorney concentrating on locating persons who have been missing for a substantial period of time or about whom little information is known. He is a consultant to law firms, corporations, government agencies and foreign governments in tracing missing witnesses, heirs, beneficiaries, relatives, debtors and others. With his worldwide contacts and many years of experience as both an attorney and an investigator, he can also assist in obtaining information and public records that are difficult to access, e.g., vital records, voter registration and court records.

Charles Eric Gordon, Esq.
5 Joyce Road
PO Box 514
Plainview, NY 11803-0514
(516) 433-5065

The following team of searchers specialize in locating birth parents, children and others who live or have lived in Germany, Austria or Switzerland. Both were born in Germany and have extensive experience and numerous contacts in Europe. For information and fees, contact:

Leonie Boehmer   Margit S. Benton
805 Alvarado, N.E.   2238 Bailey Drive
Albuquerque, NM 87108   N. Charleston, SC 29405
(505) 268-1310   (843) 747-6156

Directories of Military Installations/ Coast Guard and Navy Ships

There are 4 sections to this appendix:
1. Military Installations, United States (below).
2. Military Installations, Overseas (p. 164).
3. Phone Numbers of Overseas Military Installations (p. 175).
4. U.S. Coast Guard and Navy Ships (p. 178).

Military Installations, United States

Following is a list of military installations in the United States and its territories. They are listed by state and include all branches of the armed forces. Listed are the city (or closest city), name of installation, zip code, and the main telephone number of the installation. Most of the installations have a base or post locator. The locator can check some type of computer or manual printout of active duty personnel. Call the information number and ask for the base/post locator for military personnel. In many cases the information operator will also be the locator. The base information operator should also have phone numbers and addresses for active duty personnel living on base in military housing.

★ **TIP**: Some military installations have recently closed; some do not have a base/post locator. These will refer you to the World-Wide Locator for their branch of the service. However, if you already know to which unit the person is assigned, simply ask the base operator for the unit phone number.

For area code changes, check *www.lincmad.com/* on the Internet.

The information in this directory can be used as a complete address for mailing purposes. Use the following format:

[Name of Installation]   Fort Sam Houston
[ATTN: Base Locator]   ATTN: Base Locator
[Installation, State, Zip] Ft. Sam Houston, TX 78234

City/Town	Installation	Zip	Phone Number
Alabama			
Anniston	Anniston Army Depot	36201	(205) 235-7501
Anniston	Fort McClellan	36205	(205) 848-4611
Birmingham	Alabama Air National Guard	35217	(205) 714-2000
Daleville	Fort Rucker	36362	(334) 255-1110
Huntsville	Redstone Arsenal	35898	(205) 876-2151
Maxwell	Gunter Annex	36114	(334) 416-1110
Maxwell	Maxwell Air Force Base	36114	(334) 416-1110
Mobile	Coast Guard Aviation Trng. Cntr.	36608	(334) 441-6826
Mobile	Coast Guard Brookley Complex	36615	(334) 441-6235
Mobile	Coast Guard Marine Safety Office	36652	(334) 441-5286
Montgomery	Dannelly Field Air Natl. Guard	36125	(334) 284-7100
Alaska			
Adak	Adak Naval Air Facility	99546	(907) 592-4201
Anchorage	Elmendorf Air Force Base	99506	(907) 552-1110
Anchorage	Fort Richardson	99505	(907) 384-1110
Anchorage	Kulis Air Natl Guard Station	99502	(907) 249-1239
Anderson	Clear Air Force Base	99704	(907) 585-6113
Fairbanks	Eielson Air Force Base	99702	(907) 377-1841
Fairbanks	Fort Greely	99508	(907) 873-3255
Fairbanks	Fort Wainwright	99703	(907) 353-1110
Ketchikan	C.G. Integrated Support Command	99901	(907) 228-0210
Kodiak	Coast Guard Support Station	99619	(907) 487-5760
Kodiak	Kodiak Coast Guard Air Station	99619	(907) 487-5888
Naknek	King Salmon Airport	99613	(907) 552-1110
Sitka	Sitka Coast Guard Air Station	99835	(907) 966-5434
Arizona			
Gila Bend	Gila Bend Air Force Aux. Field	85337	(520) 683-6261
Litchfield Park	Luke Air Force Base	85309	(602) 856-7411
Sierra Vista	Fort Huachuca	85613	(520) 538-7111
Tucson	Davis-Monthan Air Force Base	85707	(520) 228-3900

Yuma	Yuma Marine Corps Air Station	85369	(520) 341-2011
Yuma	Yuma Proving Ground	85365	(520) 328-3287

Arkansas

Fort Smith	Fort Chaffee	72905	(501) 484-2141
Jacksonville	Little Rock Air Force Base	72099	(501) 987-3131
Pine Bluff	Pine Bluff Arsenal	71602	(501) 540-3000

California

Alameda	Alameda C.G. Support Center	94501	(510) 437-2900
Barstow	Barstow M.C. Logistical Base	92311	(760) 577-6211
Barstow	Ft. Irwin Natl. Training Center	92310	(760) 256-1071
China Lake	China Lk. Naval Air Weapons Stn.	93555	(760) 939-9011
Concord	Concord Naval Weapons Stn.	94520	(510) 246-5000
Coronado	Coronado Naval Amphibious Base	92135	(619) 545-8123
Costa Mesa	Costa Mesa Air Natl. Guard Stn.	92627	(714) 668-2300
El Centro	El Centro Naval Air Facilty	93524	(619) 339-2524
El Segundo	Los Angeles Air Force Base	90245	(310) 363-1110
Eureka	Coast Guard Group Humboldt Bay	95521	(707) 839-6123
Fairfield	Travis Air Force Base	94535	(707) 424-1110
Fresno	Fresno Air National Guard Base	93727	(559) 251-2501
Hayward	Hayward Air National Guard	94545	(510) 264-5600
Herlong	Sierra Army Depot	96113	(530) 827-4575
Imperial Bch.	Imperial Beach Naval Station	92155	(619) 437-2011
Imperial Bch.	Imp. Bch. Outlying Landing Field	91932	(619) 437-9428
Lemoore	Lemoore Naval Air Station	93246	(559) 998-0100
Lompoc	Vandenberg Air Force Base	93437	(805) 734-8232
Los Angeles	Los Angeles Coast Guard Air Stn.	90245	(310) 215-2112
Marysville	Beale Air Force Base	95903	(530) 634-3000
Monterey	Monterey Coast Guard Group	93940	(408) 647-7300
Monterey	Monterey Naval Postgraduate Sch.	93943	(408) 656-2441
Monterey	Presidio of Monterey	93944	(408) 242-5119
Mountain View	Santa Clara Naval Air Reserve	94035	(650) 603-9527
North Island	North Island Naval Air Station	92135	(619) 545-1011
Oakland	Oakland Army Base	94626	(510) 466-3911
Oakland	Oakland Fleet & Ind. Supply Cntr.	94625	(510) 302-2000
Oceanside	Camp Pendleton M.C. Base	92055	(760) 725-4111
Paso Robles	Camp Roberts Air National Guard	93451	(805) 238-3100
Petaluma	Petaluma C.G. Training Center	94952	(707) 765-7211
Point Mugu	Pt. Mugu Naval Air Weapons Stn.	93042	(805) 989-1110
Point Reyes	Point Reyes Coast Guard Station	94956	(415) 669-2000
Port Hueneme	Naval Construction Batn. Center	93043	(805) 982-4711

Port Hueneme	Pt. Hueneme Air Natl. Guard Stn.	93041	(805) 986-8000
Rosamond	Edwards Air Force Base	93524	(805) 277-1110
Sacramento	McClellan Air Force Base	95652	(916) 643-4113
Sacramento	Sacramento Coast Guard Air Stn.	95652	(916) 643-2081
San Diego	Fleet Combat Trng. Center Pacific	92147	(619) 553-8330
San Diego	Miramar Naval Air Station	92145	(619) 537-1011
San Diego	North Island Naval Air Station	92135	(619) 545-0183
San Diego	San Diego Coast Guard Air Stn.	92101	(619) 683-6330
San Diego	S.D. Marine Corp Recruit Depot	92140	(619) 524-8762
San Diego	San Diego Naval Medical Center	92134	(619) 532-6400
San Diego	San Diego Naval Station	92136	(619) 556-1246
San Diego	San Diego Naval Submarine Base	92106	(619) 222-3632
San Francisco	San Francisco Coast Guard Air Stn.	94128	(650) 876-2902
San Francisco	Treasure Island Naval Station	94130	(415) 395-1000
San Luis Obispo	Camp San Luis Obispo Trng. Cntr.	93403	(805) 594-6201
Santa Ana	El Toro Marine Corp Air Station	92709	(714) 726-2100
Seal Beach	Seal Beach Naval Weapons Station	90740	(562) 626-7011
Sunnyvale	Onizuka Air Station	94089	(408) 752-3000
Tracy	Tracy Defense Depot	95296	(209) 982-2000
29 Palms	29 Palms Air/Ground Center	92278	(760) 830-6000

Colorado

Aurora	Buckley Air National Guard Base	80011	(303) 677-9011
Aurora	Fitzsimons Army Medical Center	80045	(303) 361-8241
Colorado Spgs.	Fort Carson	80913	(719) 526-5811
Colorado Spgs.	Norad Air Force Base	80914	(719) 474-1110
Colorado Spgs.	Peterson Air Force Base	80914	(719) 556-7321
Colorado Spgs.	U.S. Air Force Academy	80840	(719) 333-1110
Denver	Air Force Reserve Personnel Cntr.	80279	(303) 676-6453
Denver	Rocky Mountain Arsenal	80022	(303) 288-0711
Colorado Spgs.	Falcon Air Force Base	80912	(719) 567-1110
Pueblo	Pueblo Army Depot	81006	(719) 549-4111

Connecticut

Groton	New London Naval Subm. Base	06349	(860) 694-4636
New Haven	Long Island Sands C.G. Base	06512	(203) 468-4450
New London	U.S. Coast Guard Academy	06320	(860) 444-8444
Orange	Air Natl. Guard Communicat. Stn.	06477	(203) 795-2900
Windsor Locks	Bradley Air National Guard Base	06026	(860) 623-4551

Delaware

Dover	Dover Air Force Base	19902	(302) 677-3000

District of Columbia

Washington	U.S. Army Headquarters	20310	(703) 545-6700
Washington	Bolling Air Force Base	20332	(703) 545-6700
Washington	U.S. Air Force Headquarters	20593	(703) 545-6700
Washington	U.S. Coast Guard Headquarters	20593	(202) 267-2320
Washington	D.C. Air National Guard	20762	(301) 981-1110
Washington	Fort McNair	20319	(202) 685-3089
Washington	Marine Corps Barracks	20390	(202) 433-4073
Washington	U.S. Marine Headquarters	20310	(703) 545-6700
Washington	Washington National Guard	20310	(703) 695-6987
Washington	U.S. Navy Headquarters	20310	(703) 545-6700
Washington	Pentagon	20310	(703) 545-6700
Washington	Walter Reed Army Medical Center	20307	(202) 782-3501
Washington	Washington Naval Security Station	20393	(202) 764-0211
Washington	Naval Station, Anacostia Annex	20373	(703) 545-6700
Washington	Washington Naval Yard	20374	(703) 545-6700

Florida

Avon Park	Avon Park Air Force Range	33825	(941) 452-4191
Cape Canaveral	Cape Canaveral Air Force Station	32925	(407) 494-1110
Cocoa Beach	Patrick Air Force Base	32925	(407) 494-1110
Crestview	Duke Field	32542	(850) 882-1110
Homestead	Homestead Air Reserve Station	33039	(305) 224-7000
Jacksonville	Cecil Field Naval Air Station	32215	(904) 778-5627
Jacksonville	Jacksonville Naval Air Station	32212	(904) 542-2345
Jacksonville	Mayport Naval Station	32228	(904) 270-5011
Key West	Coast Guard Group	33040	(305) 292-8700
Key West	Key West Naval Air Station	33040	(305) 293-2268
Mary Esther	Hurlburt Field	32544	(850) 882-1110
Mayport	Mayport Coast Guard Base	32233	(904) 247-7301
Milton	Whiting Field Naval Air Station	32570	(850) 623-7011
Opa Locka	Miami Coast Guard Air Station	33054	(305) 953-2100
Orlando	Orlando Naval Training Center	32813	(407) 646-4501
Panama City	Panama City Coastal Systems Stn.	32407	(850) 234-4011
Panama City	Tyndall Air Force Base	32403	(850) 283-1110
Pensacola	Pensacola Naval Air Station	32508	(850) 452-0111
Pensacola	Corry Naval Station	32511	(850) 452-2000
Pensacola	Pensacola Naval Hospital	32512	(850) 452-6601
Pensacola	Saufley Field	32509	(904) 452-1300
St. Petersburg	Clearwater Coast Guard Air Stn.	33762	(813) 535-1437
Starke	Camp Blanding	32091	(904) 533-3100
Tampa	MacDill Air Force Base	33621	(813) 828-1110
Valparaiso	Eglin Air Force Base	32542	(850) 882-1113

Georgia

Albany	Marine Corps Logistics Base	31704	(912) 439-5000
Athens	Naval Supply Corps School	30606	(706) 354-1500
Augusta	Fort Gordon	30905	(706) 791-0110
Columbus	Fort Benning	31905	(706) 545-2011
Dahlonega	Camp Merrill	30533	(706) 864-3367
East Point	Fort McPherson	30330	(404) 464-3113
Forest Park	Fort Gillem	30297	(404) 464-3113
Hinesville	Fort Stewart	31314	(912) 767-1411
Kings Bay	Kings Bay Naval Submarine Base	31547	(912) 673-2000
Marietta	Atlanta Naval Air Station	30060	(770) 919-6406
Marietta	Dobins Air Reserve Base	30069	(770) 919-5000
Savannah	Hunter Army Airfield	31409	(912) 767-1411
Savannah	Savannah Coast Guard Air Station	31409	(912) 652-4646
Valdosta	Moody Air Force Base	31699	(912) 257-4211
Warner Robins	Robins Air Force Base	31098	(912) 926-1110

Hawaii

Hilo	Pohakuloa Training Area	96720	(808) 471-7110
Honolulu	Barbers Point Naval Air Station	96862	(808) 684-6266
Honolulu	Camp Smith Marine Corps Base	96861	(808) 477-6231
Honolulu	Fort Kamehameha	96653	(808) 523-6200
Honolulu	Fort Shafter	96858	(808) 471-7110
Honolulu	Hickam Air Force Base	96853	(808) 471-7110
Honolulu	Pearl Harbor Naval Complex	96860	(808) 471-7110
Honolulu	Tripler Army Medical Center	96859	(808) 433-2778
Honolulu	Wheeler Army Air Field	96857	(808) 471-7110
Honolulu	Fort DeRussey	96815	(808) 955-0060
Kailua	Kaneohe Bay Marine Corps Base	96863	(808) 471-7110
Kapolei	Barbers Point Naval Air Station	96862	(808) 684-6266
Kekaha, Kauai	Barking Sands Pac. Missile Range	96752	(808) 335-4254
Pearl City	Smith Field	96782	(808) 477-9417
Wahiawa	E. Pacific Naval Computer Tele. Stn.	96786	(808) 653-5385
Wahiawa	Schofield Barracks	96857	(808) 471-7110
Waianae	Lualualei Naval Magazine	96792	(808) 474-4340
Waimanalo	Bellows Air Force Station	96795	(808) 259-8080

Idaho

Boise	Gowen Air National Guard Base	83705	(208) 422-5366
Mountain Home	Mountain Home Air Force Base	83648	(208) 828-2111

Illinois

Belleville	Scott Air Force Base	62225	(618) 256-1110

Chicago	Illinois Air National Guard HQ	60666	(773) 825-5601
Chicago	O'Hare Air Reserve Facility	60666	(773) 825-5647
Granite City	Price Support Center	62040	(618) 452-4212
Great Lakes	Great Lakes Naval Training Center	60088	(847) 688-3500
Marseilles	Camp Marseilles	61341	(815) 795-5701
Rock Island	Rock Island Arsenal	61299	(309) 782-6001

Indiana

Crane	Crane Naval Weapons Support Cntr	47522	(812) 854-1606
Edinburgh	Camp Atterbury	46124	(812) 526-9711
Grissom	Grissom Reserve Center	46971	(317) 688-5211
Indianapolis	Fort Benjamin Harrison	46249	(317) 510-5000
Terra Haute	Indiana Air National Guard HQ	47803	(812) 877-5210

Iowa

Des Moines	Des Moines Air Natl. Guard Base	50321	(515) 256-8210
Johnston	Camp Dodge/Iowa Natl. Grd. Base	50131	(515) 252-4011

Kansas

Junction City	Fort Riley	66442	(785) 239-3911
Leavenworth	Fort Leavenworth	66027	(913) 684-4021
Topeka	Forbes Field Air Natl Guard Base	66619	(785) 862-0711
Wichita	McConnell Air Force Base	67221	(316) 652-6100

Kentucky

Clarksville	Fort Campbell	42223	(502) 798-2151
Louisville	Naval Marine Corps Reserve Cntr.	40214	(502) 364-5011
Louisville	Stanford Field Air Natl Guard Base	40213	(502) 364-9400
Radcliff	Fort Knox	40121	(502) 624-1181
Richmond	Blue Grass Army Depot	40475	(316) 421-7400

Louisiana

Belle Chasse	New Orleans Naval Air Station	70143	(504) 678-3253
Bossier City	Barksdale Air Force Base	71110	(318) 456-2252
Leesville	Fort Polk	71459	(318) 531-2911
New Orleans	Jackson Barracks, Natl. Guard Base	70146	(504) 271-6262
New Orleans	Naval Reserve Personnel Center	70149	(504) 678-6738
New Orleans	Coast Guard Support Center	70117	(504) 678-3033
New Orleans	N.O. Naval Support Activity	70142	(504) 678-2655
Pineville	Camp Beauregard	71360	(318) 640-2080

Maine

Augusta	Camp Keys	04333	(207) 622-9331
Bangor	Bangor Air National Guard Base	04401	(207) 990-7700
Brunswick	Naval Air Station, Brunswick	04011	(207) 921-1110

Cutler	Naval Computer & Telecom Station	04626	(207) 259-8229
South Portland	Air Natl. Guard Stn. South Portland	04106	(207) 756-7800
South Portland	Coast Guard Base, South Portland	04106	(207) 767-0320
S.W. Harbor	Coast Guard Base, S.W. Harbor	04679	(207) 244-5517
Winter Harbor	Winter Harbor Naval Security Grp.	04693	(207) 963-5534

Maryland

Aberdeen	Aberdeen Proving Ground	21005	(410) 278-5201
Adelphi	Army Research Laboratories	20783	(301) 394-2515
Annapolis	Annapolis Naval Station	21402	(410) 293-1000
Annapolis	U.S. Naval Academy	21402	(410) 293-1000
Baltimore	Curtis Bay Coast Guard Yard	21226	(410) 789-1600
Baltimore	Fort Meade	20755	(301) 677-6261
Bethesda	Bethesda Naval Medical Center	20889	(301) 295-4611
Camp Springs	Andrews Air Force Base	20762	(301) 981-1110
Cascade	Fort Ritchie	21702	(301) 878-1300
Edgewood	Edgewood Arsenal	21010	(410) 278-5201
Frederick	Fort Detrick	21702	(301) 619-8000
Indian Head	Indian Head Naval Ordinance Stn.	20640	(301) 743-4000
Patuxent River	Naval Air Station, Patuxent River	20670	(301) 342-3000
Solomons	Solomons Navy Recreation Center	20688	(410) 326-4216

Massachusetts

Ayer	Fort Devens	01432	(978) 772-4825
Bedford	Hanscom Air Force Base	01731	(781) 377-4441
Boston	Boston Coast Guard Support Cntr.	02109	(617) 223-3257
Bourne	Camp Edwards	02542	(508) 968-1000
Cape Cod	Cape Cod Coast Guard Air Station	02542	(508) 968-1000
Chicopee	Westover Air Reserve Base	01022	(413) 557-1110
Falmouth	Otis Air National Guard Base	02542	(508) 968-1000
Natick	Natick Army R&D Eng. Center	01760	(508) 233-4000
So. Weymouth	South Weymouth Naval Air Station	02190	(781) 682-2500
Worcester	Worcester Air National Guard Base	01605	(508) 799-6963

Michigan

Alpena	Collins Air National Guard Base	49707	(517) 354-6550
Grand Haven	Grand Haven Coast Guard	49417	(616) 850-2500
Grayling	Camp Grayling Training Center	49739	(517) 348-7621
Mt. Clemens	Detriot Coast Guard Air Station	48045	(810) 307-6700
Slt. Sainte Marie	Slt. Sainte Marie Coast Guard Base	49783	(906) 635-3217
Selfridge	Detroit Naval Air Reserve	48045	(810) 307-4011
Traverse City	Traverse City Coast Guard Air Stn.	49684	(616) 922-8212

Minnesota

Little Falls	Camp Ripley	56345	(320) 632-7000

Twin Cities	Twin City Air Force Reserve Base	55450	(612) 713-1000

Mississippi

Bay St. Louis	NASA - Stennis Space Center	39529	(228) 688-2211
Biloxi	Keesler Air Force Base	39534	(228) 377-1110
Columbus	Columbus Air Force Base	39701	(601) 434-7322
Gulfport	Naval Construction Btn. Center	39501	(601) 871-2555
Jackson	Mississippi Air National Guard HQ	39202	(601) 313-6123
Jackson	Thompson Field	39208	(601) 939-3633
Meridian	Naval Air Station, Meridan	39309	(601) 679-2211
Pascagoula	Naval Station, Pascagoula	39595	(601) 761-2140

Missouri

Kansas City	Marine Corps Finance Center	64197	(816) 926-7652
Kansas City	Richards-Gebaur M.C. Activities	64147	(816) 843-3800
Knob Noster	Whiteman Air Force Base	65305	(816) 687-1110
St. Louis	Army Publications Center	63114	(314) 263-7305
St. Louis	Army Reserve Personnel Center	63132	(314) 263-3566
St. Louis	St. Louis Coast Guard Group HQ	63103	(314) 539-3090
Waynesville	Fort Leonard Wood	65473	(573) 596-0131

Montana

Great Falls	Malmstrom Air Force Base	59405	(406) 731-1110
Great Falls	Montana Air National Guard Base	59404	(406) 791-6220

Nebraska

Bellevue	Offutt Air Force Base	68113	(402) 294-1110
Lincoln	Nebraska Air National Guard HQ	68524	(402) 474-0518

Nevada

Fallon	Naval Air Station, Fallon	89496	(702) 426-5161
Indian Springs	Indian Springs Air Force Aux. Field	89018	(702) 879-0201
Las Vegas	Nellis Air Force Base	89191	(702) 652-1110
Reno	Nevada Air National Guard Base	89502	(702) 788-4500

New Hampshire

Amherst	New Boston Air Station	03031	(603) 471-2000
Portsmouth	Pease Air National Guard Base	03803	(603) 430-2467
Portsmouth	Portsmouth Naval Shipyard	03804	(207) 438-1000

New Jersey

Bayonne	Bayonne Military Ocean Terminal	07002	(201) 823-5111
Cape May	Cape May Coast Guard Trng. Cntr.	08204	(609) 898-6900

Colts Neck	Earle Naval Weapons Station	07722	(732) 866-2000
Dover	Picatinny Arsenal	07806	(973) 724-4021
Eatontown	Fort Monmouth	07703	(732) 532-9000
Lakehurst	Lakehurst Naval Air Eng. Station	08733	(732) 323-2011
Trenton	Naval Warfare Center, Trenton	08628	(609) 538-6613
Wrightstown	Fort Dix	08640	(609) 562-1011
Wrightstown	McGuire Air Force Base	08641	(609) 724-1100

New Mexico

Alamogordo	Holloman Air Force Base	88330	(505) 475-6511
Albuquerque	Kirtland Air Force Base	87117	(505) 846-0011
Clovis	Cannon Air Force Base	88103	(505) 784-3311
Las Cruces	White Sands Missile Range	88002	(505) 678-2121

New York

Brooklyn	Brooklyn Coast Guard Air Station	11234	(718) 258-0338
Brooklyn	Fort Hamilton	11252	(718) 630-4101
Buffalo	Buffalo Coast Guard Group	14203	(716) 843-9504
East Meadow	Mitchell Complex	11554	(516) 483-3405
Geneva	Stewart Air National Guard Base	12550	(914) 563-2000
Latham	New York Air National Guard HQ	12110	(518) 786-4502
Niagara Falls	Niagara Falls Air Force Res. Base	14304	(716) 236-2000
Romulus	Seneca Army Depot Activity	14541	(607) 869-1110
Roslyn	Roslyn Air National Guard Station	11576	(516) 299-5229
New Windsor	Stewart Army Subpost	12553	(914) 938-4011
New York	Fort Totten	11359	(718) 352-5700
New York	Governors Island Coast Guard Base	10004	(212) 668-7789
Scotia	Scotia Naval Administrative Unit	12302	(518) 395-3600
Staten Island	New York Coast Guard Activities	10004	(212) 618-7114
Watertown	Fort Drum	13602	(315) 772-6011
Watervliet	Watervliet Arsenal	12189	(518) 266-5111
West Point	U.S. Military Academy	10996	(914) 938-4011

North Carolina

Atlantic Beach	Fort Macon Coast Guard Base	28512	(919) 247-4598
Cape Hatteras	Cape Hatteras Coast Guard Group	27943	(919) 986-2175
Charlotte	North Carolina Air National Guard	28208	(704) 391-4100
Elizabeth City	Elizabeth City Coast Guard Air Stn.	27909	(252) 335-6000
Fayetteville	Pope Air Force Base	28308	(910) 394-1110
Fayetteville	Fort Bragg	28307	(910) 396-0011
Goldsboro	Seymour Johnson Air Force Base	27531	(919) 736-5400
Havelock	Marine Corps Air Stn., Cherry Pt.	28533	(919) 466-2811

Jacksonville	Camp Geiger	28542	(910) 450-0348
Jacksonville	Camp Lejeune Naval Hospital	28542	(910) 451-4300
Jacksonville	Camp Lejeune Marine Corps Base	58542	(910) 451-1113
Jacksonville	Marine Corps Air Stn, New River	28545	(910) 451-1113
Wilmington	Sunny Pt. Military Ocean Terminal	28461	(910) 457-8000

North Dakota

Devils Lake	Camp Crafton ANG Training Site	58301	(701) 662-0200
Edinburg	Cavalier Air Force Base	58220	(701) 993-3297
Emerado	Grand Forks Air Force Base	58205	(701) 747-3000
Fargo	North Dakota Air Natl. Guard HQ	58102	(701) 241-7101
Minot	Minot Air Force Base	58705	(701) 723-1110

Ohio

Cincinnatti	Blue Ash Air Natl. Guard Station	45242	(513) 792-2840
Cleveland	Coast Guard Marine Safety Office	44114	(216) 522-4405
Cleveland	Navy Finance Center	44199	(216) 522-5630
Columbus	Columbus Def. Con. Supply Cntr.	43216	(614) 692-3131
Fairborn	Wright-Patterson Air Force Base	45433	(937) 257-1110
Lockbourne	Rickenbacker Air Natl. Guard Base	43137	(614) 492-4595
Port Clinton	Perry Air National Guard Station	43452	(419) 635-4021
Vienna	Youngstown Air Reserve Station	44473	(330) 609-1000

Oklahoma

Altus	Altus Air Force Base	73523	(580) 482-8100
Braggs	Camp Gruber	74423	(918) 487-6001
Enid	Vance Air Force Base	73705	(580) 213-5000
Lawton	Fort Sill	73503	(580) 422-8111
McAlester	McAlester Army Ammunition Plant	74501	(918) 421-3490
Oklahoma City	OK City Air National Guard Base	73159	(405) 686-5210
Oklahoma City	Tinker Air Force Base	73145	(405) 732-7321
Tulsa	Oklahoma Air National Guard	74115	(918) 832-8300

Oregon

Hermiston	Umatilla Army Depot	97838	(541) 564-8632
Klamath Falls	Kingsley Field Air National Guard	97603	(541) 885-6350
North Bend	North Bend Coast Guard Air Stn.	97459	(541) 756-9222
Portland	Portland Air National Guard Base	97218	(503) 335-4000
Warrenton	Astoria Coast Guard Air Station	97146	(503) 861-6192
Warrenton	Camp Rilea	97146	(503) 861-4000

Pennsylvania

Annville	Penn. Air National Guard HQ	17003	(717) 861-8550
Carlisle	Carlisle Barracks	17013	(717) 245-3131
Chambersburg	Letterkenny Army Depot	17201	(717) 267-8111
Coraopolis	Pittsburgh Air Reserve Station	15108	(412) 474-8000
Lebanon	Fort Indiantown Gap	17003	(717) 861-2000
Mechanicsburg	Naval Ships Parts Center	17055	(717) 790-2000
New Cumberlnd	Defense Distribution Region East	17070	(717) 770-6011
Oakdale	Charles E. Kelly Support Facility	15071	(412) 693-1844
Philadelphia	Coast Guard Marine Safety Group	19147	(215) 271-4800
Philadelphia	Defense Industrial Supply Center	19111	(215) 697-2000
Philadelphia	Defense Personnel Support Center	19145	(215) 737-2411
Philadelphia	Naval Aviation Supply Office	19111	(215) 697-2000
Philadelphia	Philadelphia Naval Station	19112	(215) 897-7000
Philadelphia	Philadelphia Naval Info. Center	19112	(215) 897-6303
Philadelphia	Philadelphia Naval Shipyard	19112	(215) 897-5000
Scranton	Tobyhanna Army Depot	18466	(717) 895-7000
Willow Grove	Naval Air Station/Joint Res. Base	19090	(215) 443-1000

Rhode Island

Coventry	Coventry Air National Guard Stn.	02816	(401) 392-0800
Cranston	Rhode Island Air Natl. Guard HQ	02920	(401) 457-4100
Newport	Naval Undersea Warfare Cntr. Div.	02840	(401) 832-3124
Newport	Newport Naval Ed. & Trng. Center	02840	(401) 841-3456

South Carolina

Beaufort	Beaufort Naval Hospital	29902	(843) 525-5600
Beaufort	Marine Corp Air Station, Beaufort	29904	(843) 522-7100
Charleston	Naval Weapons Station, Charleston	29408	(843) 764-7000
Charleston	Charleston Air Force Base	29404	(843) 963-1110
Charleston	Charleston Coast Guard Base	29401	(843) 724-7600
Charleston	Charleston Naval Hospital	29405	(803) 743-7000
Columbia	Fort Jackson	29207	(803) 751-7511
Eastover	McEntire Air National Guard Base	29044	(803) 776-5121
Parris Island	P.I. Marine Corps Recruit Depot	29905	(803) 525-2111
Sumter	Shaw Air Force Base	29152	(803) 668-8110

South Dakota

Rapid City	Ellsworth Air Force Base	57706	(605) 385-1000
Sioux Falls	Foss Field Air National Guard Base	57117	(605) 988-5700

Tennesee

Manchester	Arnold Air Force Base	37389	(931) 454-3000
Maryville	McGhee Tyson Air Natl. Grd. Base	37777	(423) 985-4540
Millington	Millington Naval Air Station	38054	(901) 874-5111

Texas

Abilene	Dyess Air Force Base	79607	(915) 696-3113
Bastrop	Camp Swift	78602	(512) 303-1919
Boerne	Camp Stanley	78015	(210) 295-7408
Corpus Christi	Corpus Christi Army Depot	78419	(512) 961-2811
Corpus Christi	Corpus Christi Coast Guard Air Stn.	78419	(512) 961-2251
Corpus Christi	Naval Air Station, Corpus Christi	78419	(512) 961-2811
Del Rio	Laughlin Air Force Base	78843	(830) 298-3511
El Paso	Beaumont Army Medical Center	79920	(915) 569-2121
El Paso	Fort Bliss	79916	(915) 568-2121
Ft. Worth	Naval Air Station, Fort Worth	76127	(817) 782-5000
Galveston	Galveston Coast Guard Base	77553	(409) 766-5620
Garland	Garland Army Recruiting Reserve	75040	(972) 530-2575
Houston	Houston Coast Guard Air Station	77034	(281) 481-0025
Ingleside	Naval Station, Ingleside	78362	(512) 776-4200
Killeen	Fort Hood	76544	(254) 287-1110
Kingsville	Naval Air Station, Kingsville	78363	(512) 516-6136
La Porte	La Porte Air National Guard Stn.	77571	(281) 471-5111
Leon Springs	Camp Bullis	78257	(210) 295-7510
San Angelo	Goodfellow Air Force Base	76908	(915) 654-3231
San Antonio	Brooke Army Medical Center	78234	(210) 916-3400
San Antonio	Brooks Air Force Base	78235	(210) 536-1110
San Antonio	Fort Sam Houston	78234	(210) 221-1211
San Antonio	Kelly Air Force Base	78241	(210) 925-1110
San Antonio	Lackland Air Force Base	78236	(210) 671-1110
San Antonio	Wilford Hall Medical Center	78236	(210) 292-7100
Texarkana	Red River Army Depot	75507	(903) 334-2141
Universal City	Randolph Air Force Base	78150	(210) 652-1110
Wichita Falls	Sheppard Air Force Base	76311	(940) 676-2511

Utah

Clearfield	Hill Air Force Base	84056	(801) 777-7221
Ogden	Ogden Defense Distribution Depot	84404	(801) 399-7834
Riverton	Camp W. G. Williams	84065	(801) 253-5402
Salt Lake City	Air National Guard Base	84116	(801) 595-2200
Salt Lake City	Dugway Proving Ground	84022	(801) 831-2151
Tooele	Tooele Army Depot	84074	(801) 833-3211

162 HOW TO LOCATE ANYONE...MILITARY

Vermont

| Montpelier | Vermont National Guard HQ | 05043 | (802) 233-7296 |

Virginia

Alexandria	C.G. Information Systems Center	22315	(703) 313-5400
Alexandria	Fort Belvoir	22060	(703) 545-6700
Arlington	Fort Myer	22211	(703) 545-6700
Arlington	Marine Corps HQ, Henderson Hall	22214	(703) 545-6700
Bowling Green	Fort A. P. Hill	22427	(804) 633-8760
Chesapeake	Chesapeake Naval Security Group	22332	(757) 421-8000
Dahlgren	Naval Surface Warfare Center	22448	(540) 653-8531
Hampton	Fort Monroe	23651	(757) 727-2111
Hampton	Langley Air Force Base	23665	(757) 764-9990
Newport News	Fort Eustis	23604	(757) 878-1212
Norfolk	Little Creek Naval Amphibious Base	23521	(757) 464-7385
Norfolk	Naval Air Station, Norfolk	23511	(757) 444-0000
Petersburg	Fort Pickett	23824	(804) 292-8621
Portsmouth	Norfolk Naval Shipyard	23709	(757) 396-3000
Portsmouth	Portsmouth Coast Guard Sup. Cntr.	23703	(757) 686-4002
Portsmouth	Portsmouth Naval Medical Center	23708	(757) 953-5008
Prince George	Fort Lee	23801	(804) 765-3000
Quantico	Marine Corps Combat Command	22134	(703) 784-2121
Richmond	Defense Supply Center	23297	(804) 279-3861
Sandston	Virginia Air National Guard HQ	23150	(804) 328-3014
Virginia Beach	Dam Neck Fleet Com. Trng. Center	23461	(757) 433-6234
Virginia Beach	Fort Story	23459	(757) 422-7305
Virginia Beach	Naval Air Station, Oceana	23460	(757) 444-0000
Wallops Island	Wallops Isl. Aegis Comb. Sys. Ctr.	23337	(757) 824-1979
Warrenton	Vint Hill Farms Station	20186	(540) 341-7298
Yorktown	Yorktown Naval Weapons Station	23690	(757) 887-4000
Yorktown	Coast Guard Reserve Trng. Center	23690	(757) 898-3500

Washington

Airway Heights	Fairchild Air Force Base	99011	(509) 247-1212
Bremerton	Bremerton Naval Hospital	98312	(360) 479-6600
Bremerton	Puget Sound Naval Shipyard	98314	(360) 476-3711
Everett	Naval Station, Everett	98207	(425) 304-3000
Oak Harbor	Naval Air Station, Whidbey Island	98278	(360) 257-2211
Port Angeles	Port Angeles Coast Guard Air Stn.	98362	(360) 457-2226
Seattle	Seattle Air National Guard Base	98108	(206) 764-5600
Seattle	Coast Guard Intergrated Sup. Com.	98134	(206) 217-6400
Silverdale	Bangor Naval Submarine Base	98315	(360) 396-4840

Tacoma	Fort Lewis	98433	(253) 967-1110
Tacoma	McChord Air Force Base	98259	(253) 984-1910
Tacoma	Washington Air Natl. Guard HQ	98430	(253) 512-8000

West Virginia

| Charleston | W.V. Air National Guard HQ | 25311 | (304) 341-6300 |
| Sugar Grove | Naval Security Group Activity | 26815 | (304) 249-6304 |

Wisconsin

Camp Douglas	Volk Field Air Natl. Guard Base	54618	(608) 427-3341
Madison	Truax Field	53704	(608) 245-4500
Milwaukee	General Mitchell Air Reserve Stn.	53207	(414) 482-5000
Milwaukee	Milwaukee Coast Guard Group	53207	(414) 747-7100
Sparta	Fort McCoy	54656	(608) 388-2222

Wyoming

| Cheyenne | Frances E. Warren Air Force Base | 82005 | (307) 773-1110 |
| Guernsey | Camp Guernsey | 82214 | (307) 836-2823 |

Military Installations, Overseas

The following is a list of overseas APO and FPO addresses that can help you determine the geographic location of an overseas base, or be used as a complete mailing address.

To make a complete address, write the rank and name of the person on the first line. On the next line, add the unit and box number, followed by APO or FPO, followed by AA or AE or AP, and finally the zip. The city or country is not included.

Example:

Sgt. John Doe, Unit 20501, Box 4444, APO, AE 09795

Under Rgn. (region), AE indicates APOs and FPOs in Europe; AP indicates APOs and FPOs in the Pacific area; AA is for Central and South America. Br. (4th column) = Branch of service. A = Army; F = Air Force; M = Marine Corps; N = Navy.

APO/ FPO	Rgn.	Zip	Br.	City	Country	Installation
APO	AE	09007	A	Heidelberg	Germany	Heidelberg
APO	AE	09009	F	Ramstein	Germany	Ramstein AB (South Side)
APO	AE	09012	F	Ramstein	Germany	Ramstein AB (North Side)
APO	AE	09014	A	Heidelberg	Germany	Campbell Barracks
APO	AE	09023	F	Kapaun	Germany	Kapaun Air Station
APO	AE	09028	A	Sandhofen	Germany	Coleman Barracks
APO	AE	09031	A	Kitzingen	Germany	Harvey Barracks
APO	AE	09033	A	Schweinfurt	Germany	Ledward Barracks
APO	AE	09034	A	Baumholder	Germany	H.D. Smith Barracks
APO	AE	09036	A	Wurzburg	Germany	3 Inf. Div., Leighton Brks.
APO	AE	09042	A	Schwetzingen	Germany	208 FSU Tompkins Brks.
APO	AE	09045	A	Kirchgoens	Germany	Ayers Kaserne
APO	AE	09046	A	Boblingen	Germany	Panzer Kaserne
APO	AE	09050	F	Rhein Main	Germany	Rhein Main Air Base
APO	AE	09053	A	Garmisch	Germany	Sheridan Barracks
APO	AE	09054	A	Kaiserslautern	Germany	Daenner Kaserne
APO	AE	09056	A	Worms	Germany	Taukenen Barracks
APO	AE	09058	A	Worms	Germany	Taukenen Barracks
APO	AE	09059	A	Miesau	Germany	Miesau Army Depot
APO	AE	09060	F	Frankfurt Int'l. Airport	Germany	Frankfurt (AMT)

APO	AE	09063	A	Heidelberg	Germany	Campbell Barracks
APO	AE	09067	A	Kaiserslautern	Germany	Kaiserslautern
APO	AE	09069	A	Bremerhaven	Germany	Carl-Schurz
APO	AE	09074	A	Friedberg	Germany	Ray Barracks
APO	AE	09076	A	Buedingen	Germany	Armstrong Barracks
APO	AE	09080	F	Bonn	Germany	American Embassy
APO	AE	09081	A	Schwetzingen	Germany	CDR 1st Perscom
APO	AE	09086	A	Kaefertal	Germany	Taylor/Sullivan Barracks
APO	AE	09089	A	Babenhausen	Germany	Babenhausen Kaserne
APO	AE	09090	A	Roedelheim	Germany	Roedelheim
APO	AE	09094	F	Ramstein	Germany	CDR USAFE Airps.
APO	AE	09095	A	Germershiem	Germany	Germersheim Sub Com.
APO	AE	09096	A	Wiesbaden	Germany	Wiesbaden Air Base
APO	AE	09098	A	Bad Aibling	Germany	Bad Aibling Field Station
APO	AE	09099	A	Heidelberg	Germany	Patton Barracks
APO	AE	09100	A	Heidelberg	Germany	Campbell Barracks
APO	AE	09102	A	Heidelberg	Germany	Patton Barracks
APO	AE	09103	A	Rhinedahlen	Germany	Reichel Bldg.
APO	AE	09104	F	Geilenkirchen	Germany	Geilenkirchen Site
APO	AE	09107	A	Mohringen	Germany	Kelley Barracks
APO	AE	09110	A	Dexheim	Germany	Dexheim Military Com.
APO	AE	09111	A	Bad Kreuznach	Germany	1st ARMD Div/Rose Bks.
APO	AE	09112	A	Sorghof	Germany	Rose Barracks Sorghof
APO	AE	09114	A	Grafenwohr	Germany	Grafenwohr Training Area
APO	AE	09123	F	Spangdahlem	Germany	Spangdahlem Air Base
APO	AE	09126	F	Spangdahlem	Germany	Spangdahlem AB
APO	AE	09128	A	Vaihingen	Germany	Vaihingen
APO	AE	09131	A	Vaihingen	Germany	Patch Barracks
APO	AE	09136	F	Sembach	Germany	Semback Air Base
APO	AE	09137	F	Bitburg	Germany	Bitburg Annex
APO	AE	09138	A	Pirmasens	Germany	Husterhoeh Kaserne
APO	AE	09139	A	Bamberg	Germany	Warner Barracks
APO	AE	09140	A	Illesheim	Germany	Stark Barracks
APO	AE	09142	F	Sembach	Germany	Sembach Air Base
APO	AE	09143	A	Giessen	Germany	AAFES Warehouse
APO	AE	09154	A	Stuttgart	Germany	Robinson Barracks
APO	AE	09157	A	Augsburg	Germany	Sheridan Kaserne
APO	AE	09165	A	Hanau	Germany	Pioneer Kaserne
APO	AE	09166	A	Mannheim	Germany	Turley/Spinelli Barracks
APO	AE	09169	A	Giessen	Germany	Pendelton Barracks
APO	AE	09172	A	Oberammergau	Germany	Nato School
APO	AE	09173	A	Hohenfels	Germany	Hohenfels
APO	AE	09175	A	Darmstadt	Germany	Cambrai-Fristch

APO	AE	09177	A	Ansbach	Germany	Barton Barracks
APO	AE	09178	A	Augsburg	Germany	Reese Barracks
APO	AE	09180	A	Landstuhl	Germany	Landstuhl Med Ctr.
APO	AE	09182	A	Giebelstadt	Germany	Giebelstadt
APO	AE	09183	A	Mainheim	Germany	Sullivan Barracks
APO	AE	09185	A	Mainz	Germany	Lee Barracks
APO	AE	09186	A	Kaiserslautern	Germany	Postal Finance Supply
APO	AE	09211	A	Darmstadt	Germany	Stars & Stripes Kaserne
APO	AE	09212	F	Rhein Main	Germany	64 Repl. BN Rhein-Main AB
APO	AE	09213	F	Frankfurt	Germany	American Consulate
APO	AE	09214	F	Buchel	Germany	Buchel Air Base
APO	AE	09225	A	Kitzingen	Germany	Larson Barracks
APO	AE	09226	A	Schweinfurt	Germany	Conn Barracks
APO	AE	09227	A	Kaiserslautern	Germany	Equipment Supply Center
APO	AE	09229	A	Kaiserslautern	Germany	AAFES Central Credit Payment
APO	AE	09237	A	Frankfurt	Germany	Casual Mail Directory
APO	AE	09244	A	Wurzburg	Germany	Faulenburg Kaserne
APO	AE	09245	A	Mainz Kastell	Germany	AAFES
APO	AE	09250	A	Katterbach	Germany	Katterbach Kaserne
APO	AE	09252	A	Bad Kreuznach	Germany	Bad Kreuznach Hospital
APO	AE	09262	A	Idar-Oberstein	Germany	Strausburg Kaserne
APO	AE	09263	A	Kaiserslautern	Germany	Panzer Kaserne
APO	AE	09264	A	Ansbach	Germany	1 ARMD, Hindenburg Kaserne
APO	AE	09265	F	Berlin	Germany	US Embassy
APO	AE	09266	A	Seckenheim	Germany	Hammond Barracks
APO	AE	09267	A	Mannheim	Germany	Taylor Barracks
APO	AE	09409	M	St. Mawgan	U.K.	JMCC
FPO	AE	09419	N	Edzell Scotland	U.K.	Naval Security Group Act.
FPO	AE	09421	N	London	U.K.	RAF West Ruislip
APO	AE	09447	F	Bedford	U.K.	GEO Sep Units (GSU)
APO	AE	09448	F	Burtonwood	U.K.	Res. Stor. Acty. Burtonwood
APO	AE	09454	F	Cheltenham	U.K.	SUSLO
APO	AE	09456	F	Fairford	U.K.	RAF Fairford
APO	AE	09459	F	Bury-St. Edmunds, Suffolk	U.K.	RAF Mildenhall
APO	AE	09461	F	Thetford	U.K.	RAF Feltwell
APO	AE	09463	F	Bedford Amt	U.K.	Bedford (AMT)
APO	AE	09464	F	Lakenheath, Suffolk	U.K.	RAF Lakenheath
APO	AE	09468	F	Harrogate Yorkshire	U.K.	Menwith Hill Field Station
APO	AE	09469	F	Alconbury	U.K.	RAF Molesworth
APO	AE	09470	F	Huntingdon, Cambridgeshire	U.K.	RAF Alconbury

APO	AE	09494	F	Croughton, Northamptonshire	U.K.	RAF Crougton
APO	AE	09496	F	Flyingdales, Yorkshire	U.K.	Flyingdales
FPO	AE	09498	N	London	U.K.	American Embassy
FPO	AE	09499	N	London	U.K.	Comnavactsuk
APO	AE	09501	N	Various	U.S.	East Coast Navy Squad.
APO	AE	09502	M	Atlantic	U.S.	USMC Mobile Units
APO	AE	09503	M	Atlantic	U.S.	USMC Mobile Units
APO	AE	09504	N	NAS Oceana	U.S.	East Coast Navy Squad.
APO	AE	09506	N	NAS Norfolk	U.S.	East Coast Navy Squad.
APO	AE	09507	N	NAS Norfolk	U.S.	East Coast Navy Squad.
FPO	AE	09508	N	Guantanamo Bay	Cuba	Naval Air Station
APO	AE	09510	M	Atlantic	U.S.	USMC Mobile Units
APO	AE	09582	N	Bayonne NJ	U.S.	USNS Patuxent
APO	AE	09586	N	Norfolk VA	U.S.	USS Rivers Mendel L.
FPO	AE	09593	N	Guantanamo Bay	Cuba	Naval Station
FPO	AE	09596	M	Guantanamo Bay	Cuba	Marine Barracks
APO	AE	09601	F	Aviano	Italy	Aviano Air Base
APO	AE	09603	F	Aviano	Italy	Aviano Air Base
FPO	AE	09609	N	Gaeta	Italy	Naval Support Act. Det.
APO	AE	09610	F	Ghedi	Italy	Ghedi Air Base
FPO	AE	09612	N	La Maddalena, Sardinia	Italy	Naval Support Office
APO	AE	09613	A	Livorno	Italy	Camp Darby
APO	AE	09617	N	Naples	Italy	US Naval Hospital
APO	AE	09618	N	Aversa It	Italy	US Navy Support Site
FPO	AE	09619	N	Naples	Italy	Naval Support Activity
FPO	AE	09620	N	Naples	Italy	Navsuppact Det (AFSouth)
FPO	AE	09621	N	Naples	Italy	US Navcamsmed
FPO	AE	09622	N	Naples Capodichino	Italy	Naval Support Activity
FPO	AE	09623	N	Sigonella It	Italy	Sigonella One Postal
APO	AE	09624	F	Rome	Italy	American Embassy
FPO	AE	09625	N	Naples	Italy	FMC Det Rome IT
FPO	AE	09626	N	Naples	Italy	Naples (FMC)
FPO	AE	09627	N	Sigonella	Italy	Naval Air Station
APO	AE	09628	A	Verona	Italy	Nato Land South
APO	AE	09630	A	Vicenza	Italy	Caserma Eberle
APO	AE	09631	N	Sigonella IT	Italy	Sigonella Two Postal
APO	AE	09636	F	Sigonella	Italy	US Naval Hospital
APO	AE	09638	N	Bari	Spain	Forward Logistic Site
APO	AE	09642	F	Madrid	Spain	American Embassy

APO	AE	09643	F	Moron	Spain	Moron Air Base
FPO	AE	09644	N	Rota	Spain	Naval Communication Sta.
FPO	AE	09645	N	Rota	Spain	Naval Station
APO	AE	09647	F	Madrid Int'l. Airprt.	Spain	Madrid (AMT)
APO	AE	09703	A	Brunssum	Netherlands	Brunssum
APO	AE	09704	F	Thule	Greenland	Thule Air Force Base
APO	AE	09705	A	Shape Casteau	Belgium	Nato Hqtrs
APO	AE	09706	F	Stavanger	Norway	724 Air Base Station
APO	AE	09707	F	Oslo	Norway	American Embassy
APO	AE	09708	A	Chievres	Belgium	Chievres Air Base
APO	AE	09709	F	Rotterdam	Netherlands	MTMC
APO	AE	09710	F	Brussels	Belgium	US Embassy Brussels
APO	AE	09713	A	Kleine Borgel	Belgium	Kleine Borgel
APO	AE	09714	F	Brussels City	Belgium	Brussels (AMT)
APO	AE	09715	F	The Hague	Netherlands	American Embassy
APO	AE	09716	F	Copenhagen	Denmark	American Embassy
APO	AE	09717	F	Volkel	Netherlands	Volkel Air Base
APO	AE	09718	F	Rabat	Morocco	American Embassy
APO	AE	09720	F	Terceira Azores	Portugal	Lajes Field
APO	AE	09721	F	Helsinki	Finland	American Embassy
APO	AE	09722	F	Karup	Denmark	Nato
APO	AE	09723	F	Helsinki	Finland	American Embassy
APO	AE	09724	F	Brussels ITY	Belgium	Nato
APO	AE	09725	F	Keflavik	Iceland	AFI Keflavik
APO	AE	09726	F	Lisbon	Portugal	American Embassy
FPO	AE	09728	N	Keflavik	Iceland	Naval Station
FPO	AE	09729	N	HOFN	Iceland	Commander 667th ACWS
APO	AE	09732	F	North Bay	Canada	CFB North Bay
APO	AE	09733	N	Halifax Nova Scotia	Canada	PEP Halifax
APO	AE	09735	F	Winnipeg, Manitoba	Canada	Winnipeg, Manitoba
APO	AE	09777	F	Paris	France	American Embassy
APO	AE	09779	F	Zagreb	Croatia	Joint Endeavor
APO	AE	09780	F	Sarajevo	Yugoslavia	Joint Endeavor
APO	AE	09781	F	Split	Croatia	Joint Endeavor
APO	AE	09782	F	Kiseljac	Yugoslavia	Joint Endeavor
APO	AE	09783	F	Belgrade	Yugoslavia	Joint Endeavor
APO	AE	09785	F			Joint Endeavor
APO	AE	09786	F			Joint Endeavor
APO	AE	09787	F		Yugoslavia	Joint Endeavor
APO	AE	09788	F	Tuzla	Bosnia	Joint Endeavor
APO	AE	09789	F	Tuzla	Bosnia	Joint Endeavor
APO	AE	09790	F	Skopje	Macedonia	Able Sentry
APO	AE	09791	F	Istres	France	Joint Endeavor

APO	AE	09792	F	San Vito	Italy	Joint Endeavor
APO	AE	09793	F	Taszar	Hungary	Joint Endeavor
APO	AE	09794	F	Taszar	Hungary	Joint Endeavor
APO	AE	09795	F			Joint Endeavor
APO	AE	09796	F			Joint Endeavor
APO	AE	09802	F	Taif	Saudi Arabia	TAIF SA
APO	AE	09803	F	Riyadh	Saudi Arabia	Riyadh SA
APO	AE	09804	F	Dhahran	Saudi Arabia	Dhahran (AMT)
APO	AE	09805	F	Al-Jubail	Saudi Arabia	Al-Jubail SA
APO	AE	09808	A	Dhahran	Saudi Arabia	Camp Lucky
APO	AE	09809	F	Khamis Mushayt	Saudi Arabia	Khamis Mushayt SA
APO	AE	09810	F	Tabuk	Saudi Arabia	Tabuk SA
APO	AE	09811	F	Jeddah	Saudi Arabia	Jeddah SA
APO	AE	09812	F	Islamabad	Pakistan	American Embassy
APO	AE	09813	A	Monrovia	Liberia	US Mission Liberia
APO	AE	09814	F	Karachi	Pakistan	American Consultate
APO	AE	09819	F	Izmir	Turkey	Izmir Air Station
APO	AE	09821	F	Izmir	Turkey	Izmir Air Station
APO	AE	09822	F	Ankara	Turkey	Ankara Air Station
APO	AE	09823	F	Ankara	Turkey	American Embassy
APO	AE	09824	F	Adana	Turkey	Incirlik Air Base
APO	AE	09826	F	Riyadh	Saudi Arabia	Riyadh Amt
APO	AE	09827	F	Istanbul	Turkey	Istanbul Amt
APO	AE	09828	A	Kinshasa	Zaire	US Mission Zaire
APO	AE	09829	F	Khartoum	Sudan	American Embassy
APO	AE	09830	F	Tel Aviv	Israel	American Embassy
APO	AE	09831	F	Nairobi	Kenya	American Embassy
APO	AE	09832	A	El Gorah	Egypt	North Site
APO	AE	09833	A	Sharm El Shiek	Egypt	South Site
FPO	AE	09834	N	Jufair	Bahrain	Manama Ba
FPO	AE	09835	N	Cairo	Egypt	Namru III
FPO	AE	09836	N	Nicosia	Cypress	USDAO
APO	AE	09837	N	Jujairah UAE	United Arab Emirates	Forward Logistic Site
APO	AE	09838	N	Maharraq	Bahrain	Fleet Mail Center
APO	AE	09839	F	Cairo	Egypt	American Embassy
APO	AE	09841	F	Athens	Greece	Athens Amt/APO
APO	AE	09842	F	Athens	Greece	American Embassy
APO	AE	09843	F	Araxos	Greece	Araxos Installation
APO	AE	09852	F	Riyadh	Saudi Arabia	Riyadh SA
APO	AE	09853	F	Al-Dhafra UAE	Saudi Arabia	Al Dhafra UAE
APO	AE	09854	F	QA	Qatar	Doha QA
APO	AE	09855	A	Kuwait City	Kuwait	Kuwait KU

APO	AE	09858	F	Dhahran	Saudi Arabia	Dhahran SA
FPO	AE	09865	N	Souda Bay Crete	Greece	Naval Support Activity
APO	AE	09867	F	Amman	Jordan	Amman JO
APO	AE	09868		Cairo	Egypt	Cairo EG
APO	AE	09871	F	Riyadh	Saudi Arabia	Riyadh SA
APO	AE	09872	F	King Khalid	Saudi Arabia	King Khalid SA
APO	AE	09873	F	Tabuk	Saudi Arabia	Tabuk SA
APO	AE	09875	F	Al Ain UAE	United Arab Emirates	Al Ain UAE
APO	AE	09876		Thumrait Oman	Oman	Thumrait OM
APO	AE	09877	F	Masirah Oman	Oman	Masirah OM
APO	AE	09879			United Arab Emirates	Abu Dhabi UAE
APO	AE	09880	F	Kuwait City	Kuwait	American Embassy
APO	AE	09881	F	Eskan Village	Saudi Arabia	Riyadh SA
APO	AE	09882		Al Kharj	Saudi Arabia	Al Kharj
APO	AE	09883		Al-Jubail	Saudi Arabia	Al-Jubail
APO	AE	09884		Khamis Myshayt	Saudi Arabia	Khamis Myshayt
APO	AE	09885		Al Minhad UAE	Saudi Arabia	Al Minhad UAE
APO	AE	09886	F	King Abdul SA	Saudi Arabia	King Abdul SA
APO	AE	09887	F	King Fahd SA	Saudi Arabia	King Fahd SA
APO	AE	09888	F	Al Jaber KU	Kuwait	Al Jaber KU
APO	AE	09889	A	Camp Doha KU	Kuwait	Camp Doha KU
APO	AE	09890	F	Seeb OM	Kuwait	Seeb OM
APO	AE	09891	F	Bateen UAE	United Arab Emirates	Bateen UAE
APO	AE	09892	F	Amman	Jordan	Amman JO
APO	AE	09893	F	Khobar Towers	Saudi Arabia	Dharan SA
APO	AE	09894	F	Khobar Towers	Saudi Arabia	Dharan SA
APO	AE	09895	A	Riyadh	Saudi Arabia	Riyadh SA
APO	AE	09896	A	TAIF	Saudi Arabia	Riyadh SA
APO	AE	09897	F	Bahrain	Bahrain	TAIF
APO	AE	09898	A	Doha	Qatar	Doha QA
APO	AE	09899	F	Nairobi	Kenya	Nairobi KE
APO	AA	34001	F	Veracruz	Panama	Howard AFB Olad
APO	AA	34002	F	Diablouz	Panama	Albrook AFS
APO	AA	34003	F	Ancon	Panama	Quarry Heights
APO	AA	34004	F	Corozal	Panama	Ft. Clayton
APO	AA	34005	F	Margarita	Panama	Ft. Sherman
APO	AA	34006	F	Veracruz	Panama	Ft. Kobbe
APO	AA	34009	F	Corozal	Panama	Panama Area Exchange
APO	AA	34011	F	Balboa	Panama	Panama Canal Commission
APO	AA	34012	M	Veracruz	Panama	Marine Forces Liaison

APO	AA	34020	F	San Jose	Costa Rica	American Embassy
APO	AA	34021	F	Managua	Nicaragua	American Embassy
APO	AA	34022	F	Tegucigalpa	Honduras	American Embassy
APO	AA	34023	F	San Salvador	El Salvador	American Embassy
APO	AA	34024	F	Guatemala City	Guatemala	American Embassy
APO	AA	34025	F	Belize City	Belize	American Embassy
APO	AA	34030	F	Rio De Janerio	Brazil	American Consulate
APO	AA	34031	F	Lima	Peru	American Embassy
APO	AA	34032	F	La Paz	Bolivia	American Embassy
APO	AA	34033	F	Santiago	Chili	American Embassy
APO	AA	34034	F	Buenos Aires	Argentina	American Embassy
APO	AA	34035	F	Montevideo	Uraguay	American Embassy
APO	AA	34036	F	Asuncion	Paraguay	American Embassy
APO	AA	34037	F	Caracas	Venezuela	American Embassy
APO	AA	34038	F	Bogota	Columbia	American Embassy
APO	AA	34039	F	Quito	Ecuador	American Embassy
APO	AA	34040	A	San Juan	Puerto Rico	Fort Buchanan
APO	AA	34041	F	Santo Domingo	Dominican Republic	American Embassy
APO	AA	34042	F	Comayagua	Honduras	Soto Cano AB
APO	AA	34045	A	Patuka ES	Ecuador	JTF Safe Border
FPO	AA	34050	C	Boringuen	Puerto Rico	Coast Guard Air Station
FPO	AA	34051	N	Roosevelt Roads	Puerto Rico	Naval Station
FPO	AA	34053	N	Sabana Seca	Puerto Rico	Naval Security Group Act.
FPO	AA	34055	N	Barbados	Barbados	American Embassy
FPO	AA	34058	N	Andros Island	The Bahamas	Navunderwater Sys Cen Det.
FPO	AA	34061	N	Cocoli	Panama	Naval Station Panama
FPO	AA	34077	F	Port-Au-Prince	Haiti	
APO	AA	34091	N	Ingleside TX	U.S.	USS Inchon
APO	AA	34098	M	Atlantic	U.S.	USMC Mobile Units
APO	AA	34099	N	Miami Gateway	U.S.	Mobile Units (USN)
APO	AP	96201	A	Kimpo	South Korea	Kimpo MMT
APO	AP	96203	A	Yongsan	South Korea	Yongsan (JUSMAG)
APO	AP	96204	A	Yongsan	South Korea	Yongsan (PSC 303)
APO	AP	96205	A	Yongsan	South Korea	CDR 8th Perscom TAPD
APO	AP	96205	A	Yongsan	South Korea	Yongsan
APO	AP	96206	A	Yongsan	South Korea	Yongsan (PSC 450)
APO	AP	96207	A	Yongsan	South Korea	Yongsan (Casual Mail Dir)
APO	AP	96208	A	Chunchon	South Korea	Camp Page
APO	AP	96212	A	Taegu	South Korea	Camp Henry (19 SPT CMD)
APO	AP	96214	F	Kimhae	South Korea	Kimhae Air Base
APO	AP	96215	A	Pohang	South Korea	Team Sprit
APO	AP	96217	A	Pohang	South Korea	Team Sprit

APO	AP	96218	A	Taegu	South Korea	Camp Henry
APO	AP	96219	A	Pohang	South Korea	Team Sprit
APO	AP	96220	A	Cheju-Do	South Korea	Camp Mcnab
APO	AP	96221	A	Pohang	South Korea	Team Sprit
APO	AP	96224	A	Tongduchon-NI	South Korea	Camp Casey
APO	AP	96251	A	Yono-Te-Ri	South Korea	Camp Edwards
APO	AP	96257	A	Uijongbu	South Korea	Camp Stanley
APO	AP	96258	A	Uijongbu	South Korea	Camp Red Cloud
APO	AP	96259	A	Pusan	South Korea	Hialeah Compound
APO	AP	96260	A	Waegwan	South Korea	Camp Carroll
APO	AP	96262	F	Kwang Ju Ab	Korea	Kwang Air Base
APO	AP	96264	F	Kunsan	South Korea	Kunsan Air Base
APO	AP	96266	F	Osan	South Korea	Osan Air Base
APO	AP	96267	F	Osan	South Korea	Osan Air Base
FPO	AP	96269	N	Chinhae	South Korea	Chinhae Fleet Activity
APO	AP	96271	A	Pyongteak	South Korea	Camp Humphreys
APO	AP	96275	A	Suwon Korea	South Korea	Suwon Air Base
APO	AP	96276	F	Seoul	South Korea	Kimpo Int'l. Airport
APO	AP	96278	F	Song Tansi	South Korea	Osan Air Base
APO	AP	96283	A	Bupyeong	South Korea	Camp Market
APO	AP	96284	A	Bupyeong	South Korea	Camp Market (AAFES)
APO	AP	96297	A	Wonju	South Korea	Camp Long
FPO	AP	96306	N	Atsugi	Japan	Naval Air Facility
FPO	AP	96309	F	Osaka Japan	Japan	Kansai Int'l. Airport
FPO	AP	96310	M	Iwakuni	Japan	MCAS
FPO	AP	96313	N	Kami Seya	Japan	Naval Radar Rec Facility
APO	AP	96319	F	Misawa	Japan	Misawa Air Base
FPO	AP	96321	N	Sasebo	Japan	Hario Family Housing Area
FPO	AP	96322	N	Sasebo	Japan	Fleet Activity
APO	AP	96323	F	Yokota	Japan	Yokota AB (PAC S & S)
APO	AP	96325	F	Yokota	Japan	Yokota Air Base East
APO	AP	96326	F	Yokota	Japan	Yokota AB Japan
APO	AP	96328	F	Yokota	Japan	Yokota Air Base
APO	AP	96330	F	Yokota	Japan	Yokota Air Base PMOJ
APO	AP	96336	F	Tokyo	Japan	Narita Airport
APO	AP	96337	A	Tokyo	Japan	Camp Zama
APO	AP	96338	A	Tokyo	Japan	Camp Zama
APO	AP	96339	A	Camp Zama	Japan	Orient Shield
APO	AP	96343	A	Tokyo	Japan	CDR USAR Japan
APO	AP	96343	A	Tokyo	Japan	Camp Zama
FPO	AP	96347	N	Yokohama	Japan	Yokohama (FMC)
FPO	AP	96348	N	Yokohama	Japan	Yokohama Housing
FPO	AP	96349	N	Yokosuka	Japan	Yokosuka Fleet Activity

FPO	AP	96350	N	Yokosuka	Japan	Yokosuka Naval Hospital
FPO	AP	96362	N	Camp Kuwae	Japan	Okinawa Naval Hospital
APO	AP	96364	F	Kadena	Japan	Kadena Air Base
APO	AP	96365	F	Naha	Japan	Naha Int'l. Airport
APO	AP	96367	F	Kadena	Japan	Kadena Air Base
APO	AP	96368	F	Kadena	Japan	Kadena Air Base
FPO	AP	96370	N	Kadena Naha	Japan	Fleet Activity
FPO	AP	96372	M	Makiminato, Okinawa	Japan	USMC Futenma
FPO	AP	96373	N	Makiminato Okinawa	Japan	USMC Camp Foster
APO	AP	96374	N	Makiminato Okinawa	Japan	USMC Camp Butler
APO	AP	96375	N	Makiminato Okinawa	Japan	USMC Camp Kinser
APO	AP	96376	N	Yomitan, Okinawa	Japan	USMC Tori Station
FPO	AP	96377	M	Tengan, Okinawa	Japan	USMC Camp Courtney
APO	AP	96378	M	Makiminato Okinawa	Japan	USMC Camp Foster
APO	AP	96379	M	Makiminato Okinawa	Japan	USMC Camp Foster
APO	AP	96384	M	Tengan, Okinawa	Japan	USMC Camp Hansen
APO	AP	96386	M	Makiminato Okinawa	Japan	USMC Futenma
APO	AP	96387	M	Mainland Japan	Japan	USMC Camp Fuji
APO	AP	96388	M	Tengan, Okinawa	Japan	USMC Camp Schwab
APO	AP	96440	F	Manila	Philippines	US Embassy
FPO	AP	96506	N	Adak	U.S.	Naval Air Station
APO	AP	96508	A	Big Delta	U.S.	Fort Greely
APO	AP	96511	N	CFB Esquimalt, BC	Canada	Canadian Forces Station
APO	AP	96515	N	Manila	Philippines	US Embassy
APO	AP	96517	N	Manila	Philippines	US Embassy
APO	AP	96520	F	Jakarta	Indonesia	US Embassy Jakarta
FPO	AP	96521	N	Hong Kong	Hong Kong	American Consulate
FPO	AP	96522	N	Hong Kong	Hong Kong	Naval Contracting Dep
FPO	AP	96530	F	Perth	Australia	American Consulate
FPO	AP	96531	F	Christchurch	New Zealand	Navsuppforantarctica Det
FPO	AP	96534	N	Singapore	Singapore	US Navy Office
FPO	AP	96535	F	Kuala Lampur	Malaysia	US Embassy
FPO	AP	96536	N	Agana	U.S.	Comnavmarianas GQ
FPO	AP	96537	N	Agana	U.S.	NCTAMS
FPO	AP	96538	N	Agana	U.S.	US Naval Hospital
FPO	AP	96540	N	Agana	U.S.	Naval Station

APO	AP	96543	F	Agana	U.S.	Anderson Air Base
APO	AP	96545	A	Brisbane	Australia	Tandem Thrust 1997
APO	AP	96546	F	Bangkok	Thailand	US Embassy
APO	AP	96547	F	Bangkok	Thailand	Cobra Gold
APO	AP	96548	F	Alice Springs	Australia	Alice Springs
APO	AP	96549	F	Canberra A.C.T.	Australia	Canberra
APO	AP	96551	F	Melbourne, Victoria	Australia	US Consulate
APO	AP	96552	F	Woomera	Australia	Woomera Site
APO	AP	96553	F	Sydney	Australia	US Consulate
APO	AP	96554	F	Sydney	Australia	US Consulate
APO	AP	96555	A	Kwajalein	Marshall Isl.	Kwajalein Missile Range
APO	AP	96556	A	Pohakuloa	U.S.	Pohakuloa Training Area
APO	AP	96557	A	Kwaja Atoll	Marshall Isl.	ROI-Namur Island
APO	AP	96558	C	Johnston Island	U.S.	Johnston Island
APO	AP	96580	A	Rockhampton	Australia	Tandem Thrust 1997
APO	AP	96594	A	Townsville	Australia	Tandem Thrust 1997
APO	AP	96595	N	Diego Garcia Isl.	Indian Ocean	Naval Support Facility
APO	AP	96596	A	Sam Hill	Australia	Tandem Thrust 1997
APO	AP	96597	A	Williamson Airfield	Australia	Tandem Thrust 1997
FPO	AP	96598	F	Amundsen-Scott	Antarctica	South Pole Station
FPO	AP	96599	F	McMurdo Station	Antarctica	Navsuppforantarctica Det.
APO	AP	96601	N	Various	U.S.	West Coast Navy Squads.
APO	AP	96602	M	Okinawa (Mobile)	Japan	3rd Mar Div
APO	AP	96603	M	Okinawa (Mobile)	Japan	3rd MAW
APO	AP	96604	M	Okinawa (Mobile)	Japan	3rd FSSG
APO	AP	96605	N	W. Coast MSC Ships	U.S.	MSC Ships
APO	AP	96606	M	Okinawa (Mobile)	Japan	3rd MEF
APO	AP	96607	M	Hawaii	U.S.	USMC Mobile Units
APO	AP	96608	M	California	U.S.	USMC Mobile Units
APO	AP	96609	M	California	U.S.	USMC Mobile Units
APO	AP	96610	M	California	U.S.	USMC Mobile Units
APO	AP	96611	M	California	U.S.	USMC Mobile Units
APO	AP	96613	M	Hawaii	U.S.	USMC Mobile Units
APO	AP	96662	N		U.S.	MV Cape Washington
APO	AP	96679	N	Pacflt	U.S.	USNS Tippecanoe

Phone Numbers of Overseas Military Installations

Numbers in parentheses (example: first line, below) are U.S. area codes. Dial these numbers as you would any long distance number in the U.S. All other numbers require dialing "011" and then the number.

Br. = Branch. A = Army; F = Air Force; N = Navy; M = Marines.

Zip	Br.	Country	Phone Number	Installation
00934	A	Puerto Rico	(787) 273-3869	Fort Buchanan
09014	A	Germany	49-6221-57-8916	Stuttgart
09014	A	Germany	49-6221-57-8916	US Army Europe
09031	A	Germany	49-9321-305509	Kitzingen Community
09031	A	Germany	49-931-889-7103	Wuerzberg Community
09033	A	Germany	49-9721-96-6751	Scheinfurt Community
09034	A	Germany	49-6783-6-6252	Baumholder Community
09045	A	Germany	49-6033-82-113	Kirch-Goens/Butzbach Com.
09050	F	Germany	49-69-699-7992	Rhein-Main Air Base
09053	A	Germany	49-8821-750-712	Garmisch Community/Rec Cntr.
09074	A	Germany	49-6031-81-3528	Friedberg Community
09086	A	Germany	49-621-730-4475	Mannheim Community
09094	F	Germany	49-6371-47-5100	Ramstein Air Base
09096	A	Germany	49-611-705-5034	Wiesbaden Community
09098	A	Germany	49-8051-803-172	Chiemsee Recreation Ctr
09098	A	Germany	49-8061-38-5016	USA Bad Aibling
09102	A	Germany	49-6221-57-6883	Heidelberg Community
09104	F	Germany	49-2451-63-3791	Geilenkirchen Air Base
09111	A	Germany	49-671-60-9-113	Bad Kreuznach Community
09112	A	Germany	49-9662-83-1500	Vilseck Community
09114	A	Germany	49-9641-83-8371	Grafenwoehr Community
09126	F	Germany	49-6565-61-7491	Spangdahlem Air Base
09139	A	Germany	49-951-300-7777	Bamberg Community
09140	A	Germany	49-9641-83-555-764	Illesheim Community
09165	A	Germany	49-6183-88-8965	Hanau Community
09169	A	Germany	49-402-7619	Giessen Depot
09173	A	Germany	49-9472-83-2861	Hohenfels Community
09175	A	Germany	49-6151-69-7113	Darmstadt Community
09177	A	Germany	49-9802-832-846	Ansbach Community
09178	A	Germany	49-821-540-113	Augsburg Community
09182	A	Germany	49-9334-8-7877	Giebelstadt Community
09227	A	Germany	49-631-536-7251	Kaiserslautern Community

Zip	Br.	Country	Phone Number	Installation
09409	M	U.K.	44-16373-2201 or -2775	RAF St. Mawgan
09420	N	U.K.	44-1437-720654	Bawdy Wales Naval Facility
09421	N	U.K.	44-171-514-1110	London Naval Activity
09421	N	U.K.	44-1895-616552	Comnavvactuk
09456	F	U.K.	44-1285-71-4110	RAF Fairford
09459	F	U.K.	44-1638-54-3406	RAF Mildenhall
09464	F	U.K.	44-1638-523847	RAF Lakenheath
09468	F	U.K.	44-1423-777730	RAF Menwith Hall
09470	F	U.K.	44-1480-823557	RAF Molesworth
09470	F	U.K.	44-1480-451898	RAF Alconbury
09494	F	U.K.	1280-708-000	RAF Croughton
09593	N	Cuba	53-99-4141	Guantanamo Bay Naval Station
09601	F	Italy	39-434-66-8256	Aviano Air Base
09609	N	Italy	39-771-709-818	Gaeta Naval Support Activity
09612	N	Italy	39-789-798-205 or -206	La Maddalena Naval Sup. Act.
09613	A	Italy	39-50-54-7084	Camp Darby/Livorno
09619	N	Italy	39-81-724-1110	Admiral Carney Park
09619	N	Italy	39-81-724-4393	Naples Naval Support Activity
09623	N	Italy	39-095-56-4291	NAS Sigonella
09630	A	Italy	39-444-51-7617	Vicenza Community
09643	F	Spain	34-95-584-8111	Moron Air Base
09645	N	Spain	34-56-82-5232	Rota Naval Station
09703	A	Netherlands	31-46-443-7512	Schinnen Community
09704	F	Denmark	299-50-636	Thule Air Base (Greenland)
09707	F	Norway	47-67-14-3030	Oslo Community
09708	A	Belgium	32-65-44-113	Shape/Chievres Air Base Com.
09720	F	Portugal	351-95-540100	Lajes Field
09724	F	Belgium	32-2-728-1769	Brussels Nato Community
09724	F	Belgium	32-2-502481	Tri-Mission Association
09726	F	Portugal	351-1-443-1791	Reducto Gomes Freire
09728	N	Iceland	354-425-4401	Keflavik Naval Air Station
09803	A	S. Arabia	966-1-498-7006	U.S. Military Training Mission
09803	F	S. Arabia	966-1-891-119	Riyadh Community
09811	F	S. Arabia	966-2-682-0951 or-0942	Jeddah Community
09821	F	Turkey	90-232-484-5360	Izmir Air Station
09824	F	Turkey	90-322-316-6755	Incirlik Air Base
09834	N	Bahrain	973-724-046	Bahrain Naval Support Unit
09839	F	Egypt	20-2-355-7371	Cairo East Air Base Community
09858	F	S. Arabia	966-3-899-1119	Dhahran Community
09865	N	Greece	30-821-63388	Souda Bay Naval Sup. Facility
09880	F	Kuwait	965-242-4151	Kuwait Community Int. Airport

Zip	Br.	Country	Phone Number	Installation
32925	N	Antigua	(809) 462-0368	Antigua Air Station
34001	F	Panama	507-284-5650	Howard Air Force Base
34004	F	Panama	507-288-9235	Fort Clayton
34042	F	Honduras	504-33-51-01	Soto Cano Air Base
34051	N	Puerto Rico	(787) 865-4975	Roosevelt Roads
34061	F	Panama	507-283-1110	Rodman Naval Station
96205	A	Korea	82-2-7918-7999	Yongsan Community
96218	A	Korea	82-53-470-8698	Camp Henry-Taego
96224	A	Korea	82-351-869-3436	Camp Casey
96259	A	Korea	82-51-801-3571	Camp Hialeah-Pusan
96264	F	Korea	82-654-470-5644	Kunsan Air Base
96269	A	Korea	82-533-540-5385	Comfleacts Chinhae Installation
96271	A	Korea	82-333-690-8401	Camp Humphreys
96278	F	Korea	82-333-661-5440	Osan Air Base
96306	N	Japan	81-3117-64-3628	Atsugi Naval Air Facilty
96310	M	Japan	81-6117-53-3311	Iwakuni Marine Corps Air Station
96319	F	Japan	81-3117-66-9366	Misawa Air Base
96322	N	Japan	81-956-24-6111	Sasebo Fleet Activities
96328	F	Japan	81-423-77-7009	Tama Outdoor Recreation Area
96328	F	Japan	81-3117-55-8725	Yokota Air Base
96337	A	Japan	81-3-3440-7871	The New Sanno U.S. Forces Center
96337	A	Japan	81-3117-29-3270	Tokyo Administration Facility
96343	A	Japan	81-3117-63-8089	Camp Zama
96349	N	Japan	81-311-743-9626	Yokosuka Fleet Activities
96364	F	Japan	81-611-734-3366	Kadena Air Base
96368	F	Japan	81-98-041-5164	Okuma Beach Resort-Okinawa
96370	N	Japan	81-642-2264 or -2266	White Beach Recreation Services
96373	N	Japan	81-611-745-3155	Camp Butler Marine Corps Base
96376	N	Japan	81-611-744-4385	Torii Station
96531	F	New Zealand	64-3-358-1475	Christchurch Naval Station
96534	N	Singapore	65-724-2387	Singapore Community
96540	N	Guam	(671) 333-2056	USN Forces Marianas
96543	F	Guam	(671) 366-8136	Anderson AFB
96546	F	Thailand	66-2-287-1036	Bangkok Community
96548	F	Australia	61-89-530-570	Alice Springs Airport
96552	F	Australia	61-86-739-911	Woomera Air Station
96554	F	Australia	61-45-70-2340	RAAF Richmond
96659	N	Hong Kong	852-2-861-0063	Hong Kong Community

U.S. Coast Guard and Navy Ships

The following lists provide the names, hull numbers, and zip codes of Coast Guard and Navy ships. Homeports and states are also provided for Navy ships.

To make a complete mailing address, write the rank and name of the person on the first line. On the next line, add the unit and box number, followed by FPO, followed by AA or AE or AP, and finally the zip code. The state or homeport should not be included.

Example:

LTJG John Doe, USS Nimitz (CVN 88), FPO, AP 96697

The two-letter abbreviation of AE indicates APOs and FPOs in Europe. AP indicates APOs and FPOs in the Pacific area. AA is for Central and South America.

U.S. Coast Guard Ships

Ship	Hull No.	Address		Zip Code
USCGC Cushing	WPB 1321	FPO	AA	34051-3823
USCGC Nunivak	WPB 1306	FPO	AA	34051-3823
USCGC Ocracode	WPB 1307	FPO	AA	34051-3823
USCGC Vashon	WPB 1308	FPO	AA	34051-3823
USCGC Munro	WHEC 724	FPO	AP	96672-3917
USCGC Sherman	WHEC 720	FPO	AP	96678-3923
USCGC Morgenthau	WHEC 722	FPO	AP	96672-3916
USCGC Rush	WHEC 723	FPO	AP	96677-3921
USCGC Jarvis	WHEC 725	FPO	AP	96669-3912
USCGC Boutwell	WHEC 719	FPO	AP	96661-3902
USCGC Kukui	WLB 203	FPO	AP	96672-3913
USCGC Walnut	WLB 205	FPO	AP	96683-3910
USCGC Polar Star	WAGB 10	FPO	AP	96698-3920
USCGC Polar Sea	WAGB 11	FPO	AP	96698-3919
USCGC Midgett	WHEC 726	FPO	AP	96698-3915
USCGC Mellon	WHEC 717	FPO	AP	96698-3914
USCGC Galveston Island	WPB 1349	FPO	AP	96540-1056

U.S. Navy Ships

Ship		Hull No.	Address		Zip Code	Homeport
USS	Abraham Lincoln	CVN 72	FPO	AP	96612-2872	Everett, WA
USS	Alabama	SSBN 731	FPO	AP	96698-2108	Bangor, WA
USS	Alaska	SSBN 732	FPO	AP	96698-2111	Bangor, WA
USS	Albany	SSN 753	FPO	AE	09564-2409	Norfolk, VA
USS	Albuquerque	SSN 706	FPO	AE	09564-2386	Groton, CT
USS	Alexandria	SSN 757	FPO	AE	09564-2413	Groton, CT
USS	Anchorage	LSD 36	FPO	AP	96660-1724	San Diego, CA
USS	Annapolis	SSN 760	FPO	AE	09564-2416	Groton, CT
USS	Antietam	CG 54	FPO	AP	96660-1174	San Diego, CA
USS	Anzio	CG 68	FPO	AE	09564-1188	Norfolk, VA
USS	Arctic	AOE 8	FPO	AE	09564-3039	Earle, NJ
USS	Ardent	MCM 12	FPO	AA	34090-1932	Ingleside, TX
USS	Arleigh Burke	DDG 51	FPO	AE	09565-1269	Norfolk, VA
USS	Arthur W Radford	DD 968	FPO	AE	09586-1206	Norfolk, VA
USS	Asheville	SSN 758	FPO	AP	96660-2414	San Diego, CA
USS	Ashland	LSD 48	FPO	AE	09564-1736	Little Creek, VA
USS	Augusta	SSN 710	FPO	AE	09564-2390	Groton, CT
USS	Austin	LPD 4	FPO	AE	09564-1707	Norfolk, VA
USS	Avenger	MCM 1	FPO	AA	34090-1921	Ingleside, TX
USS	Barry	DDG 52	FPO	AE	09565-1270	Norfolk, VA
USS	Bataan	LHD 5	FPO	AE	09554-1657	Norfolk, VA
USS	Belleau Wood	LHA 3	FPO	AP	96623-1610	Sasebo, Japan
USS	Benfold	DDG 65	FPO	AP	96661-1283	San Diego, CA
USS	Billfish	SSN 676	FPO	AE	09565-2356	Groton, CT
USS	Black Hawk	MHC 58	FPO	AA	34091-1955	Ingleside, TX
USS	Blue Ridge	LCC 19	FPO	AP	96628-3300	Yokosuka, Japan
USS	Boise	SSN 764	FPO	AE	09565-2420	Norfolk, VA
USS	Bonhomme Richard	LHD 6	FPO	AP	96617-1656	San Diego, CA
USS	Boone	FFG 28	FPO	AA	34093-1484	Mayport, FL
USS	Boston	SSN 703	FPO	AP	96661-2383	Pearl Harbor, HI
USS	Boxer	LHD 4	FPO	AP	96661-1663	San Diego, CA
USS	Bremerton	SSN6 98	FPO	AP	96661-2378	San Diego, CA
USS	Bridge	AOE 10	FPO	AP	96661-3040	Bremerton, WA
USS	Briscoe	DD9 77	FPO	AE	09565-1215	Norfolk, VA
USS	Buffalo	SSN 715	FPO	AP	96661-2395	Pearl Harbor, HI
USS	Bunker Hill	CG 52	FPO	AP	96661-1172	San Diego, CA
USS	Camden	AOE 2	FPO	AP	96698-3013	Bremerton, WA
USS	Cape St George	CG7 1	FPO	AE	09566-1191	Norfolk, VA
USS	Cardinal	MHC 60	FPO	AA	34090-1959	Ingleside, TX
USS	Carl Vinson	CVN 70	FPO	AP	96629-2840	Bremerton, WA

USS	Carney	DDG 64	FPO	AA	34090-1282	Mayport, FL
USS	Caron	DD 970	FPO	AE	09566-1208	Norfolk, VA
USS	Carr	FFG 52	FPO	AE	09566-1506	Norfolk, VA
USS	Carter Hall	LSD 50	FPO	AE	09573-1738	Little Creek, VA
USS	Champion	MCM 4	FPO	AA	34090-1924	Ingleside, TX
USS	Chancellorsville	CG 62	FPO	AP	96662-1182	Yokosuka, Japan
USS	Chandler	DDG 996	FPO	AP	96662-1268	Everett, WA
USS	Charlotte	SSN 766	FPO	AP	96662-2422	Pearl Harbor, HI
USS	Cheyenne	SSN 773	FPO	AP	96662-2429	Pearl Harbor, HI
USS	Chicago	SSN 721	FPO	AP	96662-2401	Pearl Harbor, HI
USS	Chief	MCM 14	FPO	AA	34090-1934	Ingleside, TX
USS	Chinook	PC 9	FPO	AE	09566-1968	Little Creek, VA
USS	Chosin	CG 65	FPO	AP	96662-1185	Pearl Harbor, HI
USS	Cimarron	AO 177	FPO	AP	96662-3018	Pearl Harbor, HI
USS	Corpus Christi	SSN 705	FPO	AE	09566-2385	Groton, CT
USS	Clark	FFG 11	FPO	AE	09566-1469	Norfolk, VA
USS	Cleveland	LPD 7	FPO	AP	96662-1710	San Diego, CA
USS	Cole	DDG 67	FPO	AE	09566-1285	Norfolk, VA
USS	Columbia	SSN 771	FPO	AP	96662-2427	Pearl Harbor, HI
USS	Columbus	SSN 762	FPO	AP	96662-2418	Pearl Harbor, HI
USS	Comstock	LSD 45	FPO	AP	96662-1733	San Diego, CA
USS	Connecticut	SSN 22	FPO	AE	09566-2302	Groton, CT
USS	Constellation	CV 64	FPO	AE	09558-2780	San Diego, CA
USS	Cormorant	MHC 57	FPO	AA	34090-1958	Ingleside, TX
USS	Coronado	AGF 11	FPO	AP	96662-3330	San Diego, CA
USS	Cowpens	CG 63	FPO	AP	96662-1183	San Diego, CA
USS	Crommelin	FFG 37	FPO	AP	96662-1492	Pearl Harbor, HI
USS	Curtis Wilbur	DDG 54	FPO	AP	96683-1272	Yokosuka, Japan
USS	Curts	FFG 38	FPO	AP	96662-1493	San Diego, CA
USS	Cushing	DD 985	FPO	AP	96662-1223	Yokosuka, Japan
USS	Cyclone	PC 1	FPO	AE	09566-1960	Little Creek, VA
USS	Dallas	SSN 700	FPO	AE	09567-2380	Groton, CT
USS	David R Ray	DD 971	FPO	AP	96677-1209	Everett, WA
USS	De Wert	FFG 45	FPO	AA	34090-1499	Mayport, FL
USS	Decatur	DDG 73	FPO	AP	96663-1290	San Diego, CA
USS	Defender	MCM 2	FPO	AA	34090-1922	Ingleside, TX
USS	Denver	LPD 9	FPO	AP	96663-1712	San Diego, CA
USS	Detroit	AOE 4	FPO	AE	09567-3015	Earle, NJ
USS	Devastator	MCM 6	FPO	AA	34090-1926	Ingleside, TX
USS	Dextrous	MCM 13	FPO	AA	34090-1933	Ingleside, TX
USS	Deyo	DD 989	FPO	AE	09567-1227	Norfolk, VA
USS	Dolphin	AGSS 555	FPO	AP	96663-4000	San Diego, CA
USS	Doyle	FFG 39	FPO	AA	34090-1494	Mayport, FL

USS	Dubuque	LPD 8	FPO	AP	96663-1711	Sasebo, Japan
USS	Duluth	LPD 6	FPO	AP	96663-1709	San Diego, CA
USS	Eisenhower	CVN 69	FPO	AE	09532-2830	Norfolk, VA
USS	Elliot	DD 967	FPO	AP	96664-1205	San Diego, CA
USS	Elrod	FFG 55	FPO	AE	09568-1509	Norfolk, VA
USS	Emory S Land	AS 39	FPO	AE	09545-2610	Norfolk, VA
USS	Enterprise	CVN 65	FPO	AE	09543-2810	Norfolk, VA
USS	Essex	LHD 2	FPO	AP	96643-1661	San Diego, CA
USS	Estocin	FFG 15	FPO	AE	09568-1473	Norfolk, VA
USS	Falcon	MHC 59	FPO	AA	34091-1957	Ingleside, TX
USS	Fife	DD 991	FPO	AP	96665-1229	Everett, WA
USS	Firebolt	PC 10	FPO	AE	09569-1969	Little Creek, VA
USS	Fitzgerald	DDG 62	FPO	AP	96665-1280	San Diego, CA
USS	Fletcher	DD 992	FPO	AP	96665-1230	Pearl Harbor, HI
USS	Florida	SSBN 728	FPO	AP	96698-2099	Bangor, WA
USS	Ford	FFG 54	FPO	AP	96665-1508	Everett, WA
USS	Fort Mchenry	LSD 43	FPO	AP	96665-1731	Sasebo, Japan
USS	Frank Cable	AS 40	FPO	AP	96662-2615	Guam
USS	Frederick	LST 1184	FPO	AP	96665-1805	Pearl Harbor, HI
USS	Gary	FFG 51	FPO	AP	96666-1505	San Diego, CA
USS	George Philip	FFG 12	FPO	AP	96675-1470	San Diego, CA
USS	George Washington	CVN 73	FPO	AE	09550-2873	Norfolk, VA
USS	Georgia	SSBN 729	FPO	AP	96698-2102	Bangor, WA
USS	Germantown	LSD 42	FPO	AP	96666-1730	Sasebo, Japan
USS	Gettysburg	CG 64	FPO	AA	34091-1184	Mayport, FL
USS	Gladiator	MCM 11	FPO	AA	34091-1931	Ingleside, TX
USS	Gonzalez	DDG 66	FPO	AE	09570-1284	Norfolk, VA
USS	Grapple	ARS 53	FPO	AE	09570-3223	Little Creek, VA
USS	Grasp	ARS 51	FPO	AE	09570-3220	Little Creek, VA
USS	Greeneville	SSN 772	FPO	AP	96666-2428	Pearl Harbor, HI
USS	Guardian	MCM 5	FPO	AP	96666-1925	Sasebo, Japan
USS	Gunston Hall	LSD 44	FPO	AE	09573-1732	Little Creek, VA
USS	Halyburton	FFG 40	FPO	AE	09568-1495	Norfolk, VA
USS	Hampton	SSN 767	FPO	AE	09573-2423	Norfolk, VA
USS	Harpers Ferry	LSD 49	FPO	AP	96665-1737	San Diego, CA
USS	Harry S Truman	CVN 75	FPO	AE	09524-2875	Norfolk, VA
USS	Hartford	SSN 768	FPO	AE	09573-2424	Groton, CT
USS	Hawes	FFG 53	FPO	AE	09573-1507	Norfolk, VA
USS	Hawkbill	SSN 666	FPO	AP	96667-2346	Pearl Harbor, HI
USS	Hayler	DD 997	FPO	AE	09573-1231	Norfolk, VA
USS	Helena	SSN 725	FPO	AE	09573-2405	Portsmouth, NH
USS	Henry M Jackson	SSBN 730	FPO	AP	96698-2105	Bangor, WA
USS	Heron	MHC 52	FPO	AA	34091-1951	Ingleside, TX

USS	Hewitt	DD 966	FPO	AP	96667-1204	San Diego, CA
USS	Honolulu	SSN 718	FPO	AP	96667-2398	Pearl Harbor, HI
USS	Hopper	DDG 70	FPO	AP	96667-1289	Pearl Harbor, HI
USS	Houston	SSN 713	FPO	AP	96667-2393	San Diego, CA
USS	Hue City	CG 66	FPO	AA	34091-1186	Mayport, FL
USS	Hurricane	PC 3	FPO	AP	96667-1962	San Diego, CA
USS	Hyman G Rickover	SSN 709	FPO	AE	09586-2389	Norfolk, VA
USS	Inchon	MCS 12	FPO	AE	09529-1655	Ingleside, TX
USS	Ingraham	FFG 61	FPO	AP	96668-1515	Everett, WA
USS	Jacksonville	SSN 699	FPO	AE	09575-2379	Norfolk, VA
USS	Jarrett	FFG 33	FPO	AP	96669-1489	San Diego, CA
USS	Jefferson City	SSN 759	FPO	AP	96669-2415	San Diego, CA
USS	John A Moore	FFG 19	FPO	AP	96672-1475	San Diego, CA
USS	John C Stennis	CVN 74	FPO	AP	96615-2874	San Diego, CA
USS	John F Kennedy	CV 67	FPO	AA	34095-2800	Mayport, FL
USS	John Hancock	DD 981	FPO	AA	34091-1219	Mayport, FL
USS	John L Hall	FFG 32	FPO	AA	34091-1488	Pascagoula, MS
USS	John Paul Jones	DDG 53	FPO	AP	96669-1271	San Diego, CA
USS	John S Mccain	DDG 56	FPO	AP	96672-1274	Yokosuka, Japan
USS	John Young	DD 973	FPO	AP	96686-1211	San Diego, CA
USS	Juneau	LPD 10	FPO	AP	96669-1713	San Diego, CA
USS	Kamehameha	SSN 642	FPO	AP	96670-2063	Pearl Harbor, HI
USS	Kauffman	FFG 59	FPO	AE	09576-1513	Norfolk, VA
USS	Kearsarge	LHD 3	FPO	AE	09534-1662	Norfolk, VA
USS	Kentucky	SSBN 737	FPO	AA	34091-4990	Kings Bay, GA
USS	Key West	SSN 722	FPO	AP	96683-2402	Pearl Harbor, HI
USS	Kingfisher	MHC 56	FPO	AA	34091-1956	Ingleside, TX
USS	Kinkaid	DD9 65	FPO	AP	96670-1203	San Diego, CA
USS	Kitty Hawk	CV 63	FPO	AP	96634-2770	Yokosuka, Japan
USS	Klakring	FFG 42	FPO	AE	09576-1497	Norfolk, VA
USS	L Mendel Rivers	SSN 686	FPO	AE	09586-2366	Norfolk, VA
USS	La Jolla	SSN 701	FPO	AE	09577-2381	Portsmouth, NH
USS	La Moure County	LST 1194	FPO	AE	09577-1815	Little Creek, VA
USS	La Salle	AGF 3	FPO	AE	09577-3320	Gaeta, Italy
USS	Laboon	DDG 58	FPO	AE	09577-1276	Norfolk, VA
USS	Lake Champlain	CG 57	FPO	AP	96671-1177	San Diego, CA
USS	Lake Erie	CG 70	FPO	AP	96671-1190	Pearl Harbor, HI
USS	Leyte Gulf	CG 55	FPO	AE	09570-1175	Norfolk, VA
USS	Los Angeles	SSN 688	FPO	AP	96671-2368	Pearl Harbor, HI
USS	Louisiana	SSBN 743	FPO	AE	34091-2144	Groton, CT
USS	Louisville	SSN 724	FPO	AP	96671-2404	Pearl Harbor, HI
USS	Mahan	DDG 72	FPO	AE	09578-1292	Norfolk, VA
USS	Maine	SSBN 741	FPO	AA	34092-2138	Kings Bay, GA

USS	Maryland	SSBN 738	FPO	AA	34092-2129	Kings Bay, GA
USS	Mcclusky	FFG 41	FPO	AP	96672-1496	San Diego, CA
USS	Mcfaul	DDG 74	FPO	AE	09578-1293	Norfolk, VA
USS	Mcinerney	FFG 8	FPO	AA	34092-1466	Mayport, FL
USS	Mckee	AS 41	FPO	AP	96621-2620	San Diego, CA
USS	Memphis	SSN 691	FPO	AE	09578-2371	Groton, CT
USS	Miami	SSN 755	FPO	AE	09578-2411	Groton, CT
USS	Michigan	SSBN 727	FPO	AP	96698-2096	Bangor, WA
USS	Milius	DDG 69	FPO	AP	96672-1286	San Diego, CA
USS	Minn. St Paul	SSN 708	FPO	AE	09578-2388	Norfolk, VA
USS	Mitscher	DDG 57	FPO	AE	09578-1275	Norfolk, VA
USS	Mobile Bay	CG 53	FPO	AP	96672-1173	Yokosuka, Japan
USS	Monongahela	AO 178	FPO	AE	09578-3019	Norfolk, VA
USS	Monsoon	PC 4	FPO	AP	96672-1963	San Diego, CA
USS	Monterey	CG 61	FPO	AE	09578-1181	Norfolk, VA
USS	Montpelier	SSN 765	FPO	AE	09578-2421	Norfolk, VA
USS	Moosbrugger	DD 980	FPO	AE	09578-1218	Norfolk, VA
USNS	Mount Baker	TAE 34	FPO	AE	09578-4047	Charleston, SC
USS	Mount Hood	AE 29	FPO	AP	96672-3007	Bremerton, WA
USS	Mount Vernon	LSD 39	FPO	AP	96672-1727	San Diego, CA
USS	Mount Whitney	LCC 20	FPO	AE	09517-3310	Norfolk, VA
USS	Nashville	LPD 13	FPO	AE	09579-1715	Norfolk, VA
USS	Nassau	LHA 4	FPO	AE	09557-1615	Norfolk, VA
USS	Nebraska	SSBN 739	FPO	AA	34092-2132	Kings Bay, GA
USS	Nevada	SSBN 733	FPO	AP	96698-2114	Bangor, WA
USS	Newport News	SSN 750	FPO	AE	09579-2406	Norfolk, VA
USS	Nicholas	FFG 47	FPO	AE	09579-1501	Norfolk, VA
USS	Nicholson	DD 982	FPO	AE	09579-1220	Norfolk, VA
USS	Nimitz	CVN 68	FPO	AE	09521-2820	Norfolk, VA
USS	Norfolk	SSN 714	FPO	AE	09579-2394	Norfolk, VA
USS	Normandy	CG 60	FPO	AE	09579-1180	Norfolk, VA
USS	Oak Hill	LSD 51	FPO	AE	09573-1739	Little Creek, VA
USS	O'Bannon	DD 987	FPO	AA	34092-1225	Mayport, FL
USS	O'Brien	DD 975	FPO	AP	96674-1213	Yokosuka, Japan
USS	Ogden	LPD 5	FPO	AP	96674-1708	San Diego, CA
USS	Ohio	SSBN 726	FPO	AP	96698-2093	Bangor, WA
USS	Oklahoma City	SSN 723	FPO	AE	09581-2403	Norfolk, VA
USS	Oldendorf	DD 972	FPO	AP	96674-1210	San Diego, CA
USS	Olympia	SSN 717	FPO	AP	96674-2397	Pearl Harbor, HI
USS	Oriole	MHC 55	FPO	AA	34092-1954	Ingleside, TX
USS	Osprey	MHC 51	FPO	AA	34092-1950	Ingleside, TX
USS	Parche	SSN 683	FPO	AP	96675-2363	Bangor, WA
USS	Pasadena	SSN 752	FPO	AP	96675-2408	Pearl Harbor, HI

USS	Patriot	MCM 7	FPO	AP	96675-1927	Sasebo, Japan
USS	Paul F Foster	DD 964	FPO	AP	96665-1202	Everett, WA
USS	Paul Hamilton	DDG 60	FPO	AP	96667-1278	Pearl Harbor, HI
USS	Pearl Harbor	LSD 52	FPO	AP	96667-1740	San Diego, CA
USS	Peleliu	LHA 5	FPO	AP	96624-1620	San Diego, CA
USS	Pelican	MHC 53	FPO	AA	34092-1952	Ingleside, TX
USS	Pennsylvania	SSBN 735	FPO	AA	34092-2120	Kings Bay, GA
USS	Pensacola	LSD 38	FPO	AE	09582-1726	Little Creek, VA
USS	Peterson	DD 969	FPO	AE	09582-1207	Norfolk, VA
USS	Philadelphia	SSN 690	FPO	AE	09582-2370	Groton, CT
USS	Philippine Sea	CG5 8	FPO	AA	34092-1178	Mayport, FL
USS	Pioneer	MCM 9	FPO	AA	34092-1929	Ingleside, TX
USS	Pittsburgh	SSN 720	FPO	AE	09582-2400	Groton, CT
USS	Platte	AO 186	FPO	AE	09582-3022	Norfolk, VA
USS	Pogy	SSN 647	FPO	AP	96675-2333	Bremerton, WA
USS	Ponce	LPD 15	FPO	AE	09582-1717	Norfolk, VA
USS	Port Royal	CG 73	FPO	AP	96675-1193	Pearl Harbor, HI
USS	Portland	LSD 37	FPO	AE	09582-1725	Little Creek, VA
USS	Portsmouth	SSN 707	FPO	AP	96675-2387	San Diego, CA
USS	Princeton	CG 59	FPO	AP	96675-1179	San Diego, CA
USS	Providence	SSN 719	FPO	AE	09582-2399	Groton, CT
USS	Rainier	AOE 7	FPO	AP	96698-3038	Bremerton, WA
USS	Ramage	DDG 61	FPO	AE	09586-1279	Norfolk, VA
USS	Raven	MHC 61	FPO	AA	34092-1960	Ingleside, TX
USS	Rentz	FFG 46	FPO	AP	96677-1500	San Diego, CA
USS	Reuben James	FFG 57	FPO	AP	96669-1511	Pearl Harbor, HI
USS	Rhode Island	SSBN 740	FPO	AA	34092-2135	Kings Bay, GA
USS	Robert G Bradley	FFG 49	FPO	AA	34090-1503	Mayport, FL
USS	Robin	MHC 54	FPO	AA	34092-1953	Ingleside, TX
USS	Rodney M Davis	FFG 60	FPO	AP	96663-1514	Everett, WA
USS	Ross	DDG 71	FPO	AE	09586-1288	Norfolk, VA
USS	Rushmore	LSD 47	FPO	AP	96677-1735	San Diego, CA
USS	Russell	DDG 59	FPO	AP	96677-1277	Pearl Harbor, HI
USS	Sacramento	AOE 1	FPO	AP	96678-3012	Bremerton, WA
USS	Safeguard	ARS 50	FPO	AP	96678-3221	Pearl Harbor, HI
USS	Saipan	LHA 2	FPO	AE	09549-1605	Norfolk, VA
USS	Salt Lake City	SSN 716	FPO	AP	96678-2396	San Diego, CA
USS	Salvor	ARS 52	FPO	AP	96678-3222	Pearl Harbor, HI
USS	Samuel B Roberts	FFG 58	FPO	AE	09586-1512	Norfolk, VA
USS	Samuel E. Morison	FFG 13	FPO	AA	34092-1471	Mayport, FL
USS	San Francisco	SSN 711	FPO	AP	96678-2391	Pearl Harbor, HI
USS	San Jacinto	CG 56	FPO	AE	09587-1176	Norfolk, VA
USS	San Juan	SSN 751	FPO	AE	09587-2407	Groton, CT

USNS	Santa Barbara	TAE 28	FPO	AA	34093-3006	Charleston, SC
USS	Santa Fe	SSN 763	FPO	AP	96678-2419	Pearl Harbor, HI
USS	Scout	MCM 8	FPO	AA	34093-1928	Ingleside, TX
USS	Scranton	SSN 756	FPO	AE	09587-2412	Norfolk, VA
USS	Seattle	AOE 3	FPO	AE	09587-3014	Earle, NJ
USS	Seawolf	SSN 21	FPO	AE	09587-2301	Groton, CT
USS	Sentry	MCM 3	FPO	AA	34093-1923	Ingleside, TX
USS	Shamal	PC 13	FPO	AE	09587-1972	Little Creek, VA
USS	Shiloh	CG 67	FPO	AP	96678-1187	San Diego, CA
USS	Shreveport	LPD 12	FPO	AE	09587-1714	Norfolk, VA
USS	Sides	FFG 14	FPO	AP	96678-1472	San Diego, CA
USS	Simon Lake	AS 33	FPO	AE	09536-2590	La Maddalena, Italy
USS	Simpson	FFG 56	FPO	AE	09587-1510	Norfolk, VA
USS	Sirocco	PC 6	FPO	AE	09587-1965	Little Creek, VA
USS	Springfield	SSN 761	FPO	AE	09587-2417	Groton, CT
USS	Spruance	DD 963	FPO	AA	34093-1201	Mayport, FL
USS	Squall	PC 7	FPO	AP	96678-1966	San Diego, CA
USS	Stark	FFG 31	FPO	AA	34093-1487	Mayport, FL
USS	Stephen W Groves	FFG 29	FPO	AA	34091-1485	Pascagoula, MS
USS	Stethem	DDG 63	FPO	AP	96678-1281	San Diego, CA
USS	Stout	DDG 55	FPO	AE	09587-1273	Norfolk, VA
USS	Stump	DD 978	FPO	AE	09587-1216	Norfolk, VA
USS	Supply	AOE 6	FPO	AE	09587-3037	Earle, NJ
USS	Tarawa	LHA 1	FPO	AP	96622-1600	San Diego, CA
USS	Taylor	FFG 50	FPO	AA	34093-1504	Mayport, FL
USS	Tempest	PC 2	FPO	AE	09588-1961	Little Creek, VA
USS	Tennessee	SSBN 734	FPO	AA	34093-2117	Kings Bay, GA
USS	Thach	FFG 43	FPO	AP	96679-1498	Yokosuka, Japan
USS	The Sullivans	DDG 68	FPO	AA	34093-1287	Mayport, FL
USS	Thed. Roosevelt	CVN 71	FPO	AE	09599-2871	Norfolk, VA
USS	Thomas S Gates	CG 51	FPO	AA	34091-1171	Pascagoula, MS
USS	Thorn	DD 988	FPO	AE	09588-1226	Norfolk, VA
USS	Thunderbolt	PC 12	FPO	AE	09588-1971	Little Creek, VA
USS	Ticonderoga	CG 47	FPO	AA	34093-1158	Pascagoula, MS
USS	Toledo	SSN 769	FPO	AE	09588-2425	Groton, CT
USS	Topeka	SSN 754	FPO	AP	96679-2410	Pearl Harbor, HI
USS	Tortuga	LSD 46	FPO	AE	09588-1734	Little Creek, VA
USS	Trenton	LPD 14	FPO	AE	09588-1716	Norfolk, VA
USS	Trepang	SSN 674	FPO	AP	96679-2354	Bremerton, WA
USS	Tucson	SSN 770	FPO	AP	96679-2426	Pearl Harbor, HI
USS	Typhoon	PC 5	FPO	AE	09588-1964	Little Creek, VA
USS	Underwood	FFG 36	FPO	AA	34093-1491	Mayport, FL
USS	Valley Forge	CG 50	FPO	AP	96682-1170	San Diego, CA

USS	Vandegrift	FFG 48	FPO	AP	96682-1502	Yokosuka, Japan
USS	Vella Gulf	CG 72	FPO	AE	09590-1192	Norfolk, VA
USS	Vicksburg	CG 69	FPO	AA	34093-1189	Mayport, FL
USS	Vincennes	CG 49	FPO	AP	96682-1169	Yokosuka, Japan
USS	Wadsworth	FFG 9	FPO	AP	96683-1467	San Diego, CA
USS	Warrior	MCM 10	FPO	AA	34093-1930	Ingleside, TX
USS	Wasp	LHD 1	FPO	AE	09556-1660	Norfolk, VA
USS	West Virginia	SSBN 736	FPO	AA	34093-2123	Kings Bay, GA
USS	Whidbey Island	LSD 41	FPO	AE	09591-1729	Little Creek, VA
USS	Whirlwind	PC 11	FPO	AE	09591-1970	Little Creek, VA
USS	Willamette	AO 180	FPO	AP	96683-3021	Pearl Harbor, HI
USS	William H Bates	SSN 680	FPO	AP	96661-2360	Pearl Harbor, HI
USS	Wyoming	SSBN 742	FPO	AA	34093-2141	Kings Bay, GA
USS	Yorktown	CG 48	FPO	AA	34093-1159	Pascagoula, MS
USS	Zephyr	PC 8	FPO	AP	96687-1967	San Diego, CA

Appendix **B**

Directory of State Resources

This directory is a listing of helpful information by state. Most listings are official state offices but some are not — for example, some historical and genealogical societies are not part of the state government. Department of Veterans Affairs offices, which are federal, are listed here because there is at least one per state. Anything listed in *italics* is informational or a heading and not part of the name or address.

Below is a listing and description of the categories and offices found under each state.

State Government Information Number

This is the information operator for all state offices and state agencies. Say you are looking for your old boyfriend who was a doctor in the military. You know he might have left the service to enter private practice in his home state of Texas. Call the Texas state government information operator and request the physicians licensing board agency. Then call that office to get his business address and telephone number.

State Prison Locator

If you think someone's been in trouble with the law this may be a good place to start. Check the prison locators to find out if your subject is residing in, or has been in, their facilities in the past ten years. They can search by legal name and alias. Arizona is the only state that provides this information via a 900 number and charges a per minute fee. For the military prison at Fort Leavenworth, Kansas, see p. 59.

State Archives, Genealogical/Historical Societies

These offices can help in any search, especially in a particularly difficult case. Their employees are trained searchers and can access many historical and genealogical records. Types of documents include old photographs, family history information, state military records, state census records, birth and death announcements, etc. These resources vary by state. Some states have lists of people from their state who joined the military for WWII or other wars. They may also have information on veterans who died in WWII, Korea, Vietnam or Desert Storm.

State Adjutants General Office

This is the top military office for the state. It's in charge of state Army and Air National Guards and maintains records of people who are serving or have served in these groups.

Department of Veterans Affairs Regional Office

Always check with your local Veterans Affairs Regional Office and ask if they have any information on your subject. Do they have him listed in their files? If so, do they have a current address? (If they do, they will only forward a letter.) Do they have a report of death? All Veterans Affairs Regional Offices are reached through the same number: (800) 827-1000.

When calling any office for help, hopefully whoever answers the telephone will be polite and cooperative, but if this is not the case, call back. Someone else may answer. Then start over asking the same questions.

ALABAMA
State government information number: (334) 242-8000
State prison locator: (334) 240-9500
State website: *www.state.al.us*

State of Alabama
Archives & History Department
Reference Rm. PO Box 300100
Montgomery, AL 36130-0100
(334) 242-4435, (334) 240-3433 Fax

Alabama Historical Association
PO Box 870380
Tuscaloosa, AL 35487-0380

Alabama Genealogical Society
800 Lakeshore Drive
Birmingham, AL 35229
(205) 870-2749

Southern Society of Genealogists
Stewart University
PO Box 295
Centre, AL 35960
(205) 447-2939

State Adjutant General
PO Box 3711
Montgomery, AL 36109-0711
(334) 271-7259

Veterans Affairs Regional Office
345 Perry Hill Road
Montgomery, AL 36109
(800) 827-1000

ALASKA
State government information number: (907) 465-2111
State prison locator: (907) 465-3376
State website: *www.state.ak.us*

State Archives:
Department of Education
Archives Division
141 Willoughby Avenue
Juneau, AK 99801-1720
(907) 465-2270, (907) 264-0881 Fax

Alaska Assn. for Historic Preservation
524 W. 4th Ave, Suite 203
Anchorage, AK 99501
(907) 272-2119

Alaska Historical Society
PO Box 100299
Anchorage, AK 99510-0299
(907) 276-1596

Alaska Genealogical Society
7030 Dickerson Drive
Anchorage, AK 99504

State Adjutant General
PO Box 5800
Ft. Richardson, AK 99505-5800
(907) 428-6400

Veterans Affairs Regional Office
2925 DeBarr Road
Anchorage, AK 99508-2989
(800) 827-1000

ARIZONA
State government information number: (602) 542-4900
State prison locator: (900) 226-8682 (fee charged per minute)
State website: *www.state.az.us*

State Archives:
Library, Archives & Pub. Records Dept.
1700 W. Washington, Rm 442
Phoenix, AZ 85007
(602) 542-4159, (602) 542-4402 Fax

Arizona Historical Society
949 East Second Street
Tuscon, AZ 85719
(602) 628-5774

State Historical Society
Flagstaff Branch
North Fort Valley Road
Route 4, Box 705
Flagstaff, AZ 86001
(602) 774-6272

State Historical Society
Yuma Branch
240 South Madison Avenue
Yuma, AZ 85364
(602) 782-1841

Family History Society of Arizona
PO Box 310
Glendale, AZ 85311
(602) 926-1815

State Genealogical Society
PO Box 42075
Tuscon, AZ 85733-2075

Genealogical Society of Arizona
PO Box 27237
Tempe, AZ 85282

State Adjutant General
5636 E. McDowell Road
Phoenix, AZ 65008-3495
(602) 267-2700

Veterans Affairs Regional Office
3225 N. Central Avenue
Phoenix, AZ 85012
(800) 827-1000

ARKANSAS
State government information number: (501) 682-3000
State prison locator: (870) 247-1800
State website: *www.state.ar.us*

State Archives:
Arkansas Historical Commission
State Archives
One Capitol Mall
Little Rock, AR 72201
(501) 682-6900

Arkansas Historical Assn
University of Arkansas
Fayetteville, AR 72701
(501) 575-5884

Arkansas Historical Society
422 South Sixth Street
Van Buren, AR 72956

Arkansas Genealogical Society
1411 Shady Grove Road
Hot Springs, AR 71901
(501) 262-4513 Phone/Fax

State Adjutant General
Camp Robinson
North Little Rock, AR 72199-9600
(501) 212-4001

Veterans Affairs Regional Office
PO Box 1280
North Little Rock, AR 72115
(800) 827-1000

CALIFORNIA
State government information number: (916) 657-9900
State prison locator: (916) 445-6713
State website: *www.state.ca.us*

State Archives:
Secretary of State
1020 "O" Street
Sacramento, CA 95814
(916) 653-7715, (916) 653-7134 Fax

Council for Promotion of History
California History Center
DeAnza College
21250 Stevens Creek Blvd.
Cupertino, CA 95014
(408) 996-4712

California Historical Society
2099 Pacific Avenue
San Francisco, CA 94109-2235
(415) 567-1848

California Genealogical Society
300 Brannan Street
PO Box 77105
San Francisco, CA 94107-0105
(415) 777-9936

California Genealogical Alliance
4808 East Garland Street
Anaheim, CA 92807-1005
(714) 777-0483

Professional Genealogists of Calif.
5048 "J" Parkway
Sacramento, CA 95823

State Adjutant General
PO Box 269101
Sacramento, CA 95826-9101
(916) 854-3310

Veterans Affairs Regional Office
11000 Wilshire Blvd.
Los Angeles, CA 90024
(800) 827-1000

Veterans Affairs Regional Office
8810 Rio San Diego Drive
San Diego, CA 92108
(800) 827-1000

Veterans Affairs Regional Office
1301 Clay Street
Oakland, CA 94612
(800) 827-1000

COLORADO
State government information number: (303) 866-5000
State prison locator: (719) 579-9580
State website: *www.state.co.us*

State Archives:
Colorado Info. Technology Services
Archives & Public Records Division
1313 Sherman Street, Room 1B20
Denver, CO 80203
(303) 866-2055, (303) 866-2257 Fax

State Historical Society
Colorado Historical Society
1300 Broadway
Denver, CO 80203-2137
(303) 866-2305

Colorado Genealogical Society
PO Box 9218
Denver, CO 80209-0218

State Adjutant General
6848 S. Revere Parkway
Englewood, CO 80112-6703
(303) 397-3173

Council of Genealogical Societies
PO Box 24379
Denver, CO 80224-0379

Veterans Affairs Regional Office
155 Van Gordon Street
Denver, CO 80225
(800) 827-1000

CONNECTICUT
State government information number: (860) 566-2211
State prison locator: (860) 692-7480
State website: *www.state.ct.us*

State Archives:
Connecticut State Library
History & geneaology Unit
231 Capitol Avenue
Hartford, CT 06106
(860) 566-3692, (860) 566-2133 Fax

State Historical Society
Connecticut Historical Commission
59 South Prospect Street
Hartford, CT 06106
(860) 566-3005

Connecticut Historical Society
1 Elizabeth Street at Asylum Ave.
Hartford, CT 06105
(860) 236-5621, (860) 236-2664 Fax

CT League of Historical Societies
2105 Chester Village West
Chester, CT 06412-1040

Connecticut Society of Genealogists
175 Maple Street
East Hartford, CT 06118
(960) 569-0002

State Adjutant General
360 Broad Street
Hartford, CT 06105-3795
(860) 524-4820

Veterans Affairs Regional Office
450 Main Street
Hartford, CT 06103
(800) 827-1000

DELAWARE
State government information number: (800) 273-9500
State prison locator: (302) 739-5601
State website: *www.state.de.us*

State Archives:
Delaware Public Archives
Hall of Records
PO Box 1401
Dover, DE 19903
(302) 739-5313, (302) 739-2578 Fax

Historical Society of Delaware
5050 Market Street
Wilmington, DE 19801-3091
(302) 655-7161

Delaware Genealogical Society
5050 Market Street
Wilmington, DE 19801-3091

State Adjutant General
1st Regiment Road
Wilmington, DE 19808-2191
(302) 326-7043

Veterans Affairs Regional Office
1601 Kirkwood Highway
Wilmington, DE 19805
(800) 827-1000

DISTRICT OF COLUMBIA
DC government operator: (202) 727-1000
DC website: *www.ci.washington.dc.us*

District Archives:
Secretary of District of Columbia
Archives/Public Records Office
1300 Naylor Court, N.W.
Washington, DC 20001-4225
(202) 727-2052, (202) 727-6076 Fax

The Columbia Historical Society
1307 new Hampshire Ave, N.W.
Washington, DC 20036
(202) 785-2068

U.S. Capitol Historical Society
200 Maryland Avenue, N.E.
Washington, DC 20002
(202) 543-8919

DC Washington National Guard
2001 E. Capitol St. S.E.
Washington, DC 20003
(202) 433-5100

Veterans Affairs Regional Office
1120 Vermont Ave., N.W.
Washington, DC 20421
(800) 827-1000

FLORIDA
State government information number: (850) 488-1234
State prison locator: (850) 488-2533
State website: *www.state.fl.us*

State Archives:
Library & Information Services Div.
Archives & Records
R. A. Gray Building
500 S. Bronough
Tallahassee, FL 32399-0250
(850) 487-2073, (850) 488-4894 Fax

Florida Historical Society
University of South Florida Library
4204 Fowler Avenue
PO Box 290197
Tampa, FL 33687-0197
(813) 974-3815

State Adjutant General
PO Box 1008
St. Augustine, FL 32085-1008
(904) 823-0300

Florida Genealogical Society
PO Box 18624
Tampa, FL 33679-8624

Society for Genealogical Research
8461 54th Street, North
Pinellas Park, FL 33565
(813) 391-2914

Florida State Genealogical Society
PO Box 10249
Tallahassee, FL 32302-2249

Veterans Affairs Regional Office
144 First Avenue, South
St. Petersburg, FL 33701
(800) 827-1000

GEORGIA
State government information number: (404) 656-2000
State prison locator: (404) 656-4605
State website: *www.state.ga.us*

State Archives:
Secretary of State
Archives & History Department
330 Capitol Avenue, S.E.
Atlanta, GA 30334
(404) 656-2393, (404) 651-9270 Fax

Georgia Historical Society
501 Whittaker Street
Savannah, GA 31499
(912) 651-2128

Georgia Genealogical Society
PO Box 54575
Atlanta, GA 30308-0575
(404) 475-4404

State Adjutant General
PO Box 17965
Atlanta, GA 30316-0965
(404) 624-5006

Veterans Affairs Regional Office
730 Peachtree Street, N.E.
Atlanta, GA 30365
(800) 827-1000

HAWAII
State government information number: (808) 586-2211
State prison locator: (808) 587-1258
State website: *www.state.hi.us*

State Archives:
Archives Division
Iolani Palace Grounds
Honolulu, HI 96813
(808) 586-0329, (808) 586-0330 Fax

Hawaiian Historical Society
560 Kawaiahao Street
Honolulu, HI 96813
(808) 537-6271

Sandwich Islands Genealogical Society
Hawaii State Library
478 South King Street
Honolulu, HI 96813

State Adjutant General
3949 Diamond Head Road
Honolulu, HI 96818-4495
(808) 753-4243

Veterans Affairs Regional Office
PO Box 50188
Honolulu, HI 96850-0188
(800) 827-1000

IDAHO
State government information number: (208) 334-2411
State prison locator: (208) 334-2318
State website: *www.state.id.us*

State Archives:
Idaho State Historical Society
Historical Library & Archives
450 N. 4th Street
Boise, ID 83702-6027
(208) 334-3356, (208) 334-3198 Fax

Idaho State Historical Society
Genealogical Library
450 N. 4th Street
Boise, ID 83702
(208) 334-2305

The Idaho Genealogical Society
4620 Overland Road, #204
Boise, ID 83705-2867
(208) 384-0542

State Adjutant General
4040 W. Guard Street
Boise, ID 83705-5004
(208) 422-3800

Veterans Affairs Regional Office
805 W. Franklin Street
Boise, ID 83702
(800) 827-1000

ILLINOIS
State government information number: (217) 782-2000
State prison locator: (217) 522-2666 ext. 6489
State website: *www.state.il.us*

State Archives:
Secretary of State
Archives Division
Archives Bldg, Capitol Complex
Springfield, IL 62756
(217) 782-4682, (217) 524-3930 Fax

Illinois Genealogical Society
Old State Capitol
Springfield, IL 62701
(217) 785-7938

Illinois Historic Preservation Agency
Old State Capitol
1 Old State Capitol Plaza
Springfield, IL 62701
(217) 524-6045

Illinois State Genealogical Society
PO Box 10195
Springfield, IL 62791-0195
(217) 789-1968

State Adjutant General
1301 N. MacArthur Blvd.
Springfield, IL 62702-2399
(217) 761-3540

Veterans Affairs Regional Office
536 S. Clark Street
Chicago, IL 60680
(800) 827-1000

INDIANA
State government information number: (317) 232-1000
State prison locator: (317) 232-5715
State website: *www.state.in.us*

State Archives:
Indiana State Archvies
Public Records Commission
402 W. Washington St, IGCS, W472
Indianapolis, IN 46204
(317) 232-3660, (317) 232-3154 Fax

Indiana Genealogical Society
PO Box 10507
Fort Wayne, IN 46852-0507

State Adjutant General
2002 S. Holt Road
Indianapolis, IN 46241-4839
(317) 247-3219

Indiana Historical Society
State Library & Historical Bldg.
315 West Ohio Street
PO Box 88255
Indianapolis, IN 46202
(317) 233-3157

Veterans Affairs Regional Office
575 N. Pennsylvania Street
Indianapolis, IN 46202
(800) 827-1000

IOWA
State government information number: (515) 281-5011
State prison locator: (515) 281-4816
State website: *www.state.ia.us*

State Archives:
State Historical Society of Iowa
Library/Archives
600 E. Locust, Capitol Complex
Des Moines, IA 50319
(515) 281-5111, (515) 282-0502 Fax

Iowa Genealogical Society
6000 Douglas
PO Box 7735
Des Moines, IA 50322

State Adjutant General
7700 N.W. Beaver Drive
Johnston, IA 50131-1902
(515) 252-4360

Veterans Affairs Regional Office
210 Walnut Street
Des Moines, IA 50309
(800) 827-1000

KANSAS
State government information number: (913) 296-0111
State prison locator (913) 296-7220
State website: *www.state.ks.us*

State Archives:
Historical Society
Archives Department
120 W. 10th Street
Topeka, KS 66612
(913) 296-4792, (913) 296-1005 Fax

Kansas State Historical Society
Reference Services
120 W. 10th Street
Topeka, KS 66612
(913) 296-4776

Council of Genealogical Societies
PO Box 3858
Topeka, KS 66604-6858
(913) 774-4411

State Adjutant General
2800 S.W. Topeka Blvd.
Topeka, KS 66611-1287
(913) 274-1061

Kansas Genealogical Society
Village Square Mall
700 Avenue G at Vine Street
PO Box 103 *(mail)*
Dodge City, KS 67801-0103
(316) 225-1951

Veterans Affairs Regional Office
5500 E. Kellogg
Wichita, KS 67211
(800) 827-1000

KENTUCKY
State government information number: (502) 564-3130
State prison locator: (502) 564-2433
State website: *www.state.ky.us*

State Archives:
Libraries & Archives Dept.
300 Coffee Tree Road
Frankfort, KY 40601
(502) 564-8300, (502) 564-5773 Fax

State Adjutant General
Boone Nat'l Guard Center
Frankfort, KY 40601-6168
(502) 564-8446

Historical Confed. of Kentucky
PO Box H
Frankfort, KY 40602-2108
(502) 564-3016, (502) 564-4701 Fax

Veterans Affairs Regional Office
545 S. Third Street
Louisville, KY 40202
(800) 827-1000

Kentucky Historical Society
300 Broadway, Old Capitol Annex
Frankfort, KY 40601
PO Box H *(mail)*
Frankfort, KY 40602-2108

LOUISIANA
State government information number: (504) 342-6600
State prison locator: (225) 342-6649
State website: *www.state.la.us*

State Archives:
Secretary of State
Archives & Records Division
3851 Essen Lane
Baton Rouge, LA 70809-2137
(504) 922-1184, (504) 922-0433 Fax

Louisiana Historical Society
Maritime Building
New Orleans, LA 70130
(504) 588-9044

LA Genealogical & Historical Society
PO Box 3454
Baton Rouge, LA 70821

State Adjutant General
Jackson Barracks
6400 N. Claiborne Ave.
New Orleans, LA 70146-0330
(504) 278-8317

Veterans Affairs Regional Office
701 Loyola Avenue
New Orleans, LA 70113
(800) 827-1000

MAINE
State government information number: (207) 582-9500
State prison locator: (207) 354-2535
State website: *www.state.me.us*

State Archives:
State House Station
State Archives
Augusta, ME 04333-0084
(207) 287-5790, (207) 287-5739 Fax

State Adjutant General
Camp Keys
Augusta, ME 04333-0033
(207) 626-4317

Maine Historical Society
485 Congress Street
Portland, ME 04101
(207) 774-1822

Veterans Affairs Regional Office
Route 17 East
Togus, ME 04330
(800) 827-1000

Maine Genealogical Society
PO Box 221
Farmington, ME 04938-0221

MARYLAND
State government information number: None available.
State prison locator: (410) 764-4100
State website: *www.state.md.us*

State Archives:
Hall of Records
350 Rowe Blvd.
Annapolis, MD 21401
(410) 974-3914, (410) 974-3895 Fax

State Adjutant General
5th Regiment Armory
Baltimore, MD 21201-2288
(410) 576-6011

Maryland Historical Society
201 West Monument Street
Baltimore, MD 21201
(410) 685-3750, Ext 360

Veterans Affairs Regional Office
31 Hopkins Plaza Federal Bldg.
Baltimore, MD 21201
(800) 827-1000

MASSACHUSETTS
State government information number: (617) 727-7030
State prison locator: (617) 727-3300
State website: *www.state.ma.us*

State Archives:
MA Archives at Columbia Pt..
Archives Division
220 Morrissey Blvd.
Boston, MA 02125
(617) 727-2816, (617) 727-8730 Fax

Massachusetts Historical Society
1154 Boylston Street
Boston, MA 02215
(617) 536-1608

Massachusetts Genealogical Council
PO Box 5393
Cochituate, MA 01778

Massachusetts Society of Genealogists
PO Box 215
Ashland, MA 01721-0215

State Adjutant General
50 Maple Street
Milford, MA 01757-3604
(508) 233-6621

Veterans Affairs Regional Office
JFK Federal Bldg. Govt. Ctr.
Boston, MA 02114
(800) 827-1000

MICHIGAN
State government information number: (517) 373-1837
State prison locator: (517) 335-1426
State website: *www.state.mi.us*

State Archives:
Michigan Bureau of History
Archives Section
Library & Historical Center
717 W. Allegan
Lansing, MI 48918-1837
(517) 373-1408, (517) 241-1658 Fax

Michigan Historical Commission
505 State Office Building
Lansing, MI 48913

Historical Society of Michigan
2117 Washtenaw Avenue
Ann Arbor, MI 48104
(313) 769-1828

Michigan Genealogical Council
PO Box 80953
Lansing, MI 48908-0953

State Adjutant General
2500 S. Washington Ave.
Lansing, MI 48913-5101
(517) 483-5514

Veterans Affairs Regional Office
477 Michigan Avenue
Detroit, MI 48226
(800) 827-1000

MINNESOTA
State government information number: (612) 296-6013
State prison locator: (651) 642-0322
State website: *www.state.mn.us*

State Archives:
Minnesota Hisotorical Society
Libraries & Archives
345 W. Kellogg Blvd.
St. Paul, MN 55102-1906
(612) 296-6126, (612) 297-7436 Fax

Minnesota Historical Society
345 Kellogg Blvd, W.
St. Paul, MN 55102-1906
(612) 296-2143

Minnesota Genealogical Society
1650 Carroll Avenue
St. Paul, MN 55104
PO Box 16069 *(mail)*
St. Paul, MN 55116-0069
(612) 645-3671

State Adjutant General
20 W 12th Street
St. Paul, MN 55155-2098
(612) 282-4040

Veterans Affairs Regional Office
1 Federal Drive
St. Paul, MN 55111
(800) 827-1000

MISSISSIPPI
State government information number: (601) 359-1000
State prison locator: (601) 745-6611
State website: *www.state.ms.us*

State Archives:
Archives & History Department
Archives & Library Division
PO Box 571
Jackson, MS 39205-0571
(601) 359-6850, (601) 359-6905 Fax

MS Historical & Genealogical Assn.
618 Avalon Road
Jackson, MS 39206
(601) 362-3079

Mississippi Historical Society
PO Box 571
Jackson, MS 39205-0571
(601) 359-6850

Mississippi Genealogical Society
PO Box 5301
Jackson, MS 39296-5301

State Adjutant General
PO Box 5027
Jackson, MS 39296-5027
(601) 313-6324

Veterans Affairs Regional Office
100 W. Capitol Street
Jackson, MS 39269
(800) 827-1000

MISSOURI
State government information number: (573) 751-2000
State prison locator: (573) 751-2389
State website: *www.state.mo.us*

State Archives:
Secretary of State
Archives Division
PO Box 778
Jefferson City, MO 65102-0778
(573) 751-3280, (573) 526-7333 Fax

Missouri Historical Society
Research Library & Archives
Jefferson Memorial Building
St. Louis, MO 63112-1099
(314) 746-4500

Missouri State Genealogical Assn.
PO Box 833
Columbia, MO 65205-0833

State Adjutant General
2302 Militia Drive
Jefferson City, MO 65101
(573) 526-9020

Veterans Affairs Regional Office
400 South 18th Street
St. Louis, MO 63103
(800) 827-1000

MONTANA
State government information number: (406) 444-2511
State prison locator: (406) 444-9521, (800) 456-3076
State website: *www.state.mt.us*

State Archives:
Historical Society
Archives Division
225 N. Roberts Street
Helena, MT 59620-1201
(406) 444-2694, (406) 444-2696 Fax

Montana Historical Society
Memorial Building
225 N. Roberts Street
Helena, MT 59620
(406) 444-2681

Montana State Genealogical Society
PO Box 555
Chester, MT 59522

State Adjutant General
PO Box 4789
Helena, MT 59604-4789
(406) 841-3116

Veterans Affairs Regional Office
Williams St. & Hwy. 12, West
Ft. Harrison, MT 59636
(800) 827-1000

NEBRASKA
State government information number: (402) 471-2311
State prison locator: (402) 471-2654
State website: *www.state.ne.us*

State Archives:
Historical Society, Archives
PO Box 82554
Lincoln, NE 68501-2554
(402) 471-4771, (402) 471-3100 Fax

State Adjutant General
1300 Military Road
Lincoln, NE 68508-1090
(402) 471-7210

Nebraska State Historical Society
PO Box 82554
Lincoln, NE 68501-2554
(800) 833-6747, (402) 471-4771

Veterans Affairs Regional Office
5631 S. 48th Street
Lincoln, NE 68516
(800) 827-1000

Nebraska State Historical Society Room
Chadron State College
Chadron State Library
Chadron, NE 69337

NEVADA
State government information number: (702) 687-5000
State prison locator: (702) 887-3285
State website: *www.state.nv.us*

State Archives:
State Library & Archives
100 N. Stewart Street
Carson City, NV 89710-4285
(702) 687-5160, (702) 687-8311 Fax

State Adjutant General
2525 S. Carson Street
Carson City, NV 89701-5502
(702) 887-7258

Nevada Historical Society
1650 North Virginia Street
Reno, NV 89503
(702) 688-1190

Veterans Affairs Regional Office
1201 Terminal Way
Reno, NV 89520
(800) 827-1000

Nevada State Genealogical Society
PO Box 20666
Reno, NV 89515

NEW HAMPSHIRE
State government information number: (603) 271-1110
State prison locator: (603) 271-1812
State website: *www.state.nh.us*

State Archives:
Department of State
Records Management & Archives
71 S. Fruit Street
Concord, NH 03301
(603) 271-2236, (603) 271-2272 Fax

NH Historical Society
30 Park Street
Concord, NH 03301
(603) 432-8137

State Adjutant General
4 Pembroke Road
Concord, NH 03301-5652
(603) 225-1307

Veterans Affairs Regional Office
275 Chestnut Street
Manchester, NH 03101
(800) 827-1000

NEW JERSEY
State government information number: (609) 292-2121
State prison locator: (609) 777-5753
State website: *www.state.nj.us*

State Archives:
New Jersey State Archives
185 W. State St, Box 307
Trenton, NJ 08625-0307
(609) 633-8334, (609) 396-2454 Fax

Library of NJ Historical Society
Genealogy Club
230 Broadway
Newark, NJ 07104
(201) 483-3939

New Jersey Historical Commission
20 West State Street
CN 305
Trenton, NJ 08625-0305
(609) 292-6062

State Adjutant General
Eggert Crossing Rd, CN 340
Trenton, NJ 08625-0340
(609) 562-0652

Genealogical Society of New Jersey
PO Box 1291
New Brunswick, NJ 08903
(201) 356-6920

Veterans Affairs Regional Office
20 Washington Place
Newark, NJ 07102
(800) 827-1000

NEW MEXICO
State government information number: (505) 827-9632
State prison locator: (505) 827-8677
State website: *www.state.nm.us*

State Archives:
State Records Center & Archives
1205 Camino Carols Rey
Santa Fe, NM 87505
(505) 476-7909, (505) 476-7909 Fax

State Adjutant General
47 Bataan Blvd.
Santa Fe, NM 87505-4695
(505) 474-1255

Historical Society of New Mexico
PO Box 1912
Santa Fe, NM 87504-1912

Veterans Affairs Regional Office
500 Gold Avenue, S.W.
Albuquerque, NM 87102
(800) 827-1000

New Mexico Genealogical Society
PO Box 8283
Albuquerque, NM 87198-8283
(505) 256-3217

NEW YORK

State government information number: (518) 474-2121
State prison locator: (518) 457-0034
State website: *www.state.ny.us*

State Archives:
State Archives & Records Admin.
Empire State Plaza
Cultural Education Ctr. Rm 11D40
Albany, NY 12230
(518) 474-8955, (518) 473-9985 Fax

The New York Historical Society
Library Office
170 Central Park West
New York, NY 10024-5194
(212) 873-3400

NY State Historical Assn.
Fennimore House, West Lake Rd.
PO Box 800
Cooperstown, NY 13326
(607) 547-2533

NY State Council of Genealogical
  Organizations
PO Box 2593
Syracuse, NY 13220-2593
(315) 262-2800

State Adjutant General
330 Old Niskayuna Road
Latham, NY 12110-2224
(518) 786-4570

Veterans Affairs Regional Office
111 W. Huron Street
Buffalo, NY 14202
(800) 827-1000

NORTH CAROLINA

State government information number: (919) 733-1110
State prison locator: (919) 716-3200
State website: *www.state.nc.us*

State Archives:
Cultural Resources Department
Archives & History Division
109 E. Jones Street
Raleigh, NC 27601-2807
(919) 733-3952, (919) 733-1354 Fax

NC Historical Socieities
109 East Jones Street
Raleigh, NC 27601
(919) 733-7305

NC Society of Historians
PO Box 848
Rockingham, NC 28379

NC Genealogical Society
PO Box 1491
Raleigh, NC 27602

State Adjutant General
4105 Reedy Creek Road
Raleigh, NC 27607-6410
(919) 664-6326

Veterans Affairs Regional Office
251 N. Main Street
Winston-Salem, NC 27155
(800) 827-1000

NORTH DAKOTA
State government information number: (701) 328-2000
State prison locator: (701) 328-6100
State website: *www.state.nd.us*

State Archives:
Historical Society
Archives & Historical Research Library
North Dakota Heritage Center
612 E. Boulevard Avenue
Bismarck, ND 58505
(701) 328-2666, (701) 328-3710 Fax

Bismarck-Mandan Historical
  & Genealogical Society
2708 North Fourth Street
PO Box 485
Bismarck, ND 58501
(701) 223-2929

State Adjutant General
Fraine Barracks
PO Box 5511
Bismarck, ND 58506-5511
(701) 224-5115

Veterans Affairs Regional Office
2101 Elm Street
Fargo, ND 58102
(800) 827-1000

OHIO
State government information number: (614) 466-2000
State prison locator: (614) 752-1159
State website: *www.state.oh.us*

State Archives:
Historical Society
Archives/Library
1982 Velma Avenue
Columbus, OH 43211-2497
(614) 297-2300, (614) 297-2546 Fax

Ohio Historical Society
Archives-Library Division
Interstate 71 and 17th Ave.
1982 Velma Avenue
Columbus, OH 43211-2497
(614) 297-2510, (614) 297-2411 Fax

Ohio Genealogical Society Library
34 Sturges Avenue
PO Box 2625
Mansfield, OH 44906-0625
(419) 522-9077

State Adjutant General
2825 Dublin Granville Road
Columbus, OH 43235-2789
(614) 336-7040

Veterans Affairs Regional Office
1240 E. 9th Street
Cleveland, OH 44199
(800) 827-1000

OKLAHOMA
State government information number: (405) 521-2011
State prison locator: (405) 425-2624
State website: *www.state.ok.us*

State Archives:
Libraries Department
Archives & Records Office
200 N.E. 18th Street
Oklahoma City, OK 73105-3298
(405) 521-2502, (405) 525-7804 Fax

Oklahoma Historical Society
Library Resources Division
Wiley Post Historical Bldg.
2100 N. Lincoln Blvd.
Oklahoma City, OK 73105-4997
(405) 521-2491, (405) 525-3272 Fax

Genealogial Institute of OK
3813 Cashion Place
Oklahoma City, OK 73112

Federal of Oklahoma
Genealogical Societies
PO Box 26151
Oklahoma City, OK 73126

State Adjutant General
3501 Military Circle
Oklahoma City, OK 73111-4398
(405) 425-8203

Veterans Affairs Regional Office
125 S. Main Street
Muskogee, OK 74401
(800) 827-1000

OREGON
State government information number: None available.
State prison locator: (503) 373-1595
State website: *www.state.or.us*

State Archives:
Secretary of State
Archives Division
800 Summer Street, N.E.
Salem, OR 97310
(503) 373-0701, (503) 373-0953 Fax

Oregon Historical Society
Historical Records Advisory Board
1200 S.W. Park Ave.
Portland, OR 97205
(503) 222-1741

Genealogical Forum of Oregon
Headquarters and Library
1410 S.W. Morrison St. RM 812
Portland, OR 97205
(503) 227-2398

Genealogical Heritage Council
PO Box 628
Ashland, OR 97520-0021

Oregon Genealogical Society
223 North "A" Street
Eugene, OR 97477
PO Box 10306 *(mail)*
Eugene, OR 97440-2306
(541) 746-7924

State Adjutant General
1776 Militia Way, N.E.
Salem, OR 97309-5047
(503) 945-3939

Veterans Affairs Regional Office
1220 S.W. 3rd Avenue
Portland, OR 97204
(800) 827-1000

PENNSYLVANIA
State government information number: (717) 787-2121
State prison locator: (717) 730-2721
State website: *www.state.pa.us*

State Archives:
Historical & Museum Commission
Archives & History Division
PO Box 1026
Harrisburg, PA 17108-1026
(717) 787-3281, (717) 787-4822 Fax

PA Federation of Museums
and Historical Organizations
3rd & Forster Streets
Harrisburg, PA 17120
PO Box 1026 *(mail)*
Harrisburg, PA 17108-1026
(717) 787-3253

Friends of PA Historical
and Museum Commission
PO Box 11466
Harrisburg, PA 17108-1466
(717) 183-2618

PA Historical Association
Penn State, Harrisburg
Crags Building
777 West Harrisburg Pike
Middletown, PA 17057-4898
(717) 774-4829

Heritage Society of Pennsylvania
PO Box 146
Laughlintown, PA 15655

Historical Society of PA
1300 Locust Street
Philadelphia, PA 19107-5699
(215) 545-0391

State Adjutant General
Dept. of Military & Veterans Affairs
Annville, PA 17003-5002
(717) 861-8531

Veterans Affairs Regional Office
PO Box 8079
Philadelphia, PA 19104
(800) 827-1000

Veterans Affairs Regional Office
1000 Liberty Avenue
Pittsburg, PA 15222
(800) 827-1000

RHODE ISLAND
State government information number: (401) 222-2000
State prison locator: (401) 462-5180
State website: *www.state.ri.us*

State Archives:
Secretary of State
Archives Division
337 Westminster Street
Providence, RI 02903
(401) 222-2353, (401) 222-3199 Fax

RI State Historical Society
110 Benevolent Street
Providence, RI 02906
(401) 331-8575

RI Genealogical Society
13 Countryside Drive
Cumberland, RI 02864-2601

State Adjutant General
Command Rediness Center
645 New London Ave.
Cranston, RI 02920-3097
(401) 457-4135

Veterans Affairs Regional Office
380 Westminter Mall
Providence, RI 02903
(800) 827-1000

SOUTH CAROLINA
State government information number: (803) 734-1000
State prison locator: (803) 896-8500
State website: *www.state.sc.us*

State Archives:
Archives & History Department
1430 Senate Street
Columbia, SC 29211
(803) 734-8577, (803) 734-8820 Fax

South Carolina Historical Society
Fireproof Building
100 Meeting Street
Charleston, SC 29401
(803) 723-3225

Confederation of South Carolina
  Local Historical Societies
1430 Senate Street
Columbia, SC 29201
(803) 734-8577

South Carolina Historical Assn.
Francis Marion College
Florence, SC 29501

South Carolina Genealogical Society
PO Box 16355
Greenville, SC 29606

State Adjutant General
1 National Guard Road
Columbia, SC 28201-3117
(803) 695-6205

Veterans Affairs Regional Office
1801 Assembly Street
Columbia, SC 29201
(800) 827-1000

SOUTH DAKOTA
State government information number: (605) 773-3011
State prison locator: (605) 773-3478
State website: *www.state.sd.us*

State Archives:
SD State Historical Society
Cultural Heritage Center
900 Governors Drive
Pierre, SD 57501-2217
(605) 773-3804, (605) 773-6041 Fax

SD Genealogical Society
Route 2, Box 10
Burke, SD 57523
(605) 835-9364

State Adjutant General
2823 W. Main Street
Rapid City, SD 57702-8186
(605) 399-6710

Veterans Affairs Regional Office
2501 W. 22nd Street
Sioux Falls, SD 57117
(800) 827-1000

TENNESSEE
State government information number: (615) 741-3011
State prison locator: (615) 741-2733
State website: *www.state.tn.us*

State Archives:
Secretary of State
State Library, Archives Division
403 7th Avenue North
Nashville, TN 37243-0312
(615) 741-7996, (615) 741-6471 Fax

Tennessee Historical Commission
Dept. of Environment & Conservation
701 Broadway, B-30
Nashville, TN 37243-0442
(615) 532-1550

Tennessee Historical Society
Ground Floor
War Memorial Building
300 Capitol Boulevard
Nashville, TN 37243-0084
(615) 741-8934

Tennessee Genealogical Society
PO Box 11249
Memphis, TN 38111-1249
(901) 327-3273

State Adjutant General
PO Box 41502
Nashville, TN 37204-1501
(615) 313-3125

Veterans Affairs Regional Office
1190 9th Avenue, South
Nashville, TN 37203
(800) 827-1000

TEXAS
State government information number: (512) 463-4630
State prison locator: (512) 463-9988
State website: *www.state.tx.us*

State Archives:
Library & Archives Commission
PO Box 12927
Austin, TX 78711
(512) 463-5455, (512) 463-5436 Fax

Texas State Historical Assn.
2306 SRH, University Station
Austin, TX 78712
(512) 471-1525

Texas State Genealogical Society
2507 Tannehill
Houston, TX 77008-3052
(713) 723-1762

State Adjutant General
PO Box 5218
Austin, TX 78763-5218
(512) 465-5031

Veterans Affairs Regional Office
6900 Almeda Road
Houston, TX 77030
(800) 827-1000

Veterans Affairs Regional Office
1 Veterans Plaza
701 Clay Avenue
Waco, TX 76799
(800) 827-1000

UTAH
State government information number: (801) 538-3000
State prison locator: (801) 265-5525
State website: *www.state.ut.us*

State Archives:
Utah State Archives
PO Box 141021
Salt Lake City, UT 84114-1021
(801) 538-3013, (801) 538-3354 Fax

Utah State Historical Society
Dept. of Community & Economic Dev.
Division of State History
300 Rio Grande
Salt Lake City, UT 84101-1182
(801) 533-3500

Utah Genealogical Association
PO Box 1144
Salt Lake City, UT 84110
(801) 262-7263, (801) 531-2091

State Adjutant General
PO Box 1776
Draper, UT 84020-1776
(801) 595-2000

Veterans Affairs Regional Office
125 S. State Street
Salt Lake City, UT 84147
(800) 827-1000

VERMONT
State government information number: (802) 828-1110
State prison locator: (802) 241-2442
State website: *www.state.vt.us*

State Archives:
Secretary of State
State Papers Archives Division
109 State Street
Montpelier, VT 05609-1103
(802) 828-2308, (802) 828-2496 Fax

Vermont Historical Society
Pavilion Office Building
109 State Street
Montpelier, VT 05609-0901
(802) 828-2291

Genealogical Society of Vermont
PO Box 422
Pittsford, VT 05763
(802) 483-2900

State Adjutant General
Green Mountain Armory
Camp Johnson
Colchester, VT 05446
(802) 654-0130

Veterans Affairs Regional Office
215 N. Main Street
White River Junction, VT 05009
(800) 827-1000

VIRGINIA
State government information number: (804) 786-0000
State prison loctor: (804) 674-3209
State website: *www.state.va.us*

State Archives:
State Library of Virginia
800 E. Broad Street
Richmond, VA 23219-1905
(804) 692-3500, (804) 692-3556 Fax

Virginia Historical Society
PO Box 7311
Richmond, VA 23211-0311
(804) 342-9677

Genealogical Research Institute of VA
PO Box 29178
Richmond, VA 23242-0178

Virginia Genealogical Society
5001 W. Broad St, #115
Richmond, VA 23230-3023
(804) 285-8954

State Adjutant General
600 E. Broad Street
Richmond, VA 23219-1832
(804) 775-9116

Veterans Affairs Regional Office
210 Franklin Road, S.W.
Roanoke, VA 24011
(800) 827-1000

WASHINGTON
State government information number: (360) 753-5000
State prison locator: (360) 753-1573
State website: *www.state.wa.us*

State Archives:
Secretary of State
State Archives
PO Box 40238
Olympia, WA 98504-0238
(360) 753-5485, (360) 664-8814 Fax

Washington State Historical Society
Special Collections Division
315 N. Stadium Way
Tacoma, WA 98403
(206) 593-2830

WA State Genealogical Society
PO Box 1422
Olympia, WA 98507
(206) 352-0595

State Adjutant General
PO Box 339501
Ft. Lewis, WA 98433-9501
(253) 967-0642

Veterans Affairs Regional Office
915 2nd Avenue
Seattle, WA 98174
(800) 827-1000

WEST VIRGINIA

State government information number: (304) 558-3456
State prison locator: (304) 558-2036
State website: *www.state.wv.us*

State Archives:
Division of Culture and History
Archvies & History Section
1900 Kanawha Blvd. East
Charleston, WV 25305-0300
(304) 558-0220, (304) 558-2779 Fax

WV Genealogical Society
5238 Elk River Rd, North
PO Box 249
Elkview, WV 25071

State Adjutant General
1703 Coonskin Drive
Charleston, WV 25311-1085
(304) 341-6404

Veterans Affairs Regional Office
640 Fourth Avenue
Huntington, WV 25701
(800) 827-1000

WISCONSIN

State government information number: (608) 266-2211
State prison locator: (608) 266-2471
State website: *www.state.wi.us*

State Archives:
Historical Society
Archives Department
816 State Street
Madison, WI 53706
(608) 264-6450, (608) 264-6577 Fax

State Historical Society of WI
816 State Street
Madison, WI 53706
(608) 264-6535 (Library)
(608) 264-6460

Wisconsin Genealogical Council
Route 3, Box 253
Black River Falls, WI 54615-9405
(608) 378-4388, (608) 378-3006 Fax

Wisconsin State Genealogical Society
PO Box 516
Madison, WI 53705-0106
(608) 325-2609

State Adjutant General
2400 Wright Street
Madison, WI 53708-8111
(608) 242-3444

Veterans Affairs Regional Office
5000 W. National Ave. B-6
Milwaukee, WI 53295
(800) 827-1000

WYOMING

State government information number: (307) 777-7011
State prison locator: (307) 777-7401
State website: *www.state.wy.us*

State Archives:
Dept. of Commerce
Archives Division
6101 Yellowstone Road
Cheyenne, WY 82002
(307) 777-7826, (307) 777-7044 Fax

State Adjutant General
5500 Bishop Blvd.
Cheyenne, WY 82009-3320
(307) 772-5203

Veterans Affairs Regional Office
2360 E. Pershing Blvd.
Cheyenne, WY 82001
(800) 827-1000

State-Held Military Records

There are a wide variety of military records held at the state level. This chart details these records, and refers to state historical societies, state archives, state adjutant general's offices, and state Veterans Affairs offices. Appendix B lists all these offices except the VA offices. For the phone number of a state VA office, call the state information operator listed at the beginning of each state listing.

Column A: Has Selective Service System copies of reports of separation (WWII and later unless otherwise shown).

Column B: Has National Guard records which often contain verification of service.

Column C: Has state bonus records which often contain verification of active service.

Column D: Has case files on VA and state claims. May contain verification of service.

Numbers within the chart, below:

    1 = Records in custody of state adjutant general.

    2 = Records in custody of state department of veterans affairs of similar office.

    3 = Records in custody of state library, archives, records center, etc.

A	B	C	D
Alabama			
Yes 3	Yes 1	No	Yes 2*, from 1945

*The Department of Veterans Affairs advises that additional military records may be located in one or more of 67 county field offices. Inquires should include all known Alabama address elements.

A	B	C	D
Alaska			
No	Yes 1, from May 1949	No	No
Arizona			
No	Yes 1, from prior to WWI	No	No

A	B	C	D

Arkansas

| No | Yes 1, incomplete | No | Yes 2, active claims only |

California

| No | Yes 1* | No | No* |

*Records for last names beginning with A, B, C, E, K, and P were lost in a fire in Dec. 1972.Copies of the California Military Benefit Index Cards for WWI, WWII and Korea were furnished to the NPRC (MPR). These records are identified in the registry file index as "QTD."

Colorado

| No | Yes 1, from 1869 | No | No |

Connecticut

| Yes 1 from prior WWII | Yes 1 from Rev. War | WWII, Korea 3 | Yes 2, from 1940 |

Delaware

| Yes 3 | Yes 1, from Civil War | WWII & Korea 3* | No |

*The Delaware Public Archives Commission furnished NPRC a copy of *Delaware's Role in World War II, 1940–46* and microfilmed separation documents for WWI and Korea.

District of Columbia

| Yes 1, from 1940 | Yes 1, from 1882 | No | No |

Records in column A & B are held at the Army/Air National Guard offices.

Florida

| No | Yes 1, from 1914 | No | No |

The Adjutant General's Office has publications on fatal casualties for WWII & Korea.

Georgia

| Yes 3, from 1960 | Yes 3, full span | No | Yes 2, from 1923 |

Hawaii

| Yes 1, from 1940 | Yes 1, from 1940 | WWII | Yes 2 |

Records in column A & B are held at the Veterans Affairs counselor's offices on each island; column D records are held at the Department of Human Services in Honolulu.

Idaho

| No | Yes 1, from 1926–41; 1947–current | No | Yes 2, from 1966 |

Illinois

| Yes 2 | Yes 1, from 1862 | WWII & Korea 3 | Yes 2, from WWI |

The Dept. of Veterans Affairs maintains a complete record on all veterans, living and deceased. Also maintains a card file, alphabetically, on all veterans buried in Illinois.

A	B	C	D

Indiana
Yes 1*, 2*   Yes 1, from 1922   WWII & Korea 2   No
*The Adjutant General has WWII Honor List of Army only. The SSS copies of Reports of Separation are on microfilm and in most cases are very poor copies. Some are in alphabetical order, some not. Also has separation forms for Korean veterans from Indiana, and rosters showing name, branch of service, and home address at time of service. Alphabetical by county. These records are all in addition to regular National Guard records.

Iowa
Yes 1, from WWI   Yes 1, from 1800's   WWII & Korea 2*   Yes 1, limited info
*The Veterans Affairs Division advises it has Armed Forces Grave Registration records on veterans buried in Iowa thru the Vietnam War. These show name, date of birth, date of death, names of next of kin/survivor, place of death, place of burial, general service information and undertaker.

Bonus claims files covering WWI, WWII, & Korea were furnished to NPRC.

The Veterans Affairs Division has DD214's in Korean Bonus Files.

Kansas
Yes 1*   Yes 1, from 1930s   No   Yes 2, from 1944
*The State Adjutant General advises that the SSS copies of Report of Separation are exclusive of veterans of WWII, however statements of service are available on WWII veterans.

Kentucky
Yes 1   Yes 1, from late 1800s   WWII & Korea 1   Yes 2

Louisiana
Yes 2, from 1950   Yes 1, from 1900   WWII & Korea 3   Yes 2
The SSS copies of Report of Separation have been broken out to the Parish Veteran's Affairs Offices, however, all inquiries should be directed to the Dept. of Veterans Affairs Office at Baton Rouge. That office will check with the parish offices.

Maine
Yes 2   Yes 1, from 1947   No   No
The Bureau of Veteran Services has an incomplete collection of DD214's from WWII & Korea. However, they do have Selective Service Cards relating to those veterans whose DD214's were missing.

Maryland
No   Yes 1   No   No
WWII records in book form have been obtained from the Maryland Historical Society.

The Maryland Veteran's Commission has a WWII book which lists veterans names, service numbers & residence at time of entry.

Inquiries pertaining to WWII records should be sent to the War Memorial Commission.

A	B	C	D

Massachusetts

Yes 1*	Yes 1	WWII & Korea 1	No

*The Military Records Section of the Adjutant General's Office has DD214's from 1950–55
& 1958–75. Also, the Military Records Section has Bonus Locator Cards only. The bonus
records are under the jurisdiction of the Treasurer & Receiver General, Bonus Div., Rm.
1203, McCormack State Office Bldg., Boston, MA 02108. Records for columns A & C are
held at the Adjutant General's office in Boston.

Michigan

No	Yes 1	WWII & Korea 2	Yes 2, from 1946

Minnesota

Yes *	Yes 1* & 2*	WWII & Korea 2	Yes 2, from 1940

*The Reports of Separation were broken out to each County Veterans Service Officer.

The Adjutant General's Office advises it has Army National Guard records for the following:
1946–1978, Officer Records
1950–1978, Enlisted Records

The Dept. of Veterans Affairs has National Guard records from 6-27-1950 to 7-27-1953, for
those veterans who were called to active duty during Korea and who received a state bonus.

Mississippi

Yes 2, from 1948	Yes 1, from before WWI	No	No

Missouri

Yes 1, from 1941	Yes 1, from 1900	WWI 3	No

Montana

Yes 1, from WWI	Yes 1, from 1904	WWII & Korea 1	Yes 1

Nebraska

Yes 2, from WWI	Yes 1, from 1860	No	Yes 2, from WWI

Nevada

Yes 3, from 1950	No	No	No

The State Archivist indicates good coverage, alphabetically arranged dating from 1864 for
records of the National Guard, State Militia, and Adjutant General.

New Hampshire

Yes 1, from 1939	Yes 1, from 1947	WWII & Korea 1	No

New Jersey

No	Yes 1, from 1913	No	Yes 2, from WWI

New Mexico

No	Yes 1	WWII, & Korea 2*	Yes 2

*Bonus records are available from the Veterans Service Commission only if veteran has ap-
plied for a tax exemption.

A	B	C	D

New York

No   Yes 1, from 1921   WWI & WWII 2   Yes 2*

*The Div. of Veterans Affairs has Veterans Readjustment Allowance Records (52-20 & 26-26 Clubs) for WWII and Korea. These records pertain to unemployment insurance payments made to veterans by the state of NY. A verification from the Div. of Veterans Affairs that an individual received this benefit is proof of honorable military service. However, the dates of service cannot by verified. In order to search these records the SSN is needed.

North Carolina

Yes 3,   Yes 1   No   Yes 2
from 1940–48

The Adjutant General's Office has NG records from prior to WWI, and 1947 to present.

North Dakota

Yes 1*,   Yes 1, from 1903   WWII & Korea 1   Yes 2
1912–46, 2,
from 1950–64

*Adjutant General has records prior to 1950. Dept. of Veterans Affairs has records after 1950.

Rosters of WWI, WWII, and Korea (in book form) have been furnished to NPRC (MPR).

Ohio

Yes 1 & 2   Yes 1, from 1925   WWI 1   No

The Adjutant General's Office has service records of Ohioans who served on extended active duty during World War II and Korea (certificates of discharge and Reports of Separation).

The Division of Soldiers Claims & Veterans Affairs advises it has copies of discharge papers/ separation documents for the following periods:
WWII: 12-7-1941 to 9-2-1945
Korea: 6-25-1950 to 7-19-1953; & early 1960s (if served in Vietnam)

Oklahoma

No   Yes 1   No   No

The Adjutant General's Office records begin in late 1946 & 1952 when units were federally recognized. NPRC (MPR) was furnished discharge documents from 1940 thru 1951. These records are identified in the registry file index as "QMD."

Oregon

No   Yes 1   WWI & WWII 2   Yes 2

Pennsylvania

No   Yes 3*   WWII, Korea 1, 3*   No

*The Adjutant General's Office has state bonus applications for WWI, WWII, and Korea. In order to search Korean bonus applications, the AG's office needs a service number.

The Div. of Archives & Manuscripts has Muster Rolls from 1916 to 1917; Service Records & Bonus Applications from 1917 to 1948; Draft Board Registration & Induction Records from 1917 to 1948; Veterans Compensation & Bonus File Records c. 1950; & National Guard Records from 1867 to 1969. When requesting information from this source, furnish complete name;

A	B	C	D

township or county or residence at time of entering service; approximate period of service; & date of birth. Information concerning company, battalion, or regiment with which an individual served is helpful. Most Pennsylvania veterans were urged to record their discharges with their county records officer. This was free and most veterans took advantage, particularly for WWII.

Puerto Rico

A	B	C	D
No	Yes 1	No	No

Rhode Island

A	B	C	D
Yes	Yes 1	WWII, & Korea 1	Yes 2

South Carolina

A	B	C	D
Yes 1*, from 1940–46	Yes 1*, from 1947; 3, from 1919–41	No	Yes 2, from 1927

*The SSS copies of Reports of Separation that were furnished to the Adjutant General were used to compile an "Official Roster" for WWII. A copy has been furnished to NPRC (MPR).

The Dept. of Archives and History advises it has the following records:
- Company files after induction, 1940–43, transferred from the office of the A.G.
- Discharge and releases from service,1941–43, transferred from the office of the A.G.
- S. Carolina State Guard Enlistment Records, 1941–47.

South Dakota

A	B	C	D
No	Yes 1, from prior WWI	WWII, & Korea 2	Yes 2

Tennessee

A	B	C	D
Yes 1, from 1941	Yes 1, from 1900	No	No

Texas

A	B	C	D
No	Yes 1, from 1922	No	Yes 2, from 1940

The AG's office has a list of Texans killed in WWI, WWII, & Korean conflict.

Utah

A	B	C	D
Yes 3	Yes 1, from WWII	No	No

Vermont

A	B	C	D
Yes 2, from 12-1941	Yes 2, from 1946	WWII, & Korea 2*	No

*Bonus information consists of amount and date received.

Virginia

A	B	C	D
No	Yes 1, from 1946	No	No

Virgin Islands

A	B	C	D
Yes 2	No	No	Yes 2

A	B	C	D

Washington
No — Yes 1, from 1890 — WWII & Korea 2 — Yes 2

West Virginia
Yes 1, — Yes 1, from 1921 — WWII & Korea 2 — No
from 1940–46
& 1949–77

Wisconsin
Yes 2, from WWI — Yes 1, from 1880 — WWI 2 — Yes 2, from 1943
The Dept. of Veterans Affairs advises it has Grave Registration records of veterans buried in Wisconsin which include military records information.

Wyoming
Yes 1, from WWII — Yes 1, from 1880s — No — No

Directory of Military & Patriotic Organizations

Following is a list of some of the largest military and patriotic organizations in the United States. Some include only certain branches of the military while others include all branches. Each organization has its own rules for locating a member of the organization. The majority will forward a letter. If the organization is large, you should speak with the membership office to first find out if the person is even a member. It is important to have all identifying information available before contacting these organizations for assistance.

Air Force Association
1501 Lee Highway
Arlington, VA 22209
www.afa.org
(165,000 members)

(703) 247-5800
(703) 247-5853 Fax

Air Force Sergeants Association
PO Box 50
Temple Hills, MD 20757
www.afsahq.org
(155,000 members)

(301) 899-8136 Fax

American Ex-Prisoners of War
3201 East Pioneer Parkway, #40
Arlington, TX 76010-5396
www.ax-pow.org
(30,000 members)

(817) 649-2979
(817) 649-0109 Fax

American GI Forum of the U.S.
421 S. Mitchell Avenue
San Marcos, TX 78666
www.incacorp.com/agif
(150,000 members)

(512) 353-8000
(512) 353-8002 Fax

American Gulf War Veterans Association   (800) 231-7631
3506 Highway 6 South, #117
Sugarland, TX 77478-4401
www.gulfwarvets.com

The American Legion   (317) 630-1200
PO Box 1055   (317) 630-1241 Fax
Indianapolis, IN 46206
www.legion.org
(2,900,000 members)

American Military Retirees Assn.   (518) 563-9479 Phone/fax
426 U.S. Oval, Suite 1200
Plattsburgh, NY 12903
(5,000 members)

American Retirees Association   (909) 389-0014
PO Box 2333   (909) 794-7168 Fax
Redlands, CA 92373
(1,400 members)

American Veterans of WWII,   (301) 459-9600
    Korea and Vietnam   (301) 459-7924 Fax
AMVETS
4647 Forbes Boulevard
Lanham, MD 20706-4380
www.amvets.org
(180,000 members)

Army and Air Force Mutual Aid Assn.   (800) 336-4538
468 Sheridan Avenue   (703) 522-3060
Fort Myer, VA 22211-5002   (703) 875-0076 Fax
www.aafmaa.com
(60,000 members)

Army and Navy Union   (330) 673-9373
2002 Tallmadge Road   (330) 673-8371 Fax
Kent, OH 44240
www.armynavy.net
(15,000 members)

Association of the United States Army
2425 Wilson Boulevard
Arlington, VA 22201
www.ausa.org
(110,000 members)

(800) 336-4570
(703) 841-4300
(703) 525-9039 Fax

Association of Graduates of the
   U.S. Air Force Academy
3116 Academy Drive
Colorado Springs, CO 80840-4475
www.aog-usafa.org

(719) 472-0300
(719) 333-4194 Fax

Association of Graduates of the
   U.S. Military Academy
West Point, NY 10996-1611
www.aog.usma.edu
(39,000 members)

(914) 938-4600
(914) 446-5325 Fax

Aviation Cadet Alumni Association
2665 Chestnut Street, #11
San Francisco, CA 94123

(415) 567-4717 or
(216) 355-4201

Blinded Veterans Association
477 "H" Street, N.W.
Washington, DC 20001-2694
www.bva.org
(9,000 members)

(202) 371-8880
(202) 371-8258 Fax

Catholic War Veterans USA, Inc.
441 N. Lee Street
Alexandria, VA 22314
www.va.gov/vso/cwv.htm
(24,000 members)

(703) 549-3622
(703) 684-5196 Fax

Congressional Medal of Honor Society
40 Patriots Point Road
Mount Pleasant, SC 29464
www.awod.com/gallery/probono/cmhs
(162 members)

(843) 884-8862
(843) 884-1471 Fax

Disabled American Veterans   (606) 441-7300
PO Box 14301   (606) 442-2088 Fax
Cincinnati, OH 45250-0301
www.dav.org
(1,000,000 members)

Fleet Reserve Association   (703) 683-1400
125 N. West Street   (703) 549-6610 Fax
Alexandria, VA 22314-2754
www.fra.org
(160,000 members)

Gold Star Wives of America   (609) 696-1882
1964 E. Oak Road, Unit I-4   (609) 691-1688 Fax
Vineland, NJ 08360
(13,000 members)

Jewish War Veterans of the USA   (202) 265-6280
1811 "R" Street, N.W.   (202) 234-5662 Fax
Washington, DC 20009
www.penfed.org/jwv/home.htm
(100,000 members)

Korean War Veterans Association   (703) 522-9629
PO Box 10806   (410) 828-7953 Fax
Arlington, VA 22210
www.kwva.org
(15,000 members)

Marine Corps Association   (800) 336-0291
715 Broadway Street
Quantico, VA 22134
www.mca-marines.org
(100,000 members)

Marine Corps Aviation Association   (800) 280-3001
715 Broadway Street, Box 296   (703) 630-2713 Fax
Quantico, VA 22134
www.flymcaa.org
(4,000 members)

Marine Corps League   (703) 207-9588
8626 Lee Highway, Suite 201   (703) 207-0047 Fax
Fairfax, VA 22031
www.mcleague.org
(44,000 members)

Marine Corps Reserve Officers Assn   (703) 548-7607
110 North Royal Street #406   (703) 519-8779 Fax
Alexandria, VA 22314
www.mcroa.com
(5,500 members)

Military Chaplains Association   (202) 574-2423
PO Box 42660   (202) 574-2423 Fax
Washington, DC 20015-0660

Military Order of the Purple Heart   (703) 642-5360
5413-B Backlick Road   (703) 642-2054 Fax
Springfield, VA 22151
www.purpleheart.org
(32,000 members)

Military Order of the World Wars   (703) 683-4911
435 North Lee Street   (703) 683-4501 Fax
Alexandria, VA 22314
www.moww.org
(12,000 members)

National Assn for Uniformed Services   (703) 750-1342
5535 Hempstead Way   (703) 354-4380 Fax
Springfield, VA 22151
www.naus.org
(156,000 members)

National Association of Atomic Veterans   (800) 784-NAAV
PO Box 4424   (978) 740-9267 Fax
Salem, MA 01970
www.naav.com
(4,000 members)

National Association of Fleet Tug Sailors   (415) 331-7757
PO Box 1507   (415) 331-3909 Fax
Sausalito, CA 94965-1507
(1,000 members)

National Chief Petty Officers' Association   (336) 778-2482
Charles Claybourn, Secretary
5800 Sir Knight Circle
Clemmons, NC 27012
(2,000 members)

National Gaurd Association of the U.S.   (202) 789-0031
1 Massachusetts Ave, N.W.   (202) 682-9358 Fax
Washington, DC 20001
www.ngaus.org
(51,000 members)

Natl. League of Families of American   (202) 223-6846
   Prisoners & Missing in SE Asia   (202) 785-9410 Fax
1001 Connecticut Avenue, N.W., #219
Washington, DC 20036-5504
www.pow-miafamilies.org
(2,000 members)

National Military Family Association   (703) 823-6632
6000 Stephenson Avenue #304   (703) 751-4857 Fax
Alexandria, VA 22304-3526
www.nmfa.org
(6,000 members)

National Veterans Organization, Inc.   (915) 759-6233
2001 E. Lohman, Suite 110-248   (915) 759-6322 Fax
Las Cruces, NM 88801-3167
www.nvo.org

Naval Enlisted Reserve Association   (800) 776-9020
6703 Farragut Avenue   (703) 534-3617 Fax
Falls Church, VA 22042
www.nera.org/nera
(16,000 members)

Naval Reserve Association   (703) 548-5800
1619 King Street   (703) 683-3647 Fax
Alexandria, VA 22314-2793
www.navy-reserve.org
(22,000 members)

Navy League of the United States   (703) 528-1775
2300 Wilson Boulevard   (703) 528-2333 Fax
Arlington, VA 22201-3308
www.navyleague.org
(70,000+ members)

Navy Mutual Aid Association   (800) 628-6011
Henderson Hall   (703) 614-1638
29 Carpenter Road   (703) 695-4635 Fax
Arlington, VA 22212
www.navymutual.org
(82,000 members)

Non-Commissioned Officers Association   (210) 653-6161
10635 IH35 North   (210) 637-3337 Fax
San Antonio, TX 78233
www.ncoausa.org
(148,000 members)

Paralyzed Veterans of America   (202) 872-1300
801 18 Street N.W.   (202) 785-4452 Fax
Washington, DC 20006
www.pva.org
(18,000 members)

Pearl Harbor Survivors Association, Inc.   (909) 585-3448
PO Box 442
Big Bear City, CA 92314-0442
(10,750 members)

Polish Legion of American Veterans   (860) 589-7942
59 Willis Street
Bristol, CT 06010-6861
(16,000 members)

Regular Veterans Assn. of the U.S., Inc.
5200 Wilkinson Boulevard
Charlotte, NC 28205-5450
(18,000 members)

Reserve Officers Assn. of the U.S.   (202) 646-7715
One Constitution Ave, N.E.
Washington, DC 20002
www.roa.org
(128,000 members)

Retired Enlisted Association   (800) 338-9337
1111 S. Abilene Court   (303) 752-0835 Fax
Aurora, CO 80012
www.trea.org
(77,000 members)

The Retired Officers Association   (703) 549-2311
201 N. Washington Street   (703) 838-8173 Fax
Alexandria, VA 22314-2539
www.troa.org
(400,000 members)

The Tailhook Association   (619) 689-9223
9696 Businesspark Avenue   (619) 578-8839 Fax
San Diego, CA 92131-1643
www.tailhook.org
(11,000 members)

Uniformed Service Disabled Retirees   (800) 349-0365
PO Box 2841
South Bend, IN 44680

U.S. Army Warrant Officers Association   (703) 742-7727
462 Herndon Parkway,#207   (703) 742-7728 Fax
Herndon, VA 22070
www.penfed.org/usawoa
(5,000 members)

U.S. Coast Guard Alumni Services   (860) 444-8237
U.S. Coast Guard Academy   (860) 443-4917 Fax
47 Mohegan Avenue
New London, CT 06320-8111
(6,500 members)

U.S. Coast Guard Chief Petty Officers   (703) 941-0395
5520-G Hempstead Way   (703) 941-0397 Fax
Springfield, VA 22151
www.uscgcpoa.com

U.S. Naval Academy Alumni Association   (410) 263-4448
247 King George Street   (410) 269-0151 Fax
Annapolis, MD 21402-5068
www.usna.com
(40,000 members)

U.S. Submarine Veterans of WWII   (630) 834-2718
862 Chatham Avenue
Elmhurst, IL 60126-4531
(15,000+ members)

Veterans of the Battle of the Bulge   (703) 528-4058
PO Box 11129   (703) 528-5403 Fax
Arlington, VA 22210-2129
www.battleofbulge.com
(11,000 members)

Veterans of Foreign Wars (VFW)   (816) 756-3390
406 West 34th Street   (816) 968-1157 Fax
Kansas City, MO 64111
www.vfw.org
(2,000,000 members)

Veterans of the Vietnam War, Inc.   (717) 825-7215
760 Jumper Road   (717) 825-8223
Wilkes-Barre, PA 18702-8033
www.vvnw.org
(25,000 members)

Veterans of WWI of the USA, Inc.   (703) 780-5660
PO Box 8027   (703) 780-8465 Fax
Alexandria, VA 22306-8027
(6,000 members)

Vietnam Helicopter Pilots Association   (800) 505-VHPA
494 University Avenue, #210   (916) 648-1072 Fax
Sacramento, CA 95825
www.vhpa.org
(9,500 members)

Vietnam Veterans of America, Inc.   (202) 628-2700
1224 "M" Street, N.W.   (202) 628-5880 Fax
Washington, DC 20005
www.vva.org
(45,000 members)

Vietnam Veterans Wives   (509) 826-4530
PO Box 396   (509) 826-9360 Fax
Republic, WA 99166
(200 members)

Directory of Military Reunions

There are over 7,000 military reunions held every year in the U.S. Following is a list of the largest reunion groups or associations for all branches of the military. Check the Internet at *www.militaryusa.com* or *www.vets.org* for more listings of military reunions.

U.S. AIR FORCE REUNIONS

5TH AF/90TH BG (H)
425 S 39TH ST
LINCOLN, NE 68510-1622

5TH BOMBARDMENT GROUP (H)
39685 RAMSHORN DR
MURRIETA, CA 92563-5563

5TH COMBAT COMM GRP
PO BOX 8025
WARNER ROBINS, GA 31905-8025

7TH BW/B-36 ASSN OFFICE
PO BOX 330279
FORT WORTH, TX 76163-0279

8TH AF HISTORICAL SOCIETY
PO BOX 7215
ST. PAUL, MN 55107-7215

8TH AF/303RD BG(H) ASSN INC
12700-54 RED MAPLE CIR
SONORA, CA 95370-5269

8TH AF/384TH BG(H)
650 SNUG HARBOR DR # G-402
BOYNTON BEACH, FL 33435-6140

8TH AF/94TH BG MEM ASSN
433 NW 33RD ST
CORVALLIS, OR 97330-5036

13TH BOMB SQDN ASSN
110 SILK ST
BREWER, ME 04412-1858

17TH ABN DIV ASSN OFFICE
2903 REVERE PL
DELAND, FL 32720-1459

19TH BOMB GROUP ASSN
3574 WELLSTON CT
SIMI VALLEY, CA 93063-1145

20TH AF/73RD BW ASSN
706 STARCREST
NEW BRAUNFELS, TX 78130-5363

28TH BW ASSN/28TH BG
PO BOX 3092
RAPID CITY, SD 57709-3092

36TH TACTICAL FIGHTER WING
1225 S ALMAR CIR
MESA, AZ 85204-6469

40TH BW (M)
3513 LEAWOOD DR
BELLEVUE, NE 68123-2138

55TH AIR WEATHER (VLR) SQDN
101 E MEADOWLARK RD
DERBY, KS 67037-2937

73RD BOMB WING ASSN
649 BALMORAL RD
WINTER PARK, FL 32789-5204

81ST FIGHTER WING
70 RILLA LANE
SEQUIM, WA 98382-9277

70TH AIR REFUELING ASSN
9204 PEACH TREE ST
SHERWOOD, AR 72120-3901

90TH SRW ASSN
735 NE POPLAR
TOPEKA, KS 66616-1320

100TH BW/B47/KC97
PO BOX 192
SHALIMAR, FL 32579-0192

301ST VETERANS ASSN OFFICE
6422 HANDSOME LAKE DR
SAN ANTONIO, TX 78238-1522

307TH BW B-47/KC97 ASSN
2706 NORTHCREST DR
COLO. SPRINGS, CO 80918-4316

320TH BOMB GROUP
108 ASPEN ST
HEREFORD, TX 79045-4116

330TH BOMB GROUP ASSN
413 E CENTER ST
GERMANTOWN, OH 45327-1301

351ST BOMB GROUP ASSN
PO BOX 281
MECHANICSBURG, PA 17055-0281

375TH TROOP CARRIER GROUP
625 S. WHEATON AVE
WHEATON, IL 60187-5215

376TH BOMB GROUP/WW2
1660 N. 2000 E. RD.
STONINGTON, IL 62567-9602

381ST BG MEMORIAL ASSN
1260 MAIN ST
NEW PARK, PA 17352-9376

385TH BG MEMORIAL ASSN
7442 ONTARIO ST
OMAHA, NE 68124-3563

401ST BOMB GROUP
PO BOX 15356
SAVANNAH, GA 31416-2056

424TH ASG/88TH ASS
7442 ONTARIO ST
OMAHA, NE 68124-3563

446TH BG ASSN REUNION
13382 WHEELER PLACE
SANTA ANA, CA 92705-1934

450TH BOMB GROUP
5695 IRELAND RD NE
LANCASTER, OH 43130-9478

451ST BOMB GROUP
1032 S. STATE ST
MARENGO, IL 60152-3578

459TH BOMB GROUP ASSN
90 KIMBARK RD
ROCHESTER, NY 14610-2738

483RD BG/566TH AE
4729 NW 70TH ST
OKLAHOMA CITY, OK 73132-6839

484TH BOMB GROUP ASSN
1122 YSABEL ST
REDONDO BCH, CA 90277-4453

508TH, 509TH, 510TH, 511TH BS
PO BOX 281
MECHANICSBURG, PA 17055-0281

511TH AC&W GROUP
7 ANGELA DR
DRY RIDGE, KY 41035-9678

613TH AC&W GROUP
7 ANGELA DR
DRY RIDGE, KY 41035-9678

735TH AC&W SQDNS
109 WILLOWSIDE DR
MOUNT HOLLY, NC 28120-9006

847TH AC&W GROUP
7 ANGELA DR
DRY RIDGE, KY 41035-9678

848TH AC&W GROUP
7 ANGELA DR
DRY RIDGE, KY 41035-9678

AFCEA TECHNET ASIA-PACIFIC 98
4400 FAIR LAKES CT
FAIRFAX, VA 22033-3899

AIR RESCUE ASSN
4853 DELAIRE DR
DEL CITY, OK 75115-4803

B-24 GROUPS MEMORIAL
132 PENINSULA DR
MEDICINE LAKE, MN 55441-4112

BAD 2 ASSN
527 QUARTERFIELD RD
NEWPORT NEWS, VA 23602-6140

BURTONWOOD ASSN/3RD AF
4515 W 55TH ST
CHICAGO, IL 60632-4721

CAD CL 43-K
17545 DRAYTON HALL WAY
SAN DIEGO, CA 92128-2032

CAD CL 52-G
PO BOX 1238
MT. PLEASANT, TX 75455-1238

PACIFIC AIR WEATHER SQDNS
2300 OAK KNOLL CT
COLLEYVILLE, TX 76034-4488

RF 101 VOODOO PILOTS
730 GOLF CREST LN
AUSTIN, TX 78734-4642

SELMAN FLD HISTORICAL ASSN
1726 SPENCER AVE
MONROE, LA 71201

STALAG IV & VI OFFICE
8103 E 50TH ST
LAWRENCE, IN 46226-2018

TUSKEGEE AIRMEN INC
1501 LEE HIGHWAY STE 130
ARLINGTON, VA 22209-1137

USAF HONOR GUARD
50 DUNCAN AVE STE 1
BOLLING AFB, DC 20332-5000

U.S. ARMY REUNIONS

1ST ARMORED DIV ASSN
PO BOX 2088
ELIZABETHTOWN, KY 42702-2088

1ST INFANTRY DIV
1933 MORRIS RD
BLUE BELL, PA 19422-1422

2ND ARMORED DIV ASSN
8053 HIGHPOINT BLVD
BROOKSVILLE, FL 34613-7346

2ND INFANTRY DIV/KOREA
PO BOX 1049
TIBURON, CA 94920-0980

3RD ARMORED DIV ASSN
PO BOX 61743
PHOENIX, AZ 85082-1743

3RD INF DIV SOCIETY REUNION
201 CHEROKEE TRAIL
HINESVILLE, GA 31313-5701

4TH ARMORED DIV ASSN
1823 SHADY DR
FARRELL, PA 16121-1342

5TH ARMORED DIV ASSN
13344 LUTHMAN RD
MINSTER, OH 45865-9375

5TH US CAV ASSN/BLK KNIGHTS
PO BOX 822
COLUMBIA, MO 65205-0822

6TH ARMORED DIV ASSN
PO BOX 5011
LOUISVILLE, KY 40255-0011

7TH ARMORED DIV ASSN
23218 SPRINGROOK DR
FARMINGTON HILLS, MI 48336-3371

7TH INFANTRY DIV ASSN
2937 BRUCE DR
FREMONT, CA 94539-5009

8TH ARMORED DIV ASSN
PO BOX 427
JEFFERSON CITY, TN 37760-0427

9TH INFANTRY DIV/VIETNAM
12 SUMMITT KNOLLS DR
WEBSTER, NY 14580-2816

11TH ARMORED CAV VETS OF VN
1602 LORRIE DR
RICHARDSON, TX 75080-3409

11TH INFANTRY DIV ASSN
8000 SARGENT RD
INDIANAPOLIS, IN 46256-1836

12TH ARMORED DIV ASSN
6420 MIDDLESHIRE
COLUMBUS, OH 43229-2031

13TH ABN DIV ASSN
PO BOX 1372
SHAWNEE MISSION, KS 66222-0372

14TH ARMORED DIV ASSN
PO BOX 42831
CINCINNATI, OH 45242-0831

15TH CAV GROUP
450 HIGHLAND AVE
ATHENS, GA 30606-4316

16TH ARMORED DIV ASSN
PO BOX 222
LAKE ALFRED, FL 33850-0222

22ND IR SOCIETY
600 E MAIN ST
PILOT POINT, TX 76258-9311

23RD INFANTRY DIV ASSN
1676 SW 33RD ST
REDMOND, OR 97758-9612

24TH INFANTRY DIV ASSN
1385 TERRI ST
KEYSER, WV 26726-2119

25TH INFANTRY DIV ASSN
PO BOX 746
ROCKLIN, CA 95677-0746

28TH INFANTRY DIV ASSN
329 MANSION DR
ALEXANDRIA, VA 22302-2904

29TH INFANTRY DIV ASSN
5928 ROBINDALE RD
BALTIMORE, MD 21228-1224

30TH FA ASSN
4204 BERKELEY DR
SHEF. VILLAGE, OH 44054-2916

30TH INFANTRY DIV ASSN
PO BOX 886
SPARTANBURG, SC 29304-0886

31ST IR ASSN/POLAR BEARS
3728 HIGHLAND AVE
SKANEATELES, NY 13152-9356

33RD INFANTRY DIV ASSN
PO BOX 13618
MILL CREEK, WA 98082-1618

34TH INFANTRY DIV ASSN
RT 1 BOX 68A
GRANGER, IA 50109-9801

35TH INFANTRY DIV ASSN
4311 WOMACK DR
COLO. SPRINGS, CO 80915-2721

40TH INFANTRY DIV ASSN
210 HIGHLAND AVE
MAYBROOK, NY 12543-1012

42ND INFANTRY DIV/WW2
311 OAKWOOD CIR
WAUSAU, WI 54403-7068

63RD INFANTRY DIV ASSN
19W 565 D00RPATH LN
LEMONT, IL 60439-8832

65TH INFANTRY DIV ASSN
7300 MARSHALL RD
UPPER DERBY, PA 19082-4820

66TH INF DIV/PANTHER VETS
167 JEFFERSON AVE
RAHWAY, NJ 07065-2806

68TH AAA GUN BN/KOREA
416 EDGEWOOD AVE
TRAFFORD, PA 15085-1119

69TH INFANTRY DIV ASSN
144 NASHUA CT
SAN JOSE, CA 95139-1236

70TH INFANTRY DIV ASSN
8214 E HIGHLAND AVE
SCOTTSDALE, AZ 85251-1731

71ST INFANTRY DIV ASSN
1 BRIARBROOK TRL
DES PERES, MO 63131-3900

78TH INFANTRY DIV VETS ASSN
2306 COMBURG CASTLE WAY
AUSTIN, TX 78748-5214

80TH INFANTRY DIV VETS ASSN
630 PENNSYLVANIA AVE
OAKMONT, PA 15139-1574

82ND ABN DIV ASSN
5459 NORTHCUTT PL
DAYTON, OH 45414-3742

86TH INF DIV ASSN/BLACKHAWK
1930 W SAN MARCOS BLVD #139
SAN MARCOS, CA 92069-3919

87TH INF DIV ASSN REUNION
2374 N DUNDEE CT
HIGHLAND, MI 48357-3716

88TH INF DIV BLUE DEVILS
PO BOX 6411
ALBANY, CA 94706-0411

89TH INF DIV SOCIETY OF WWII
818 SAN ANTONIO PL
COLO. SPRINGS, CO 80906-4907

90TH INFANTRY DIV ASSN
PO BOX 730
SOUTH HILL, VA 23970-0730

91ST BG(H) MEMORIAL ASSN
590 ALOHA DR
LAKE HAVASU CITY, AZ 86406-4559

91ST INFANTRY DIV ASSN
6109 ST JOHNS AVE
MINNEAPOLIS, MN 55424-1853

92ND INFANTRY DIV ASSN
PO BOX 453
AQUEBOGUE, NY 11931-0453

95TH INFANTRY DIV ASSN
8032 S 86TH CT
JUSTICE, IL 60458-1445

96TH INFANTRY DIV ASSN
7634 FIELDING
DETROIT, MI 48228-3232

99TH INFANTRY DIV ASSN
PO BOX 99
MARION, KS 66861-0099

100TH INFANTRY DIV ASSN
1503 CRESWOOD RD
PHILADELPHIA, PA 19115-3110

101ST ABN DIV ASSN
9836 RAINLEAF CT
COLUMBIA, MD 21046-1822

U.S. COAST GUARD REUNIONS

USCG HONOR GUARD
7323 TELEGRAPH RD
ALEXANDRIA, VA 22315-3911

USCG 165 CUTTERS CONVOY GRP
1020 COUCH AVE
ST. LOUIS, MO 63122-6902

USCG 255 CUTS/OWASCO CLASS
PO BOX 33523
JUNEAU, AK 99803-3523

USCG AVN & SUPPORT
317 JESSE AVE
ROSEVILLE, CA 95678-2035

USCG BERING STRAIT PATROL
4601 ALLENDE AVE
OCEANSIDE, CA 92057-6147

USCG CAMPBELL WAGC 32
77 GARDEN HILLS DR
CRANSTON, RI 02920-3315

USCG COMBAT VETS ASSN
14334 THORNWOOD TR
HUDSON, FL 34669-3639

USCG DUANE W/WPG/WHEC 33
PO BOX 3268
S. ATTLEBORO, MA 02703-0930

USCG EASTWIND SAGB 279
37C JEFFERSON DR
MAPLE SHADE, NJ 08052-1421

USCG GREENLAND PATROL
1533 WALES AVE
BALDWIN, NY 11510-1743

USCG OSC CL4-56
7617 W TAPPS DR E
SUMNER, WA 98390-8686

USCG RES TNG CTR YORKTOWN
998 RIDGEWOOD LN
W. CHESTER, PA 19382-5251

USCG STN ST AUGUSTINE FL
18 ST AUGUSTINE BLVD
ST. AUGUSTINE, FL 32084-3753

USCGC BIBB WHEC 31
505 E HENRY CLAY ST
MILWAUKEE, WI 53217-5640

USCGC BITTERSWEET WLB 389
USCG GROUP/30 LITTLE
WOODS HOLE, MA 02543-1099

USCGC CAMPBELL ASSN
8341 SANDS PT BLVD
TAMARAC, FL 33321-3854

USCGC CASCO WAVP 370
PO BOX 141
LYONS, WI 53148-0141

USCGC CAYNE WPC 105
1743 GLEN RIDGE RD
BALTIMORE, MD 21234-5211

USCGC CEDAR
PO BOX 695
DOS PALOS, CA 93620-0965

USCGC CHAUTAUQUA WPG 41
3212 N GOLETA DR
LAS VEGAS, NV 89108-4735

USCGC COURIER WAGR 410
PO BOX 1319
PEPERELL, MA 01463-3319

USCGC FINCH WDE 428
5510 SOUTHAMPTON DR
SPRINGFIELD, VA 22151-1431

USCGC FIREBUSH WLB 393
PO BOX 190653
KODIAK, AK 99619-0653

USCGC INGHAM W 35
PO BOX 145
LANCASTER, VA 22503-0145

USCGC MACKINAC
7204 N E 185TH ST
BOTHELL, WA 98011-2721

USCGC MARQUETTE
400 COAST GUARD DR
MARQUETTE, MI 49855-3864

USCGC MINNETONKA WHEC 67
299 NW STAATS ST
BEND, OR 97701-3272

USCGC MODOC W 46
18 NINTH AVE
HALIFAX, MA 02338-1313

USCGC MOJAVE WPG 47
16122 S GRAHAM RD
PLEASANT HILL, MO 64080-8316

USCGC ONONDAGA WPG 79
1770 STUART ST
CAMBRIA, CA 93428-5832

USCGC RED CEDAR WLM 688
4000 COAST GUARD BLVD
PORTSMOUTH, VA 23703-2195

USCGC ROCKAWAY WAGO 377
STAR RT 2 BOX 416
CRESCENT CITY, FL 32112-9731

USCGC SUMAC WLR 311
PO BOX 18640
ST. LOUIS, MO 63118-9998

USCGC SUNDREW/BOUY TNDR
1201 MINNESOTA AVE
DULUTH, MN 55802-2492

USCGC SWEETGUM W 309
201 W. CUTHBERT RD A
OAKLYN, NJ 08107-1057

USCGC TAMPA WPG 48
8125 RIVERTOWN RD
FAIRBURN, GA 30213-2343

USCGC WHITE HEATH WLM 545
427 COMMERCIAL ST/US
BOSTON, MA 02109-1081

USCGC WHITE SUMAC WLM 540
600 8TH AVE SE
ST. PETERSBURG, FL 33701-5030

USCGC WINNEBAGO WPG 40
3212 N GOLETA DR
LAS VEGAS, NV 89108-4735

USCGC WOODBINE
725 HUBBARD ST NE
GRAND RAPIDS, MI 49505-2539

USS LST 26 LST 26
88 GLENBROOK RD
LEOLA, PA 17540-1301

USS LST 261 LST 261
PO BOX 693
E. LIVERPOOL, OH 43920-0693

USS LST 763 LST 763
1972 GRAYS INN RD
COLUMBIA, SC 29210-7135

USS LST 769 LST 769
590 HARTFORD ST
WORTHINGTON, OH 43085-4120

USS LST 886 LST 886
89 JEANNETTE AVE
STATEN ISLAND, NY 10312-3610

USS MACHIAS PF 53/ED 33
806 HELENE ST
WANTAGH, NY 11793-1622

USS MILLS DE 383
145 HIGHVIEW DR
VERSAILLES, KY 40383-1145

USS MUSKOGEE PF 49
4605 S HEATHERWOOD DR
ST. JOSEPH, MO 64506-4992

USS PEORIA PF 67
1856 RIDGEWAY DR
CLEARWATER, FL 34615-2237

USS SELLSTROM DE 255
6922 W JONQUIL TER
NILES, IL 60641-3222

USS PETERSON DE 152
1914 W PARKER
MC HENRY, IL 60050-8008

USS SHELIAK AK 62/WPC 140
2123 SUSSEX LN
COLORADO SPRINGS, CO 80909-1526

USS PETTIT DE 253
1254 UPLAND HILLS DR
UPLAND, CA 91786-9176

USS SPENCER CG ASSN
100 CAMBRIDGE ST
MANCHESTER, CT 06040-3508

USS RICHEY DE 385
18437 UNIVERSITY PARK
LIVONIA, MI 48152-2629

USS THEENIM AKA 63
14 MAPLE DR
SANDY HOOK, CT 06482-1168

USS SAMUEL CHASE APA 26
106 VANCE DR
BRISTOL, CT 06010-3736

USS WAKEFIELD AP 21
6 BRASSIE WAY
N. READING, MA 01864-3434

USS SAN PEDRO PF 37
1206 HAZEL AVE
PINOLE, CA 94564-1935

USS WOONSOCKET PF 32
7948 BENZIE HWY
BENZONIA, MI 49616-9729

U.S. MARINE CORPS REUNIONS

1ST MAW ASSN/VN
PO BOX 3532
ALLENTOWN, PA 18106-0532

3RD MD/11TH ENG BN (FMF)
8451 S KILBOURN AV
CHICAGO, IL 60652-3043

1ST MD ASSN
14325 WILLARD RD STE 107
CHANTILLY, VA 20151-2110

3RD MD/2ND BN
24151 OXFORD ST
DEARBORN, MI 48124-2445

2ND MD ASSN OFFICE
PO BOX 8180
CAMP LEJEUNE, NC 28547-8081

3RD MD/3RD MAR/1ST BN
7622 HIGHLAND ST
SPRINGFIELD, VA 22150-3931

3RD MD ASSN
2363 WHISPER WALK DR
SPRING HILL, FL 34606-7246

3RD MD/3RD MED BN/DANANG
712 BESSIE DR
WHITE HALL, AR 71602-3524

3RD MD/9TH MAR/1ST BN
1152 KENSINGTON AVE
PLAINFIELD, NJ 07060-2633

4TH MD ASSN/LA CHAP 2 OFFICE
PO BOX 595
LAUREL, FL 34272-0595

6TH MD ASSN
233 N DEAN DR
PALATINE, IL 60067-5539

MARINE BKS/NAD HAWTHORNE
PO BOX 833
HAWTHORNE, NV 89415-0833

MARINE BKS/SUBIC BAY
8184 SHIPS CURVE LN
SPRINGFIELD, VA 22153-1833

MARINE CORPS AVIATION ASSN
PO BOX 296
QUANTICO, VA 22134-0296

MARINE MUSTANGS
PO BOX 1314
DELRAN, NJ 08075-0142

NAT MARINE CORPS LEAGUE
PO BOX 3070
MERRYFIELD, VA 22116-3070

USMC MUSTANG ASSN
108 GENOA DR
HAMPTON, VA 23664-1793

USMC VIETNAM HELI ASSN
72 LORRAINE ST
WEYMOUTH, MA 02189-2610

USS MISSISSIPPI/MAR DET
3 CONNELL DR
WESTFORD, MA 01886-2520

WOMEN MARINES ASSN
2537 REYNOLDS
N. LAS VEGAS, NV 89030-7326

U.S. NAVY REUNIONS

USS ALABAMA BB 60/SSBN 731
PO BOX 501
KELLER, TX 76244-0501

USS ARKANSAS BB 33
6837 EASTSIDE AVE
WOODRIDGE, IL 60517-1833

USS ATTU CVE 102
286 MOORE RD
HACKBERRY, LA 70645-3408

USS BELLEAU WOOD CVL 24
2732 S US 23
OSCODA, MI 48750-9583

USS BENNINGTON CV/CVA/CVS 20
6 MCKEE AVE
MONESSEN, PA 15062-1227

USS BISMARCK SEA CVE 95/VC 86
5902 WALTON RD
BETHESDA, MD 20817-2517

USS BRETON CVE 23
5130 S DEARBORN ST
INDIANAPOLIS, IN 46227-6677

USS COLORADO ALUMNI ASSN
16436-14TH AVE SW
SEATTLE, WA 98166-2820

USS COLUMBUS ASSN OFFICE
CA 74/CG 12/SSN 762
726 W COVINA BLVD
COVINA, CA 91722-2955

USS CORREGIDOR CVE 58
HC 2, BOX 284
BLUE EYE, MO 65611-9627

USS DIAMONDHEAD AE 19
HC 63 BOX 32
MIFFLINTOWN, PA 17059-9024

USS ENTERPRISE CV 6
22800 FAST CT
BAKERSFIELD, CA 93312-9258

USS FRANKLIN D ROOSEVELT
4213 HARRY ST
CORPUS CHRISTI, TX 78412-2933

USS IOWA VETS ASSN BB 61
418 HICKORY ST
BROOMFIELD, CO 80020-2902

USS KITTY HAWK CVA 63
1401 N MARKET
SHAWNEE, OK 74801-4927

USS LEXINGTON ASSN
1904 WESTMINSTER DR
LEXINGTON, KY 40504-1343

USS LONG BEACH CGN 9/AK 9
PO BOX 69
CLYMER, NY 14724-0069

USS LUNGA POINT CVE 94
5400 KIRKSIDE DR #C
BAKERSFIELD, CA 93309-3664

USS MANILA BAY & AIR CREWS
4837 FROSTBURG LN
VIRGINIA BEACH, VA 23455-5305

USS MARCUS ISLAND CVE 77
5450 GRAPE ST
SAN DIEGO, CA 92105-5524

USS MARYLAND BB 46
471 VIVIENNE DR
WATSONVILLE, CA 95076-3652

USS MASSACHUSETTS ASSN BB 59
PO BOX 455
WALTHAM, MA 02254-0455

USS MIDWAY & MAR DET CV 41
911 NEW GULPH RD
BRYN MAWR, PA 19010-2933

USS MISSOURI/JAP SURRENDER
66 LYNMOOR PL
HAMPDEN, CT 06517-3623

USS MOUNT BAKER AE 4
HC 63 BOX 32
MIFFLINTOWN, PA 17059-9024

USS NATOMA BAY CVE 62
242 CATHEY LN
CANTON, NC 28716-9803

USS NAVASOTA REUNION ASSN
501 E ORANGETHORPE AVE #71
ANAHEIM, CA 92801-1002

USS NEVADA BB 36/SSBN 733
27224 CORNELL ST
HEMET, CA 92344-8264

USS NEW JERSEY BB 62
PO BOX 4131
BAYONNE, NJ 07002-8131

USS NEW ORLEANS ASSN
936 SANTIAGO AVE
LONG BEACH, CA 90804-4403

USS NEW YORK BB 34
5754 DUTCHESS ST
MOBILE, AL 36609-3305

USS NEWPORT NEWS CA 148
8337 KANTER AVE
NORFOLK, VA 23518-2223

USS NORTH CAROLINA BB 55
PO BOX 480
WILMINGTON, NC 28402-0480

USS OKLAHOMA ASSN BB 37
PO BOX 104
CUSHMAN, AR 72526-0104

USS OMMANEY BAY CVE 79
8917 NOROAD
JACKSONVILLE, FL 32210-6131

USS PHILIPPINE SEA ASSN
PO BOX 8020
PT. CHARLOTTE, FL 33949-8020

USS POINT CRUZ CVE 119
3019 40TH AVE W
BRADENTON, FL 34205-3567

USS PRINCETON VETERANS
1728 S ERIE AVE
TULSA, OK 74112-6926

USS SOUTH DAKOTA ASSN BB 57
832 S BEVERLY LN
ARLINGTON HTS, IL 60005-2706

USS TAKANIS BAY CVE 89
500 WICHITA #12
MCALLEN, TX 78503-3903

USS TEXAS BB 35
911 FREE WAY
MELBOURNE, FL 32940-6929

USS UTAH ASSN BB 31/AG 16
2326 VEGA ST
GRAND PRAIRIE, TX 75050-1745

USS VALLEY FORGE CV 45/LPH 8
2301 MELROSE ST
NATIONAL CITY, CA 91950-2060

USS WEST VIRGINIA BB 48
PO BOX 442
BIG BEAR CITY, CA 92314-0442

USS WHITE PLAINS CVE 66
2283 E 15TH ST
N. SAINT PAUL, MN 55109-2320

USS WINDHAM BAY CVE 92
3860 CIRCLE DR
ROBERTSVILLE, MO 63072-1326

USS YORKTOWN CVS 10
161 TERRACE AVE
NEWPORT, WA 99156-8326

WAVES NATIONAL CONVENTION
95-021 KUAHELANI AVE #201
MILILANI, HI 96789-1605

JOINT SERVICES REUNIONS

AFRO-AMERICANS IN NATL DEF
AFROTC DET 10, TUSKEGEE UNIV
TUSKEGEE INST., AL 36088-1645

AIR INTELLIGENCE TRNG CTR
1735 W. SUNN FORD LN I304
BREMERTON, WA 98312-5327

ALL VETERANS REUNION
PO BOX 16279
INDIANAPOLIS, IN 46216-0279

AMERICAN DEF. OF BATAAN
1231 SWEETWATER-VONORE RD
SWEETWATER, TN 37874-5945

AMERICAN EX-POW ASSN
PO BOX 523
W. SACRAMENTO, CA 95691-0523

AMERICAN FORCES NET. EUROPE
4240 SE 20TH PL #211
CAPE CORAL, FL 33904-5451

ANGLICO ASSN
PO BOX 27554
TUCSON, AZ 85726-7554

ANZIO BEACHHEAD VETS, WWII
2633 LORETTO RD
JACKSONVILLE, FL 32223-1310

ASIATIC FLEET COM. FORCES
40 SHOREWOOD DR
ASHEVILLE, NC 28804-2332

ASSN OF AVIATION ORD. MEN
8979 VIA CARACAS
SAN DIEGO, CA 92162-2723

ASSN OF GUNNERS MATES
PO BOX 247
HAMMOND, IN 46325-0247

BATTLE OF BULGE FOUND.
1522 W 5TH ST
STORM LAKE, IA 50588-3049

BERLIN AIRLIFT VETS ASSN
PO BOX 612
S. VIENNA, OH 45369-0612

BERLIN US MIL. VETS ASSN
305 SUTHERLAND CT
DURHAM, NC 27712-9464

BLACK WAR VETS OFFICE
PO BOX 24352
RICHMOND, VA 23224-0352

BURMA/BRITISH/1ST AMERICA
1469 MAGELLAN CIR
ORLANDO, FL 32818-6738

CHRISTMAS ISLAND TF
12149 KRISTY LN
SARATOGA, CA 95070-3313

COUNTER MEASURE VETS ASSN
1 COACHLIGHT DR
LITTLE ROCK, AR 72227-6435

DAKOTA BULL SESSION/MAR.
PO BOX 626
DEVIL'S LAKE, ND 58301-0626

DEFENDERS OF MIDWAY ASSN
8724 PIEDRA WAY
FAIR OAKS, CA 95628-2931

DEPT OF ILLINOIS KWVA
3502 N. WATER ST
DECATUR, IL 62526-2300

DFC SOCIETY
34552 CAMINO CAPISTRANO
CAPISTRANO BCH, CA 92624-1232

DISTING. FLYING CROSS SOC
34552 CAMINO CAPISTRANO
CAP. BEACH, CA 92624-1232

DMZ TO DELTA DANCE
PO BOX 5653
ARLINGTON, VA 22206-0653

EBEYE ISLAND
2125 SABAL PALM DR
EDGEWATER, FL 32141-3831

ESCORT CAR. SAILORS/AIRMEN
1100 HOLLY LN
ENDICOTT, NY 13760-1524

EXERCISE TIGER
2118 20TH AVE
MONROE, WI 53566-3425

FLIGHT PREP SCHOOL
7339 N HIDDEN HILLS
SAN ANTONIO, TX 78244-1503

GAMEWARDENS OF VN ASSN
PO BOX 501656
SAN DIEGO, CA 92150-1656

GAMEWARDENS OF VN ASSN
4166 WARD DR NE
SALEM, OR 97305-2187

GUADALCANAL CAMP. VETS
1309 BARCLAY DR
KALAMAZOO, MI 49004-1003

GUAM NAV & INS FORCES
6126 CHADWICK AVE
SAN DIEGO, CA 92139-3610

HEPPENHEIM POW SURVIVORS
107 PURDUE DR
WINCHESTER, VA 22602-4364

HISPANIC AMERICAN ABN ASSN
4615 E. CESAR CHAVEZ AVE
LOS ANGELES, CA 90022-1207

HOWARD COUNTY VN VETS
PO BOX 6104
KOKOMO, IN 46904-6104

HQ BALTAP/NATO
7676 IVANHOE WAY
ENGLEWOOD, CO 80112-6529

INT'L SOC. OF DYSFU
PO BOX 7181
CUT AND SHOOT, TX 77303-0181

INT'L VETS REUNION
2526 6TH AVE E
HIBBING, MN 55746-2226

IWO JIMA COMM.
625 MOONBEAM ST
PLACENTIA, CA 92870-4807

IWO JIMA SURVIVORS ASSN
PO BOX 310516
NEWINGTON, CT 06131-0516

IWO JIMA SURVIVORS OF TX
PO BOX 1657
BOWIE, TX 76230-1657

IWO JIMA SURVIVORS/NY
780 MIDWOOD ST
UNIONDALE, NY 11553-1947

IWO JIMA VETERANS REUNION
594 OLD HWY 27
VICKSBURG, MS 39180-8820

JAPANESE AM VETS ASSN/US
13222 RIPPLING BROOK DR
SILVER SPRING, MD 20906-5312

JATG SOMALIA
5521-C ED LOU LN
ST. LOUIS, MO 63128-3873

JOINT BRAZIL US MIL COMM
3262 MARYDON DR
BATON ROUGE, LA 70814-2583

JNT SEC AREA/PANMUNJOM
623 W. OGLETHORPE BLVD #A
ALBANY, GA 31701-2703

JTF 1/J4 & J32
1500 NW 64TH AVE
HOLLYWOOD, FL 33024-5906

K-9 VN SCOUT DOG HANDLERS
19385 OASIS AVE #4
PEYTON, CO 80831-7817

KOREAN WAR EX-POW ASSN
8316 N. LOMBARD ST #449
PORTLAND, OR 97203-3727

KOREAN WAR VETERANS INT'L
PO BOX 8946
VIRGINIA BEACH, VA 23450-8946

KOREAN WAR VETS/NY
15 REED ST
WATERLOO, NY 13165-1305

KOREAN WAR VETS OF NC
PO BOX 126
COGAN STATION, PA 17728-0126

KWVA OFFICE
PO BOX 1839
FAIRVIEW HTS, IL 62208-0039

KWVA/COLORADO CHAPT
8420 CANDLEFLOWER CI
COLO. SPRINGS, CO 80920-5761

KWVA/DUTCH NELSEN CHAPT
2523 MONTEREY RD
COLO. SPRINGS, CO 80910-1233

LEGION OF VALOR MUSEUM
2425 FRESNO ST
FRESNO, CA 93721-1803

LZ BLUEGRASS INC
PO BOX 16404
SHIVELY, KY 40256-0404

LZ FRIENDLY VIETNAM VETS
5048 FLORENCE ST
OAKWOOD, GA 30566-2645

MCCLOSKEY GEN HOSP/AMP
2510 HAYWARD RD
LOUISVILLE, KY 40242-6430

MILITARY MUSICIANS
201 BLUE SKY DR
MARIETTA, GA 30068-3511

MIL. ORDER OF PURPLE HEART
512 BACKLICK RD STE B
SPRINGFIELD, VA 22151-3934

MILITARY WOMEN OFFICERS
1010 AMERICAN EAGLE BLV #535
SUN CITY CENTER, FL 33573-5273

MINDANAO GUERRILLAS
2305 W. RUTHRAUFF RD
TUCSON, AZ 85705-1901

MOROCCAN REUNION ASSN
PO BOX 13362
OMAHA, NE 68113-0362

MUKDEN EX-POW 14TH REUNION
5174 E. BELMONT AVE
FRESNO, CA 93727-2401

NAT ALLIANCE OF MIA/POW FAM
12 CLIFFORD DR
FARMINGDALE, NY 11735-3305

NAT ASSN FOR UNIFORMED SERV
5535 HEMPSTEAD WAY
SPRINGFIELD, VA 22151-4094

NAT ASSN OF BATTLEFIED COM
1900 REALEZA CT
LAS VEGAS, NV 89102-2061

NAT ASSN OF FLEET TUG SAILORS
PO BOX 1507
SAUSALITO, CA 94966-1507

NAT ASSN OF FLEET TUG SAILORS
1611 WOODBRDGE CIR E
FOLEY, AL 36535-2267

NAT ASSN OF MEDICS & CORPSMN
6 LAUREL DR
ASHBURNHAM, MA 01430-1000

NAT EOD ASSN INC
5534 MERLIN DR
SAN ANTONIO, TX 78218-2821

NAT ORDER OF BATTLEFIELD COM
67 OCEAN DR
ST. AUGUSTINE, FL 32084-7451

NAT SOJOURNERS OFFICE
8301 E BOULEVARD DR
ALEXANDRIA, VA 22308-1316

NATO REUNION
RT 4, BOX 363
HARRISON, AR 72601-9149

NAV/MAR/CG PENSACOLA
PO BOX 460006
SAN ANTONIO, TX 78246-0006

NEBRASKA KOREAN WAR VETS
201 E. WALNUT AVE
NORFOLK, NE 68701-4259

NEBRASKA VN VETS
1102 N. 18TH ST
NORFOLK, NE 68701-2524

NEWFIE REUNION
3006 HEATHER LN
BIRMINGHAM, AL 35242-4115

NHA TRANG AFB
615 CHICKASAW DR
WESTMINSTER, SC 29693-6409

NOBC REUNION
1916 CATAWBA ST
FAYETTEVILLE, NC 28303-4106

N. DAKOTA KOREAN VETS
1739 4TH AVE NE
JAMESTOWN, ND 58401-2430

NROTC
1191 SWAN BEATTY RD
CAMDEN, OH 45311-8619

OPERATION DEEP FREEZE
51 HORNET RD
N. KINGSTOWN, RI 02852-2103

OPERATION LZ/DC
W 5889 DURST RD
NEW GLARUS, WI 53574-9704

PAN MUN JOM JSA
2212 GRANT DR
BISMARCK, ND 58501-2331

PARSONS SCHL OF DESIGN/VETS
66 5TH AVE 6TH FLOOR
NEW YORK, NY 10011-8878

PEARL HARBOR ATTACK VETS
PO BOX 112
SOUTHAMPTON, MA 01073-0112

PELELIU REUNION
4405 CUMBERLAND RD N
FT. WORTH, TX 76116-8107

PH SURV ASSN/FLA CHAPT
225 PARNELL ST
MERRITT ISLAND, FL 32953-4713

PRESIDENTIAL SERVICE ASSN
163 LINWOOD ST
LYNN, MA 01905-1218

PURPLE HEART RECIPIENTS
114 DAFFODIL DR
KILLEEN, TX 78542-1819

RAF RADAR
1232 S. HERITAGE DR
MARYVILLE, TN 37801-6453

RET ENLISTED VET PERS
PO BOX 340078
SAN ANTONIO, TX 78234-0078

RETIRED ENLISTED ASSN
1111 S. ABILENE CT
AURORA, CO 80012-4950

RETIRED SGM & CHIEF'S ASSN
1923 WENDOVER DR
FAYETTEVILLE, NC 28304-1429

RICHMOND REMEMBERS/TET 68
PO BOX 31885
RICHMOND, VA 23294-1885

ROLLING THUNDER VI
205 POST RD
NESHANIC STN, NJ 08853-4015

SAIGON MISSION ASSN
2716 OAKES AVE
ANACORTES, WA 98221-1317

SCOUTS/RAIDERS/UDT/SEALS
3300 NORTH A1A
FT. PIERCE, FL 34949-8520

SPECIAL OPERATIONS ASSN
PO BOX 250161
SAN FRANCISCO, CA 94125-0161

TAN SON NHUT ASSN
6203 57TH AVE
RIVERDALE, MD 20737-2856

TENNESSEE 2000
211 7TH AVE N STE 403
NASHVILLE, TN 37219-1823

TIGER SURV/KOREA/EX-POW
2257A VIA PUERTA
LAGUNA HILLS, CA 92653-2339

UDORN/ALL THAI REUNION
818 GARZA AVE
DALLAS, TX 75216-5902

USN/USMC NAV WEATHER SERV
4114 MORRELL ST
SAN DIEGO, CA 92109-5517

USTDC
9001 NEPTUNE DR
PENSACOLA, FL 32507-1409

V-12/DARTMOUTH
BLUEBERRY HILL
LEBANON, NH 03766-0374

VETS APPRECIATION BANQUET
5505-A W. 19TH AVE
STILLWATER, OK 74074-1323

VETS HOMECOMING
PO BOX 7425
BRANSON, MO 65615-7425

VETS OF UNDERAGE MILITARY SERV
100 VILLAGE LN
PHILADELPHIA, PA 19154-3602

VIETNAM HELICOPTER PILOTS ASSN
949 UNIVERSITY AVE STE 210
SACRAMENTO, CA 95825-6728

VIETNAM WOMEN VETERANS
PO BOX 9
CONOWINGO, MD 21019-0009

WAKE ISLAND DEFENDERS
1425 E. MADISON AVE #67
EL CAJON, CA 92019-1012

WHITE HOUSE MEDICAL UNIT
PO BOX 7199
BOCA RATON, FL 33431-0199

WOMENS O'SEAS SERV. LEAGUE
414 WINDCREST DR
SAN ANTONIO, TX 78239-2422

WORLD WAR II VETERANS ASSN
4218 TAVENOR LN
HOUSTON, TX 77047-1842

WYOMING VN VETS REUNION
131 S. COLORADO AVE
CASPER, WY 82601-2155

Social Security Number Allocations

This section explains the meaning of the number groups within each Social Security number. Sometimes this information can be very helpful in a search.

The Social Security Administration was formed in 1933. Between 1933 and 1972, Social Security numbers (SSNs) were assigned at field offices in each state. Since 1973, Social Security numbers have been issued by the central office.

The Social Security number consists of 9 digits. The first 3 digits are the area number. The middle 2 digits are the group number. The last 4 digits are the serial number.

Example: SSN 123-45-6789

123 = Area number
45 = Group number
6789 = Serial number

Serial Number

Within each group, the serial number (last 4 digits) runs consecutively from 0001–9999.

Area Number

The area number identifies the state indicated in the original application. The chart below shows the first 3 digits (area number) of the Social Security numbers allocated to each state and U.S. possession.

001-003	New Hampshire	433-439,	
005-007	Maine	659-665*	Louisiana
008-009	Vermont	440-448	Oklahoma
010-034	Massachusetts	449-467, 627-645	Texas
035-039	Rhode Island	468-477	Minnesota
040-049	Connecticut	478-485	Iowa
050-134	New York	486-500	Missouri
135-158	New Jersey	501-502	North Dakota
159-211	Pennsylvania	503-504	South Dakota
212-220	Maryland	505-508	Nebraska
221-222	Delaware	509-515	Kansas
223-231, 691-699*	Virginia	516-517	Montana
232-236	West Virginia	518-519	Idaho
232, 237-246,		520	Wyoming
681-690*	North Carolina	521-524, 650-653*	Colorado
247-251,		525, 585,	
654-658*	South Carolina	648-649*	New Mexico
252-260, 667-675*	Georgia	526-527, 600-601	Arizona
261-267, 589-595	Florida	528-529, 646-647*	Utah
268-302	Ohio	530, 680*	Nevada
303-317	Indiana	531-539	Washington
318-361	Illinois	540-544	Oregon
362-386	Michigan	545-573, 602-626*	California
387-399	Wisconsin	574	Alaska
400-407	Kentucky	575-576, 750-751*	Hawaii
408-415,		577-579	District of Columbia
756-763*	Tennessee	580	Virgin Islands
416-424	Alabama	580-584, 596-599	Puerto Rico
425-428, 587, 588*,		586	Guam
752-755*	Mississippi	586	American Samoa
429-432, 676-679*	Arkansas	586	Philippine Islands
		700-728**	Railroad Board

*Some of these numbers may not yet be issued.

**700-728 RRB (Railroad Board). Issuance of these numbers to railroad employees was discontinued July 1, 1963.

Note: The same area number, when shown more than once, means that certain numbers have been transferred from one state to another, or that an area number has been divided for use among certain geographic locations.

Area numbers range from 001 through 587, 589 through 649, and 700 through 728. Social Security numbers containing area numbers other than these are not valid.

Prior to converting from service numbers to Social Security numbers as a mean of identification, the military assigned dummy Social Security numbers to individuals who did not have them when they entered the service. The area numbers within these dummy Social Security numbers range from 900 through 999 and appear on some military orders and unit rosters in the late 1960s and early 1970s. The dummy numbers were later replaced with valid Social Security numbers.

Group Number

As we have seen, the first three digits indicate the area (or state) of the Social Security number. Within each area, group numbers (the middle two digits) are allocated. These numbers range from 01 to 99, but are not assigned in consecutive order. For administrative reasons, the first group numbers issued are the odd numbers from 01 through 09. Then even numbers from 10 through 98 are issued. After all even numbers in group 98 of a particular area have been issued, the even numbers 02 through 08 are used, followed by odd numbers 11 through 99 as shown:

Odd	01, 03, 05, 07, 09
Even	10 through 98
Even	02, 04, 06, 08
Odd	11 through 99

The chart below shows the highest group number allocated for each area number as of February 1997.

001-002	90	362-367	21	530	97
003	88	368-386	19	531-534	37
004-007	96	387-399	15	535-539	35
008-023	80	400-402	51	540	51
024-034	78	403-407	49	541-544	49
035-039	64	408-412	81	545-573	99
040-043	96	413-415	79	574	23
044-049	94	416	47	575	77
050-081	86	417-424	45	576	75
082-134	84	425-428	81	577	29
135-144	02	429-432	91	578-579	27
145-158	98	433	95	580	31
159-200	76	434-439	93	581-585	99
201-211	74	440-446	08	586	29
212-214	49	447-448	06	587	79
215-220	47	449-467	99	589-592	65
221-222	88	468	33	593-595	63
223-229	77	469-477	31	596-599	52
230-231	75	478-485	25	600	65
232	45	486-491	13	601	63
233-236	43	492-500	11	602-620	94
237-239	85	501-502	13	621-626	92
240-246	83	503	27	627-628	56
247-251	99	504	25	629-645	54
252-259	97	505-506	37	646	34
260	95	507-508	35	647	32
261-267	99	509-515	13	648-649	10
268-274	02	516	31	650	03
275-302	98	517	29	651-654	01
303	19	518	51	700-723	18
304-317	17	519	49	724	28
318-357	92	520	37	725-726	18
358-361	90	521-529	99	727	10
				728	14

Military Service Numbers

Service numbers were issued by the armed forces as a means of identifying individual members. These were also known as military serial numbers or, by the Coast Guard, as signal numbers. The Air Force and Army discontinued using service numbers on July 1, 1969; the Navy and Marine Corps on July 1, 1972; the Coast Guard on October 1, 1974. Social Security numbers are now used in place of service numbers.

It is not possible to derive a Social Security number from a military service number. These are two completely separate numbers issued by two different government agencies.

Using Charts One, Two, and Three (following pages)

Here's how to determine where and when a Regular Army or Air Force service number was issued (10–19 million):

- Determine from which state the service number was issued by using Chart One, Column (1).
- Determine which date the service number was issued by using Chart Two.

Example: Service number 12,250,000 was issued in Delaware, New Jersey, or New York (from Chart One) between the years 1946–1948 (from Chart Two).

Here's how to determine where and when a regular or reserve draftee service number was issued:

- Determine from which state the service number was issued by using Chart One, Column (2) or (3).
- 30–39 million service numbers were assigned between 1940–1946 and 50–57 million service numbers were assigned between 1948–1969.

Example: A service number 38,945,340 was issued in Arkansas, Louisiana, New Mexico, Oklahoma, or Texas between the years 1940–1946 (from Chart One).

Here's how to determine where and when a National Guard service number was issued:

• Determine from which state the service number was issued by using Chart Three.

Example: A National Guard service number 22,859,996 was issued in Rhode Island between the years 1946–1969.

Chart One

Service Numbers: First two numbers.

The numbers listed below represent the first two digits of an Air Force or Army service number issued between the years 1940–1969. These service numbers were assigned to Air Force and Army enlisted male personnel by state entrance stations.

(1) Regular and Reserve Air Force and Army
(2) Draftees between 1940–1946 (30–39 million)
(3) Draftees between 1948–1969 (50–57 million)
(4) State or territory

(1)	(2)	(3)	(4)	(1)	(2)	(3)	(4)
14	34	53	Alabama	17	37	55	Kansas
19	39	50	Alaska	15	35	52	Kentucky
19	39	56	Arizona	18	38	54	Louisiana
18	38	54	Arkansas	11	31	51	Maine
19	39	56	California	13	33	52	Maryland
17	37	55	Colorado	11	31	51	Massachusetts
11	31	51	Connecticut	16	36	55	Michigan
12	32	51	Delaware	17	37	55	Minnesota
14	34	53	Florida	14	34	53	Mississippi
14	34	56	Georgia	17	37	55	Missouri
10	30	50	Hawaii	19	39	56	Montana
19	39	56	Idaho	17	37	55	Nebraska
16	36	55	Illinois	19	39	56	Nevada
15	35	52	Indiana	11	31	51	New Hampshire
17	37	55	Iowa	12	32	51	New Jersey

(1)	(2)	(3)	(4)	(1)	(2)	(3)	(4)
18	38	54	New Mexico	14	34	53	Tennessee
12	32	51	New York	18	38	54	Texas
14	34	53	North Carolina	19	39	56	Utah
17	37	55	North Dakota	11	31	51	Vermont
15	35	52	Ohio	13	33	52	Virginia
18	38	54	Oklahoma	15	35	52	West Virginia
19	39	56	Oregon	19	39	56	Washington
13	33	52	Pennsylvania	16	36	55	Wisconsin
11	31	51	Rhode Island	17	37	55	Wyoming
14	34	53	South Carolina	10	30	50	Panama
17	37	55	South Dakota	10	30	50	Puerto Rico

Chart Two

Regular U.S. Air Force and U.S. Army Service Numbers.

Service numbers 10,000,000–19,999,999 were issued to regular Air Force and regular Army enlisted men for the periods indicated below. These numbers were also assigned to enlisted male reservists.

10,000,000–10,999,999	1940–1969*

* These numbers were used for initial enlistments occurring outside the continental limits: Alaska, Hawaii, Puerto Rico, and Panama.

11,000,000–11,142,500	1940–1945
11,142,501–11,188,000	1946–1948
11,188,001–11,238,500	1949–1951
11,238,501–11,283,000	1952–1954
11,283,001–11,344,500	1955–1957
11,344,501–11,384,000	1958–1960
11,384,001–11,999,999	1961–1969
12,000,000–12,242,000	1940–1945
12,242,001–12,321,000	1946–1948
12,321,001–12,393,500	1949–1951
12,393,501–12,469,000	1952–1954
12,469,001–12,553,375	1955–1957
12,553,376–12,614,900	1958–1960
12,614,901–12,999,999	1961–1969
13,000,000–13,197,500	1940–1945
13,197,501–13,299,700	1946–1948
13,299,701–13,408,700	1949–1951
13,408,701–13,511,500	1952–1954
13,511,501–13,621,140	1955–1957
13,621,141–13,705,500	1958–1960
13,705,501–13,999,999	1961–1969
14,000,000–14,204,500	1940–1945
14,204,501–14,300,770	1946–1948
14,300,771–14,454,000	1949–1951
14,454,001–14,547,500	1952–1954
14,547,501–14,661,000	1955–1957
14,661,001–14,745,000	1958–1960
14,745,001–14,999,999	1961–1969
15,000,000–15,201,000	1940–1945
15,201,001–15,280,500	1946–1948
15,280,501–15,465,760	1949–1951
15,465,761–15,530,600	1952–1954
15,530,601–15,593,615	1955–1957
15,593,616–15,639,615	1958–1960
15,639,616–15,999,999	1961–1969
16,000,000–16,201,500	1940–1945
16,201,501–16,307,000	1946–1948
16,307,001–16,398,890	1949–1951
16,398,891–16,481,925	1952–1954
16,481,926–16,600,497	1955–1957
16,600,498–16,683,100	1958–1960
16,683,101–16,999,999	1961–1969

17,000,000–17,183,500	1940–1945	18,546,001–18,607,725	1958–1960
17,183,501–17,254,500	1946–1948	18,607,726–18,999,999	1961–1969
17,254,501–17,338,840	1949–1951	19,000,000–19,235,500	1940–1945
17,338,841–17,410,300	1952–1954	19,235,501–19,324,485	1946–1948
17,410,301–17,512,785	1955–1957	19,324,486–19,420,000	1949–1951
17,512,786–17,592,940	1958–1960	19,420,001–19,520,770	1952–1954
17,592,941–17,999,999	1961–1969	19,520,771–19,590,665	1955–1957
18,000,000–18,247,100	1940–1945	19,590,666–19,597,661	1958
18,247,101–18,360,800	1946	19,597,662–19,999,999	1959–1969
18,360,801–18,546,000	1947–1957		

Chart Three

National Guard Service Numbers.

Enlisted National Guard service numbers 20,000,000–20,999,999 were assigned between the years 1940–1946. These sets of numbers had no known state of origin. Service numbers 21,000,000–29,999,999 were issued from 1946–1969 and were allocated by state. Following is the list by service number and state.

First Army

21,000,000	21,139,999	Connecticut
21,190,000	21,259,999	Maine
21,260,000	21,619,999	Massachusetts
21,620,000	21,689,999	New Hampshire
21,690,000	21,899,999	New Jersey*
21,900,000	22,699,999	New York
22,700,000	22,789,999	New Jersey*
22,790,000	22,859,999	Rhode Island
22,860,000	22,909,999	Vermont

*Note that New Jersey has two sets of numbers.

Second Army

21,140,000	21,189,999	Delaware
22,910,000	22,959,999	District of Columbia
23,170,000	23,269,999	Kentucky
23,270,000	23,379,999	Maryland
23,380,000	23,729,999	Ohio
23,730,000	24,259,999	Pennsylvania
24,260,000	24,409,999	Virginia
24,410,000	24,479,999	West Virginia

Third Army

24,480,000	24,619,999	Alabama
24,620,000	24,729,999	Florida
24,730,000	24,879,999	Georgia
24,960,000	25,109,999	North Carolina
25,110,000	25,249,999	South Carolina
25,250,000	25,409,999	Tennessee

Fourth Army

25,410,000	25,499,999	Arkansas
25,500,000	25,629,999	Louisiana
25,630,000	25,679,999	New Mexico
25,680,000	25,839,999	Oklahoma
25,840,000	26,239,999	Texas

Fifth Army

22,960,000	23,169,999	Indiana
26,240,000	26,329,000	Colorado
26,330,000	26,779,999	Illinois
26,780,000	26,919,999	Iowa
26,920,000	27,009,999	Kansas
27,010,000	27,339,999	Michigan
27,340,000	27,499,999	Minnesota
27,500,000	27,659,999	Missouri
27,660,000	27,729,999	Nebraska
27,730,000	27,789,999	North Dakota
27,790,000	27,849,999	South Dakota
27,850,000	28,019,000	Wisconsin
28,020,000	28,039,999	Wyoming

Sixth Army

28,040,000	28,089,999	Arizona
28,090,000	28,639,999	California
28,640,000	28,709,999	Idaho
28,710,000	28,759,999	Montana
28,760,000	28,769,999	Nevada
28,770,000	28,909,999	Oregon
28,910,000	28,969,999	Utah
28,970,000	29,029,999	Washington

Overseas Areas

29,030,000	29,119,999	Hawaii
29,120,000	29,239,999	Puerto Rico
29,240,000	29,249,999	Alaska
29,250,000	29,999,999	Unused

Chart Four: Dates service numbers were issued (by branch).

AIR FORCE (Air Force service numbers were discontinued on July 1, 1969.)

Officers			*Enlisted*
Begin #	Ending #	Years	
1	99,999	1947–1969*	Same as Army†
1,800,000	1,999,999	1947–1969	
2,200,000	3,999,999	1947–1969	

† Air Force shared enlisted service numbers with the Army from 1947–1969.
* Use suffix "A" or prefix "FR" for Regular Air Force.

ARMY (Army service numbers were discontinued on July 1, 1969.)

Officers			*Enlisted*		
Begin #	Ending #	Years	Begin #	Ending #	Years
1	19,999	1921–1935	1	5,999,999	1918–1919
20,000	99,999	1935–1964	6,000,000	7,999,999	1919–1940
100,000	124,999	1921–1941*	8,000,000	8,999,999	1948–1969w
125,000	499,999	1921–1941	10,000,000	10,999,999	1940–1969†
500,000	799,999	1942–1954	11,000,000	19,999,999	1940–1969x
800,000	999,999	1921–1969**	30,000,000	39,999,999	1940–1946
1,000,000	2,999,999	1942–1954	42,000,000	46,999,999	1943–1946
3,000,000	3,999,999	1957–1969wo	50,000,000	59,999,999	1948–1966
4,000,000	4,999,999	1954–1957	60,000,000	69,999,999	1966–1969
5,000,000	5,999,999	1957–1969	90,000,000	99,999,999	1940–1945#

* In 1965 Regular Army officers received numbers in the lower part of this series with prefix "OF."
** These were also given to Warrant Officers and Army Field Clerks.
† These numbers were issued for enlistments outside the continental limits.
# Approx. 20,000 of these numbers were issued to Philippine Army in WWII.
x For a more detailed listing of these numbers, see Chart Two.
wo = Warrant Officers, w = women.

COAST GUARD (Coast Guard signal nos.* were discontinued on Oct. 1, 1974.)

Officers			*Enlisted*		
Begin #	Ending #	Years	Begin #	Ending #	Years
1,000	99,999	1915–1974	100,000	199,999	1915–1930
60,000	60,393	1957–1961	200,000	254,999	1930–1942
			255,000	349,999	1945–1962
			350,000	499,999	1962–1974
			500,000	707,999	1941–1945
			2,000,000	2,199,999	1948–1974
			3,000,000	3,081,999	1942–1944
w = women			4,000,000	4,040,999	1942–1945w
* The Coast Guard			5,000,000	5,001,499	1942
called their numbers			6,000,000	6,207,999	1941–1945
signal numbers.			7,000,000	7,027,999	1943–1945

MARINE CORPS (Marine Corps service nos. were discontinued on July 1, 1972.)

Officers			*Enlisted*		
Begin #	Ending #	Years	Begin #	Ending #	Years
1	19,999	1920–1945*	20,000	50,000	1905–1917m
20,000	99,999	1941–1966*	50,001	60,000	Not used
100,000	124,999	1966–1972*	60,001	99,999	1905–1917m
			100,000	199,999	1917–1925m
			200,000	254,999	1925–1933m
			255,000	349,999	1933–1941m
			350,000	499,999	1941–1942m
			500,000	599,999	1942–1946m
			600,000	670,899	1943–1947m
			670,900	699,999	Not used
			700,000	799,999	Women
			800,000	999,999	1943–1947m
			1,000,000	1,699,999	1944–1957m
			1,700,00	1,799,999	Women
			1,800,000	1,896,265	1956–1960
			1,896,266	1,999,999	1956–1965
* Always preceded by "O"			2,000,000	2,199,999	1964–1972
m = male			4,041,000	4,999,999	WWI numbers

NAVY (Navy service numbers were discontinued on July 1, 1972.)

Officers			*Enlisted*		
Begin #	End #	Years	Begin #	End #	Years
501	124,999	1903–1941	100,000	999,999	1965–1972
125,000	199,999	1942	1,000,000	1,999,999	1885–1918
200,000	254,999	1942–1943	2,000,000	9,999,999	1918–1965
255,000	349,999	1943–1944			
350,000	499,999	1944–1947			
500,000	599,999	1947–1955			
600,000	670,899	1955–1963			
670,900	699,999	1963–1965			
700,000	707,999	1965–1966			
708,000	799,999	1966–1972			

Suffix/Prefix Chart

Coast Guard: Did not use prefixes or suffixes.

Marine Corps: Used "O" for Officers and "W" for Women.

Navy: Used "W" for women. In 1965 the navy began preceding enlisted service numbers with the letter "B" (B100000–B999999).

After "B," they used consecutive letters of the alphabet, excluding letters that might be confused with other designators. For a detailed description of Navy service numbers for 1941–1965, we suggest *Lost Shipmates,* available from the USS Whetstone Association, 302 S. Oak St, La Porte, TX 77571. $20.

Air Force: (S) = suffix; (P) = prefix
A   (S)   Regular Air Force male officers. Until 1965.
AA (P)   Women enlisted personnel (WAF).
AD (P)   Aviation cadets.
AF (P)   Male enlisted personnel other than aviation cadets.
AO (P)   Reserve officers. 1947–1965.
AR (P)   Enlisted reserve of Air Force & U.S. Air Force Dieticians. Until 1965.
AW (P)   Male reserve of Air Force & U.S. Air Force Warrant Officers. 1947–1965.
E   (S)   Regular Air Force male warrant officers. Until 1965.
FG (P)   Air National Guard officers and warrant officers, both male and female. From 10/1/1965.
FR (P)   Regular Air Force officers & warrant officers–both male and female. From 10/1/1965.
FT (P)   Officers & warrant officers without component, both male and female. From 10/1/1965.
FV (P)   Reserve & warrant officers, both male and female. From 10/1/1965.
H   (S)   Regular Air Force women warrant officers. Until 1965.
K   (S)   Air Force academy cadets. Until 1965.
W   (S)   Regular Air Force. Until 1965.

Army: (S) = suffix; (P) = prefix
A   (P)   Enlisted women (WAC) without specification of component.

ER (P) Army reserve. Includes enlisted Army National Guard transferred from AUS, RA or NGUS. From unknown to 10/3/1962.

F (P) Field clerks' numbers in 800,000 series in WWI.

FR (P) Enlisted army reservists. From 12/23/1957 to 10/3/1962.

K (P) Women officers. Except Regular Army with service numbers 100,001 or higher. Women's Army Corps, Army Nurse Corps and Army Medical Specialists Corps.

KF (P) Regular Army women officers with service numbers 100,001 and higher.

L (P) Women's Army Corps officers.

MJ (P) Occupational Therapists officers.

MM (P) Physical therapist officers.

MN (P) Male officers of Army Nurse Corps.

MR (P) Dietitians.

N (P) Female nurses (officers).

NG (P) Army National Guard enlisted personnel.

O (P) Male officers. Except regular army with service numbers 100,001 and higher after 10/28/1963. Army Nurse Corps and Army Medical Specialist Corps.

OF (P) Army male officers with service numbers 100,001 and higher after 10/28/1963.

R (P) Officer dietitians.

R (P) Army WWI enlisted numbers 1 to 5,999,999 if reenlisted.

RA (P) Regular army enlisted personnel. Since 10/1/1945.

RM (P) Regular army enlisted holding appointment as warrant officer in active army reserve.

RO (P) Regular army enlisted holding commission in active army reserve.

RP (P) Retired enlisted, recalled to active duty in retired status. Only used if transferred to Army Reserve, Retired.

RV (P) Women's Army Corps warrant officers holding commissions in active reserve.

RW (P) Warrant officers holding commissions in active reserve.

T   (P) Flight officers appointed from enlisted ranks. Numbers T10,000–T223,600. 1942 –?.

UR (P) Inductees holding commissions or warrants in active army reserve.

US (P) Enlisted men without specification of component.

V   (P) Women's Army Corps officers.

W   (P) Warrant Officers.

WA (P) Regular Army enlisted women (WAC).

WL (P) Regular army enlisted women holding commissions in active Army reserve.

WM (P) Regular army enlisted women holding warrants in the Army active reserve.

WR (P) Enlisted women reservists (WAC).

Forms and Worksheets

Freedom of Information Act Request

This is a sample letter for contacting the armed forces and federal agencies concerning a FOIA request:

```
[Date]
[Agency Head or FOIA Officer]
[Name of Agency]
[Address]

TO WHOM IT MAY CONCERN:

Under the Freedom of Information Act, 5 USC,
subsection 532, I am requesting access to, or
copies of [identify the records as clearly and
specifically as possible].

If there are any fees for copying or searching
the records please let me know before you
fulfill my request [or, please supply the
records without informing me of the cost if the
fees do not exceed $____, which I agree to pay].

[Optional:] I am requesting this information
because [state the reason(s) if you think it
will help you obtain the information].

If you deny all or any part of this request,
please cite each specific exemption that justi-
fies your refusal to release the information and
notify me of appeal procedures available under
the law.

[Optional:] If you have any questions about this
request, you may telephone me at [home phone] or
at [office phone].

        Sincerely,

        [Your name]

        [Address]
```

Individual Data Worksheet

Complete legal name, nicknames, maiden name, previous married names, and aliases _____

_____

_____

Social Security number _____

Date of birth _____

Place of birth _____

Parents' names _____

_____

Spouse and former spouse's name(s) _____

_____

Names of brothers and sisters _____

_____

Names of other relatives _____

_____

_____

Children's names and addresses_____

_____

Previous addresses _____

_____

_____

_____

Previous telephone number(s) _____

Military service number _____

VA claim number/VA insurance number _____

_____

Branch of military service _____

Dates of military service _____

Unit or ship assigned _____

Installation or base assigned _____

Assignments in Vietnam, Korea, etc._____

Rank or rating (if not known, officer or enlisted) _____

Membership in veterans and military reunion organizations _____

_____

Membership in the reserve or National Guard; units/dates of assignment:

_____

Real estate owned_____

_____

Automobiles, motorcycles and boats owned/state in which registered

_____

_____

Elementary, high schools, colleges and universities attended, locations and
dates _____

_____

_____

Previous employment/dates and locations _____

_____

_____

Church or synagogue affiliation_____
Union membership _____
Professional membership/licenses _____
Lodges, fraternal and service organization membership _____

_____

Physical description: height, weight, color of hair and eyes, tattoos, scars,
etc. (obtain photos)_____

_____

_____

Hunting, boating or fishing licenses _____

Pilot, amateur radio, driver and motorcycle licenses _____

Names, addresses and telephone numbers of friends and fellow employees

_____

_____

_____

Hobbies, talents and avocations _____

Political party affiliation and voter's registration _____
Foreign and national travel history _____

Dates and places of bankruptcy _____
Miscellaneous information_____

_____

_____

INSTRUCTIONS for Standard Form 180 (see next 2 pages)

1. Information needed to locate records. Certain identifying information is necessary to determine the location of an individual's record of military service. Please try to answer each item on this form. If you do not have and cannot obtain the information for an item, show "NA," meaning the information is "not available." Include as much of the requested information as you can.

2. Restrictions on release of information. Release of information is subject to restrictions imposed by the military services consistent with Department of Defense regulations and the provisions of the Freedom of Information Act (FOIA) and the Privacy Act of 1974. The service member (either past or present) or the member's legal guardian has access to almost any information contained in that member's own record. Others requesting information from military personnel/health records must have the release authorization in Section III of this form signed by the member or legal guardian, but if the appropriate signature cannot be obtained, only limited types of information can be provided. If the former member is deceased, surviving next of kin may, under certain circumstances, be entitled to greater access to a deceased veteran's records than a member of the public. The next of kin may be any of the following: unremarried surviving spouse, father, mother, son, daughter, sister, or brother. Employers and others needing proof of military service are expected to accept the information shown on documents issued by the military service departments at the time a service member separated.

3. Where reply may be sent. The reply may be sent to the member or any other address designated by the member or other authorized requester.

4. Charges for service. There is no charge for most services provided to members or their surviving next of kin. A nominal fee is charged for certain types of service. In most instances service fees cannot be determined in advance. If your request involves a service fee, you will be notified as soon as that determination is made.

PRIVACY ACT OF 1974 COMPLIANCE INFORMATION

Authority for collection of the information is 44 U.S.C. 2907, 3101, 3103, and E.O. 9397 of November 22, 1943. Disclosure of the information is voluntary. If the requested information is not provided, it may delay servicing your inquiry because the facility servicing the service member's record may not have all of the information needed to locate it. The purpose of the information on this form is to assist the facility servicing the records (see the address list) in locating the correct military service record(s) or information to answer your inquiry. This form is then filed in the requested military service record as a record of disclosure. The form may also be disclosed to Department of Defense components, the Department of Veterans Affairs, the Department of Transportation (Coast Guard), or the National Archives and Records Administration when the original custodian of the military health and personnel records transfers all or part of those records to that agency. If the service member was a member of the National Guard, the form may also be disclosed to the Adjutant General of the appropriate state, District of Columbia, or Puerto Rico, where he or she served.

Standard Form 180 (Rev. 4-96)
Prescribed by NARA (36 CFR 1228.162(a))

NSN 7540-00-142-9360

OMB No. 3095-0029   Expires 9/30/98.

REQUEST PERTAINING TO MILITARY RECORDS

To ensure the best possible service, please thoroughly review the instructions at the bottom before filling out this form. Please print clearly or type. If you need more space, use plain paper.

SECTION I - INFORMATION NEEDED TO LOCATE RECORDS (Furnish as much as possible.)

1. NAME USED DURING SERVICE (Last, first, and middle)	2. SOCIAL SECURITY NO.	3. DATE OF BIRTH	4. PLACE OF BIRTH

5. SERVICE, PAST AND PRESENT   (For an effective records search, it is important that ALL service be shown below.)

		DATES OF SERVICE		CHECK ONE		SERVICE NUMBER DURING THIS PERIOD
	BRANCH OF SERVICE	DATE ENTERED	DATE RELEASED	OFFICER	ENLISTED	(If unknown, please write "unknown.")
a. ACTIVE SERVICE						
b. RESERVE SERVICE						
c. NATIONAL GUARD						

6. IS THIS PERSON DECEASED?   If "YES" enter the date of death.

☐ NO   ☐ YES _____

7. IS (WAS) THIS PERSON RETIRED FROM MILITARY SERVICE?

☐ YES   ☐ NO

SECTION II - INFORMATION AND/OR DOCUMENTS REQUESTED

1. **REPORT OF SEPARATION** (DD Form 214 or equivalent) This contains information normally needed to verify military service. It may be furnished to the veteran, the deceased veteran's next of kin, or other persons or organizations if authorized in Section III, below. NOTE: If more than one period of service was performed, even in the same branch, there may be more than one Report of Separation. Be sure to show EACH year for which you need a copy.

☐ An **UNDELETED** Report of Separation is requested for the year(s) _____. This normally will be a copy of the full separation document including such sensitive items as the character of separation, authority for separation, reason for separation, reenlistment eligibility code, separation (SPD/SPN) code, and dates of time lost. An undeleted version is ordinarily required to determine eligibility for benefits.

☐ A **DELETED** Report of Separation is requested for the year(s) _____. The following information will be deleted from the copy sent: authority for separation, reason for separation, reenlistment eligibility code, separation (SPD/SPN) code, and for separations after June 30, 1979, character of separation and dates of time lost.

2. OTHER INFORMATION AND/OR DOCUMENTS REQUESTED _____

_____

_____

3. PURPOSE (OPTIONAL--An explanation of the purpose of the request is strictly voluntary. Such information may help the agency answering this request to provide the best possible response and will in no way be used to make a decision to deny the request.) _____

_____

_____

SECTION III - RETURN ADDRESS AND SIGNATURE

1. REQUESTER IS

☐ Military service member or veteran identified in Section I, above

☐ Next of kin of deceased veteran _____
(relation)

☐ Legal guardian (must submit copy of court appointment)

☐ Other (specify) _____

2. SEND INFORMATION/DOCUMENTS TO
(Please print or type. See instruction 3, below.)

3. AUTHORIZATION SIGNATURE REQUIRED (See instruction 2, below.)
I declare (or certify, verify, or state) under penalty of perjury under the laws of the United States of America that the information in this Section III is true and correct.

Name _____

Street _____ Apt. _____

City _____ State _____ ZIP Code _____

Signature of requester (Please do not print.) _____

Date of this request _____

(   ) _____
Daytime phone

STANDARD FORM 180 BACK (Rev. 4-96)

LOCATION OF MILITARY RECORDS

The various categories of military service records are described in the chart below. For each category there is a code number which indicates the address at the bottom of the page to which this request should be sent.

1. Health and personnel records. In most cases involving individuals no longer on active duty, the personnel record, the health record, or both can be obtained from the same location, as shown on the chart. However, some health records are available from the Department of Veterans Affairs (VA) Records Management Center (Code 11). A request for a copy of the health record should be sent to Code 11 if the person was discharged, retired, or released from active duty (separated) on or after the following dates: ARMY-- October 16, 1992; NAVY--January 31, 1994; AIR FORCE and MARINE CORPS--May 1, 1994. Health records of persons on active duty are generally kept at the local servicing clinic, and usually are available from Code 11 a week or two after the last day of active duty.

2. Records at the National Personnel Records Center. Note that it takes at least three months, and often six or seven, for the file to reach the National Personnel Records Center (Code 14) in St. Louis after the military obligation has ended (such as by discharge). If only a short time has passed, please send the inquiry to the address shown for active or current reserve members. Also, if the person has only been released from active duty but is still in a reserve status, the personnel record will stay at the location specified for reservists. A person can retain a reserve obligation for several years, even without attending meetings or receiving annual training.

3. Definitions and abbreviations. DISCHARGED--the individual has no current military status; HEALTH--Records of physical examinations, dental treatment, and outpatient medical treatment received while in a duty status (does not include records of treatment while hospitalized); TDRL--Temporary Disability Retired List.

4. Service completed before World War I (before 1929 for Coast Guard officers). The oldest military service records are at the National Archives (Code 6). Send the request there if service was completed before the following dates: ARMY--enlisted, 11/1/1912, officer, 7/1/1917; NAVY--enlisted, 1/1/1886, officer, 1/1/1903; MARINE CORPS--1/1/1905; COAST GUARD--enlisted, 1/1/1915, officer, 1/1/1929.

BRANCH	CURRENT STATUS OF SERVICE MEMBER	WHERE TO WRITE ADDRESS CODE ▼
AIR FORCE	Discharged, deceased, or retired with pay (See paragraph 1, above, if requesting health record.)	14
	Active (including National Guard on active duty in the Air Force), TDRL, or general officers retired with pay	1
	Reserve, retired reserve in nonpay status, current National Guard officers not on active duty in the Air Force, or National Guard released from active duty in the Air Force	2
	Current National Guard enlisted not on active duty in the Air Force	13
COAST GUARD	Discharged, deceased, or retired (See paragraph 1, above, if requesting health record.)	14
	Active, reserve, or TDRL	3
MARINE CORPS	Discharged, deceased, or retired (See paragraph 1, above, if requesting health record.)	14
	Individual Ready Reserve or Fleet Marine Corps Reserve	5
	Active, Selected Marine Corps Reserve, or TDRL	4
ARMY	Discharged, deceased, or retired (See paragraph 1, above, if requesting health record.)	14
	Reserve; or active duty records of current National Guard members who performed service in the U.S. Army before 7/1/72	7
	Active enlisted (including National Guard on active duty in the U.S. Army) or TDRL enlisted	9
	Active officers (including National Guard on active duty in the U.S. Army) or TDRL officers	8
	Current National Guard enlisted not on active duty in Army (including records of Army active duty performed after 6/30/72)	13
	Current National Guard officers not on active duty in Army (including records of Army active duty performed after 6/30/72)	12
NAVY	Discharged, deceased, or retired (See paragraph 1, above, if requesting health record.)	14
	Active, reserve, or TDRL	10

ADDRESS LIST OF CUSTODIANS (BY CODE NUMBERS SHOWN ABOVE) - where to write / send this form

1 Air Force Personnel Center HQ AFPC/DPSRP 550 C Street West, Suite 19 Randolph AFB, TX 78150-4721	**5** Marine Corps Reserve Support Command (Code MMI) 15303 Andrews Road Kansas City, MO 64147-1207	**8** U.S. Total Army Personnel Command 200 Stovall Street Alexandria, VA 22332-0400	**12** Army National Guard Readiness Center NGB-ARP 111 S. George Mason Dr. Arlington, VA 22204-1382
2 Air Reserve Personnel Center/DSMR 6760 E. Irvington Pl. #4600 Denver, CO 80280-4600	**6** Archives I Textual Reference Branch (NNR1), Room 13W National Archives and Records Administration Washington, DC 20408	**9** Commander USAEREC Attn: PCRE-F 8899 E. 56th St. Indianapolis, IN 46249-5301	**13** The Adjutant General (of the appropriate state, DC, or Puerto Rico)
3 Commander CGPC-Adm-3 U.S. Coast Guard 2100 2nd Street, SW. Washington, DC 20593-0001	**7** Commander U.S. Army Reserve Personnel Center ATTN: ARPC-VS 9700 Page Avenue St. Louis, MO 63132-5200	**10** Bureau of Naval Personnel Pers-313D 2 Navy Annex Washington, DC 20370-3130	**14** National Personnel Records Center (Military Personnel Records) 9700 Page Avenue St. Louis, MO 63132-5100
4 Headquarters U.S. Marine Corps Personnel Management Support Branch (MMSB-10) 2008 Elliot Road Quantico, VA 22134-5030		**11** Department of Veterans Affairs Records Management Center P.O. Box 5020 St. Louis, MO 63115-5020	

Helpful Publications and Resources

The following books and resources have proven to be valuable to searchers. We have divided them into the categories of General Reference, Military Reference, Search Related, and Databases and Microfilm. Many of these resources can be accessed at your local library through the Inter-Library Loan Program or from the state historical society.

General Reference

All in One Directory by Gebby Press. Contains addresses, telephone numbers and fax numbers of daily and weekly newspapers, radio and television stations, business, trade, black and Hispanic presses, and general and consumer magazines.

Directories in Print. Lists the names and addresses of where to acquire membership directories of hundreds of trade organizations and professional associations.

Directory of American Libraries with Genealogical and Local History by Ancestry, Inc. Provides a comprehensive listing of private and public libraries in the United States which have genealogical and local history sections. (*www.ancestry.com*)

Directory of Associations. Contains the addresses and telephone numbers of thousands of associations in the United States. The associations vary from business-oriented, veterans groups, professional, trade and numerous other types.

Directory of Special Libraries and Information Centers. Lists over 15,000 public libraries and over 19,000 special libraries, archives, research libraries and information centers in the United States.

Directory of United States Libraries. Lists all libraries in the country. Published by the American Library Association.

Knowing Where to Look: The Ultimate Guide to Research by Lois Horowitz. Contains numerous ideas on using libraries. Available from Writer's Digest Books.

The National Yellow Book of Funeral Directors. Lists names, addresses and telephone numbers of most funeral homes and directors in the United States. Listings are by city within each state. This is a priceless source of information for searchers who are attempting to locate information about a deceased person. Funeral directors keep files that may list names and addresses of relatives and friends of the deceased. This is a particularly valuable source if an obituary was not published or a death certificate is not obtainable. Also search for funeral homes using the Internet yellow pages: *www.switchboard.com*

National ZIP Code Directory. In addition to zip codes for every city and town in the nation, this book also lists county and civil jurisdictions and their addresses. Published by the U.S. Postal Service, this book is also available for use or sale at all post offices. Zip code information is also on the Internet at *www.usps.com*.

Newspapers in Microform: United States. A helpful print reference for locating newspapers stored on microfilm. Published by the Library of Congress.

Military Reference

Order of Battle (1939–1946, U.S. Army) by Shelby L. Stanton. Lists all major and subordinate Army units involved in WWII.

Vietnam Order of Battle: Army and Allied Ground Forces and Air Force Units (1961–1973). By Shelby L. Stanton. Lists all major and subordinate Army and Air Force units involved in the Vietnam War.

United States Army Unit Histories: A Reference and Bibliography. By James Controvich. Unit history information from 1900.

United States Army Unit Histories by George S. Pappas, U.S. Army Military History Institute. United States Army unit histories for WWI and WWII.

U.S. Military Museums, Historic Sites and Exhibits by Bruce Thompson and published by Military Living, is one of the most comprehensive books available on this subject. It includes listings of Air Force, Army, Coast Guard, Marine Corps, Navy and NOAA museums in the United States and overseas. It also lists all American military cemeteries and military sites in the National Park System. This 300-page book is a must for people doing military research, reunion planning, or who have an interest in our country's military history.

U.S. War Ships of WWII by Paul Silverstone. A complete list of Army, Navy and Coast Guard ships used during WWII. Includes date of commissioning and de-commissioning, and disposition of each de-commissioned ship. Published by the Naval Institute Press.

U.S. War Ships Since 1945 by Paul Silverstone. A complete list of Army, Navy and Coast Guard ships used since 1945. Includes dates of commissioning and de-commissioning, and disposition of each de-commissioned ship. Published by the Naval Institute Press.

Guide to United States Naval Administrative Histories of World War II. Compiled by W. Heimdahl and E. Marolda. Navy History Division. Naval histories and various information.

Officers Registers (listed below) provide a variety of useful information on officers and warrant officers. These books were published yearly by the various branches of service and include biographical information. See Chapter 5 (Military Records) for a detailed listing and how to acquire a copy.

U.S. Air Force Register. Annual list of commissioned officers, active and retired. Includes service number (pre mid-1969) or Social Security number and date of birth.

U.S. Army Register. Yearly lists of active, reserve and retired officers. Lists service number (pre mid-1969) or Social Security Number and date of birth. Pre-1969 active lists include state of birth and military training.

Register of Officers (Coast Guard). Published annually. Lists officers and warrant officers with date of birth and service number. Later editions include cadets at the U.S. Coast Guard Academy and list Social Security numbers.

Register of Commissioned and Warrant Officers—Navy and Marine Corps and Reserve Officers on Active Duty—of the United States Naval Reserve; Register of Retired Commissioned and Warrant Officers, Regular and Reserve of the United States Navy and Marine Corps. Annual lists that include service number (pre-1972) or Social Security number and date of birth.

General Officers of the Army and Air National Guard. Lists officers in the Air and Army National Guard Reserve and contain biographical information.

Each military academy publishes a register of graduates (below) which lists biographical information about the person including date of birth. See Chapter 5 (Military Records) for more information.

Register of Graduates of the United States Air Force Academy has begun to appear in a "condensed" version. The 1989 register is the most recent "complete" version. It contains date of birth, full biographical sketches listing awards, decorations and special honors. Spouse's name and notations indicating most recent place of employment may appear. Rank, reserve status, year and circumstances of leaving service also may appear. Names of deceased alumni appear in italics.

Alumni Directory of the U.S. Coast Guard Academy. Published annually. Includes name, address and class year. It does not contain biographical information such as date of birth.

Register of Graduates and Former Cadets of the United States Military Academy (Army). Includes state and date of birth. Every effort has been made to include awards, separation dates and ranks, prior military service, colleges and degrees earned, current address and current employment. Deceased graduate's names are printed in italics.

Register of Alumni: Graduates and Former Naval Cadets and Midshipmen. Includes date and place of birth, last known address, decorations and awards, special assignments, retirements and rank attained. A letter "D" denotes deceased alumni. The name and address of the widow is included, if available.

Draft Registration Records or Selective Service Cards. Some libraries have copies of draft registration records of their local county for World War I, World War II, Korea and Vietnam. These records contain legal name, address and date of birth.

Search Related

Peterson's Guide to Four-Year Colleges and Accredited Institutions of Post Secondary Education. Useful if you wish to obtain the address of a college alumni association or a college library. If either group does not have a record of your subject, you might place a "locator notice" in the alumni publication.

City Directories and Crisscross Directories. Public libraries, especially larger systems, maintain collections of city directories and crisscross directories of their city and surrounding cities. These directories can be some of your best search tools. Begin with the edition for the last year you knew your subject lived in a particular city. Check more current editions to find the last year he is listed and at which address. You can then identify neighbors or former neighbors who might know where the person now lives.

Biographic Register. Annual list (register) of civil service employees published by the Department of State. It includes biographic information on State Department employees as well as personnel of the Agency for International Development, the Peace Corps, the Foreign Agricultural Service, and the United States Information Agency. Many registers include date and place of birth, colleges attended, foreign service posts, and spouse's name.

Birthright: The Guide to Search and Reunion for Adoptees, Birthparents and Adoptive Parents. By Jean A. S. Strauss. Excellent resource for anyone trying to find a birth parent, adoptive parent or a child who was adopted. Published by Penguin Books.

Dictionary of Surnames. In the event you are not sure of the spelling of a surname, this book by Patrick Hanks and Flavia Hodges has alternate spellings of thousands of surnames. It also explains the origin and meaning of over 70,000 surnames. There is also a listing of 50,000 surnames on the Internet at *www.hamrick.com/names.*

Foreign Service Lists. These directories of Foreign Service officers are published three times a year by the Department of State. They list field staffs of the U.S. Information Agency, AID, the Peace Corps, and the Foreign Agricultural Service. A brief job title appears, as well as civil service grade. Check the Internet list at *www.state.gov.*

Registers of Doctors: *The Official ABMS Directory of Board Certified Medical Specialists 1998, Volumes 1–4,* and *The American Medical Directory* published by the American Medical Association. Medical associations are excellent resources for locating doctors. State and county medical associations often publish registers and directories of their members. In addition to names, these books also provide information on medical specialty, schooling, business address and other useful information.

Telephone Books. Many libraries maintain collections of old telephone books for their city and surrounding area. These telephone books can provide old addresses and often names and former addresses of spouses, children, and other relatives. They are also sources of names of former employers (individual and business names). Use these books in conjunction with city directories.

BRB Publications and Facts on Demand books contain many types of information which can be of great assistance for searchers. Following is a list of the available titles. Check their website for new listings at *www.brbpub.com*.

The 1999 MVR Book: Motor Services Guide.

The 1999 MVR Decoder Digest: Companion to the MVR Book.

The Sourcebook of County Court Records: A National Guide to Civil, Criminal and Probate Records.

The Sourcebook of Public Record Providers: National Guide to Companies that Furnish Automated Public Record Searches.

The Sourcebook of Federal Courts: U.S. District and Bankruptcy.

1999 Sourcebook of Local Court & County Record Retrievers.

The County Locator: The Guide to Locating Places and Finding the Right County for Public Record Searching.

The Librarian's Guide to Public Records: The Complete State, County, and Courthouse Locator.

The Public Record Research System.

The Public Record Research System (CD-ROM).

Public Records Online: National Guide to Private and Govern-ment Online Sources. Edited by Michael L. Sankey, James Flow-ers and Car R. Ernst. Authoritative guide to online access of public records and public information.

Find It Online. By Alan Schlein and Shirley Kisaichi. Has a comprehensive "how to" section combined with complete pro-files of best sites and databases available on the Internet.

Databases and Microfilm

Most of these databases or resources can be accessed at your local library, a repository library, or state historical soci-ety. The majority of libraries have Internet use available to the public.

National Telephone Directories. These are available on CD-ROM and on the Internet. Your local library may have a copy for use by the public. Following are a list of some of the most commonly used Internet telephone directories.

www.switchboard.com
www.555-1212.com
www.four11.com.

Social Security Death Index. This listing of deceased indi-viduals contains approximately 60 million names of people who have died since 1962. It's available on CD-ROM and on the Internet at *www. ancestry.com*

Voter Registration Records. Libraries may have access to years of voter registration lists from the board of elections (voter registration offices) of their local area. Most of these records contain legal name, address, date of birth and may contain the Social Security number of the registered voter.

Microfilm Files of Real Estate Owners. Lists (current and old) of real estate owners are often available in local libraries. This data is usually indexed by name and address.

Newsbank. Most libraries have access to local newspaper indexes that may list the name of the person you are seeking. In addition to news articles, names may be listed under birth, engagements, marriages, divorces, funeral, and death announcements. Many libraries can search national databases available through vendors. Searches can be made for an individual whose name appears in major newspaper or who may be an officer of a company (even a sole proprietorship). Check with your librarian concerning capabilities for searches and fees.

Newspaper Obituaries. Most libraries maintain an obituary file of local deaths. This information is usually obtained from local newspapers and goes back many years. Most libraries will perform a search for an obituary for a small fee. Others will only respond to a written request. Ancestry, a genealogical company, has some newspaper obituaries on their website at *www.ancestry.com.*

Military Rankings/Selective Service Chronology

Current American Military Rankings

Officers

Rate	Army, Air Force, Marines	Navy, Coast Guard
O-1	2nd Lieutenant	Ensign
O-2	1st Lieutenant	Lieutenant (j.g.)
O-3	Captain	Lieutenant
O-4	Major	Lieutenant Commander
O-5	Lieutenant Colonel	Commander
O-6	Colonel	Captain
O-7	Brigadier General	Rear Admiral (lower half)
O-8	Major General	Rear Admiral (upper half)
O-9	Lieutenant General	Vice Admiral
O-10	General	Admiral

Enlisted

Rate	Army	Air Force
E-1	Private	Airman Basic
E-2	Private	Airman
E-3	Private 1st Class	Airman 1st Class
E-4	Corporal, Specialist	Senior Airman
E-5	Sergeant	Staff Sergeant
E-6	Staff Sergeant	Technical Sergeant
E-7	Sergeant 1st Class	Master Sergeant
E-8	1st Sgt./Master Sgt.	Senior Master Sergeant
E-9	Sgt. Major/Command Sgt. Maj.	Chief Master Sergeant

Rate	Marines	Navy, Coast Guard
E-1	Private	Seaman Recruit
E-2	Private 1st Class	Seaman Apprentice
E-3	Lance Corporal	Seaman
E-4	Corporal	Petty Officer 3rd Class
E-5	Sergeant	Petty Officer 2nd Class
E-6	Staff Sergeant	Petty Officer 1st Class
E-7	Gunnery Sergeant	Chief Petty Officer
E-8	1st Sergeant/Master Sgt.	Senior Chief P. O.
E-9	Sgt. Major/Master Gunnery Sgt.	Master Chief P. O.

Brief Chronology of the U.S. Selective Service (Draft), WWI to Vietnam War

1917, May 18. Selective Service Act of 1917 enacted.

1917, June 5. Registration of men ages 21–30.

1939, September 8. President Roosevelt declares a limited national emergency.

1940, August 31. President orders National Guard to active duty.

1940, September 16. Selective Training and Service Act of 1940 enacted.

1940, October 7. First local draft boards appointed.

1940, October 16. Men ages 21–35 must register with Selective Service.

1940, November 18. First inductees sent to army induction centers.

1943, January 1. Voluntary enlistments prohibited for men 18–37; all* must enter armed forces through Selective Service.

1947, March 31. Selective Training and Service Act allowed to expire.

1948, June 24. Selective Service Act of 1948 enacted.

1951, April 23. First call for physicians under the "Doctor Draft" (Public Law 779, September 9, 1950).

1951, June 19. Universal Military Training and Service Act enacted; replaces 1948 Act.

1967, June 30. Military Selective Service Act of 1967 enacted; replaces 1951 Act.

1970, April 23. After this date no new occupational, agricultural or paternity deferments granted.

1971, September 28. Amendments to Military Selective Service Act phase out deferments for students; institute uniform national call based on lottery numbers with youngest men drafted first.

1972, December. Last calls for inductees received from Department of Defense.

July 1, 1973. President's authority to induct expires; armed forces rely solely on volunteers.

*All except 17-year-olds and those over 36. These were allowed to enlist. The navy had an upper age limit of 51 to enlist older men with construction skills for the Seabees.

Locator Services

Nationwide Locator

The Nationwide Locator is a professional locator service that performs computer searches to provide names, addresses and other important information to the public. They provide this information to heir searchers, attorneys, private investigators, collection agencies, reunion planners and individuals seeking to reunite with friends or family members. Their data is obtained from highly accurate, proprietary databases that contain nationwide information.

Following are the types of searches the Locator provides:

Social Security Number Search

Provide a name and Social Security number and receive the person's most current reported address, date reported, and all previous reported addresses (if the Social Security number is contained in a national credit file). If a report of death has been submitted, it will be listed. $50 per Social Security number for a nationwide search.

Address Update

Provide a name and last known address (not over ten years old) and receive the most current reported address and the names and telephone numbers of five neighbors. $50 per name and former address submitted.

National Surname Search

Provide a first name, middle initial (if known) and last name and receive a list of everyone with matching names, their addresses and telephone numbers. This search is best performed with slightly unusual names. A variety of databases are used to provide this information, not just national telephone directory listings. $50 per name submitted.

Date of Birth Search

Provide first and last name, approximate date or year of birth and Social Security number (if known) and receive all matching names, city, and state of residence. May be able to provide street address and telephone number. $149 per name and date of birth submitted.

Social Security Death Index Search

Provide either the name and date of birth, approximate date of birth, name and Social Security number, or name only and receive a list of people who are deceased, their Social Security number, date of birth, and the date and place of death as reported by the Social Security Administration. $50 per name submitted.

Active Duty Military Search

Provide first name, middle initial (if known), last name, rank (if known), branch of service and receive the most current reported duty assignment (unless stationed overseas) and current rank for active duty members. If the person has been discharged, the discharge date will be given. $50 per name submitted.

Retired Military Search

Provide first name, middle initial (if known), last name, rank (if known), branch of service and receive the date the person retired from the military, home of record, rank at retirement, date of retirement, current address and telephone number (if listed) $75 per name submitted.

Genealogical Search

Provide an unusual last name and receive every matching name contained in several nationwide databases. This list includes first name, middle initial, last name, date of birth (if available), address and death index listing by last name. $95 per last name submitted.

Information will be provided to you within 24 hours of receipt, and will be returned by mail or fax. Volume discounts are available. Prices are subject to change without notice. Other specialized searches are available. Please write or fax for more information.

If you would like the Nationwide Locator to perform any of these searches for you, please write or fax the information required to the address or fax number listed below. Please include the following in your request:

- Payment in full: check, money order or credit card. If using Visa, MasterCard or American Express, please include your card number, the expiration date, the amount charged, and your signature.
- Your name, daytime telephone number, and address.
- Include your fax telephone number, if you're requesting the information be returned by fax.

The Nationwide Locator
PO Box 17118
Spartanburg, SC 29301
(864) 595-0813 Fax

Obtaining Military Records

The U.S. Locator Service (not affiliated with the federal government) can quickly obtain records from the National Personnel Records Center and the Army Reserve Personnel Center in St. Louis, Missouri. All requests are properly prepared and hand-carried to the appropriate Center, thus assuring that you will receive the records in the quickest manner possible. The following records can be obtained:

Certified copies of Report of Separation (DD 214) for anyone discharged or retired from the armed forces, and Army Reservists who have been separated from active duty. Fee is $60. Allow 2–4 weeks for delivery.

A copy of the complete military personnel and medical records of an individual (every item in the file is copied). This can only be provided to the veteran, or his next of kin if the veteran is deceased. This includes records of individuals who are retired from the military, most individuals who are discharged and have no reserve obligation (all branches), and current members of the Army Reserve. Copies of military records of individuals on active duty, current members of the Army National Guard and Air National Guard, current members of the Navy, Marine and Air Force Reserves cannot be obtained because these records are not at the National Personnel Records Center. Fee is $110.

Note: Requests for Report of Separation (DD 214) and military records are made with the authorization form shown on page 288. It must be completed and signed by the veteran, or next of kin if deceased. Please include proof of death (e.g., death certificate, obituary or funeral card, etc.).

Certified copies of complete military personnel and medical records may also be obtained for attorneys and private investigators in four to six weeks for court cases. A court order signed by a federal or state judge is required. A sample of how the court order should be worded can be mailed or faxed upon request. Fee is $100.

Organization records can also be obtained. Write for further details.

All fees are for research and copy costs. In the event the records requested are not available or were destroyed, alternate sources will be checked. (Some records were destroyed in a 1973 fire at the NPRC.) The fee is not refundable. All requests must be prepaid and all information concerning the request should be included. All orders are shipped by First Class or Priority Mail, but can be shipped overnight at an additional cost of $20. Checks should be made payable to "U.S. Locator Service," or you may make payment by credit card. For additional information or to order records, mail or fax authorization to:

U.S. Locator Service
PO Box 2577-M
St. Louis, MO 63114-2577
(314) 423-0860 phone/Fax

Please copy the authorization form on page 288.

Military Records Authorization

I request and authorize that representatives of U.S. Locator Service be allowed to review my military and/or civilian service personnel and medical records, and/or auxiliary records in the same manner as if I presented myself for this purpose. I specifically authorize the National Personnel Records Center, St. Louis, Missouri, or other custodians of my military records, to release to U.S. Locator Service a complete copy of my military personnel and related medical records.

I am willing that a photocopy and/or fax of this authorization be considered as effective and as valid as the original.

Signature _____ Date _____

If veteran is deceased, date of death _____

   and relationship _____

<Please type or print clearly>

Name of veteran _____
                  Last   First   Middle

Social Security No. _____ Phone No. _____

Date of birth _____ Place of birth _____

Service No. _____ Branch of Service _____

Dates of service _____ Rank _____

Current military status: ☐ reserve, ☐ retired,
           ☐ separated with Army Reserve obligation, ☐ none

Please obtain: ☐ DD 214, Report of Separation, ☐ complete military
   records, ☐ other _____

Enclosed is: ☐ check, ☐ money order. Charge my ☐ Visa,
   ☐ MasterCard, ☐ American Express for $ _____

Card No. _____ Expiration Date _____

Signature _____

Name (printed) _____

Street address _____

City _____ State _____ Zip _____

Address where records are to be sent, if different from above:

_____

_____

_____

Glossary

Active Duty Member. Anyone who is currently serving in one of the armed forces.

Armed Forces. Air Force, Army, Coast Guard, Marine Corps, and Navy.

Base or Post Locator. An office or organization that has names and units of assignment of all military personnel assigned to a particular military installation, post or base.

Department of Veterans Affairs. Formerly called Veterans Administration. This government agency provides services and benefits for veterans.

Freedom of Information Act. A federal law requiring U.S. government agencies and the armed forces to release records to the public on request, unless the information is exempted by the Privacy Act or for national security reasons. Abbreviated in this book as FOIA.

Identifying Information. Information used to identify and locate someone, such as: name, Social Security number, military service number, date of birth, ship or unit assigned, physical description, and state originally from.

National Archives. The federal repository of historical documents. The National Personnel Records Center is part of the Archives.

Unit Roster. A military document that contains a list of individuals who were assigned to a particular military unit. Roster includes name (first, middle initial, and last), rank, and service number. A service number will only be listed if the person served before Social Security numbers replaced military service numbers. If the person served using a Social Security number, that will not be included on the roster.

Officers Registers. Books published by each branch of the service containing name, rank, service number or Social Security number, date of birth, and other biographical information for active duty military officers.

Privacy Act. A federal law designed to protect an individual's constitutional right to privacy. The law also allows for the disclosure to an individual of information that the federal government maintains on that person.

Rank. A grade, rating, or position in a military organization's heirarchy. See page 281.

Reserve Components. Includes the Air Force Reserve, Army Reserve, Coast Guard Reserve, Marine Corps Reserve, Navy Reserve, Army National Guard, and the Air National Guard.

Retired Military Member. A person who has completed 20 or more years of duty in any of the military components and is receiving retired pay (there are some exceptions to the 20-year service period). He may be retired from active duty or from a reserve component. A member of a reserve component is not eligible for retired pay until he reaches age 60. A military member may also retire from active duty for disability due to injury or illness, with less than 20 years of active service.

Service Number. A number formerly used by the armed forces to identify members. The Army and Air Force discontinued using service numbers on July 1, 1969; the Navy and Marine Corps on July 1, 1972; and the Coast Guard on October 1, 1974. The Social Security number is now used in place of the service number. A military service number is releasable information, unlike a Social Security number which is protected under the Privacy Act.

Ship Roster. A list of personnel assigned to a U.S. Navy ship at a particular point in time. The roster will include name (first, middle initial and last), rank and service number. A service number will only be listed if the person served before Social Security numbers replaced military service numbers. If the person served using a Social Security number, that number will not be included on the roster.

Social Security Number. The nine-digit number issued by the Social Security Administration and used by the uniformed services to identify individuals. Government agencies, including the military, are prohibited from releasing a person's Social Security number.

The Uniformed Services. The armed forces, the Public Health Service, and the National Oceanic and Atmospheric Administration.

Veterans Affairs Claim Number. The number assigned by the Department of Veterans Affairs when a veteran makes a claim for benefits. Since 1973 this number is the veteran's Social Security number with a letter attached to the front or end.

Veteran. A person who has served on active duty in one or more of the armed forces.

World-Wide Locator. An office or organization operated by each of the uniformed services which maintains records containing the name, rank, Social Security number, date of birth, unit of assignment, and location of members of their respective service. World-Wide Locators are operated for members on active duty, members of the reserves, and individuals who are retired. They normally require a name and Social Security number to search their records.

About the Authors

Lt. Col. Richard S. Johnson (Ret) retired after serving 28 years in the U.S. Army working with personnel records and management, military postal operations, and automated data processing. He processed military records and ran two army locators, which turned him into an expert at locating people in the military. When the Vietnam veteran retired in 1979, he kept up his people-finding skills in civilian life.

In 1988 he shared his extensive knowledge and research on methods of locating current and former servicemen and women in the first edition of this book. He later wrote *Secrets of Finding Unclaimed Money* and *Find Anyone Fast*.

After his retirement, Dick teamed up with his daughter, Debra Johnson Knox, to form Military Information Enterprises, which publishes books and is a licensed private detective agency in Texas and South Carolina. Debra Knox is a licensed private investigator.

Debra was quite skeptical when her father first approached her in 1987 about forming a company to publish books about locating people. But now, almost 12 years later, she admits there is nothing else she would rather do. Helping reunite people is very rewarding.

Debra Knox lives with her family in South Carolina. Lt. Col. Richard Johnson passed away in February of 1999.

Bookstore

They Also Served: Military Biographies of Uncommon Americans by Scott Baron. A fascinating collection of over 500 condensed military biographies of extraordinary Americans. The people profiled are known for their achievements outside the military. Prominent in their fields, whether it be law, medicine or the arts, their one commonality is that when our country called, they answered. Many interesting stories, facts, and trivia fill this wonderful, patriotic book. 333 pages, $15.95.

Find Anyone Fast (2nd Edition) by Richard S. Johnson and Debra Johnson Knox. Father/daughter private investigators explain how easy it is to find relatives, old romances, military buddies, dead-beat parents, or just about anyone. Includes how to use the Internet and state-of-the-art computer searches. 262 pages, $16.95.

Secrets of Finding Unclaimed Money by Richard S. Johnson. An experienced heir searcher reveals all the secrets of finding unclaimed money held by state unclaimed property offices, other state agencies, and the federal government. Also learn how to earn money by becoming a professional heir searcher. Includes sample forms and contracts. 182 pages, $11.95.

Checking Out Lawyers by Don Ray. The first in the Check 'Em Out Series of do-it-yourself investigating books. It helps you decide if you really need a lawyer, and how to find the best lawyer out of the crowd. Provides a listing of useable resources including state bar associations, secretaries of state, and bankruptcy court information. Know that you are dealing with the best! 188 pages, $15.95.

Please add $4.05 shipping/handling to all orders. Send to:

MIE PUBLISHING
PO Box 17118
Spartanburg, SC 29301

(800) 937-2133
(864) 595-0813 Fax
www.militaryusa.com

Index